Probably the oldest engine house in C
almost complete. A relic of Killicor
steep slope above Hale Mills, beside
See the note about Wheal H
(Photo by Bob Actor

Updated Information & Corrections for the Third Edition, 2006

The decade that has passed since the research for Volume 2 was carried out has inevitably brought many changes, great and small.

On 14th July 2006, as this edition was being prepared, it was announced that the Cornwall and West Devon Mining Landscape had become a World Heritage Site, recognised as having cultural importance on a global level. It remains to be seen what impact this development will have on the area featured in this guide. Meanwhile, here is a page-by-page list of the changes which have already come to my attention. Inevitably, some will have been missed; I shall be grateful to hear from any readers and users of the book who come across them.

Page 7 The Trevithick Trust has been wound up. It played a valuable part in conserving many aspects of Cornwall's industrial heritage, but was deemed at the time of its demise to have completed its work.
Page 9, penultimate paragraph The story of what has happened concerning management of the Mineral Tramways Project since Groundwork Kerrier was closed (31st March 1997) is too lengthy and complex to tell here. Suffice it to say that Cornwall County Council took it over, and for about two years it was managed by the Cornwall Archaeological Unit (CAU); in the early summer of 1999 the CAU handed it over to the Countryside Services section. In the summer of 1997 the post of Mineral Tramways Project Officer was created, financed by grant funding from European Regional Development Fund (ERDF) and the South West Regional Development Agency (SWRDA). This officer worked to complete the Coast-to-Coast Trail. This phase of works was completed in 2000. The final phase began in 2003 when a £6 million funding bid was put to Heritage Lottery, ERDF and SWRDA. This final phase will be complete in 2008, when it is planned that a further 28 km of multi-use trails will be open to the public.
Page 9, bottom Old Cowlins Mill no longer has a Mineral Tramways exhibition or sales of books etc. The unfortunate effects caused by the demise of Time Cycles, already noted in the 1997 edition, have been partially offset by the arrival of Bissoe Tramways Cycle Hire: see the note relating to pages 54 & 56.
Page 10 Maps: The Ordnance Survey "Explorer" series (1:25000) is the most useful now. All the territory dealt with in both volumes of *Tramway Trails* is covered on Explorer 104, Redruth & St Agnes. The Sustrans Cornish Way map for cyclists could also prove useful.

Page 11 The leaflet described here and referred to in connection with most of the walk routes in the first half of the book is no longer available. Instead now there is an attractively illustrated folded A3 sheet entitled *Mineral Tramways - Tracking Cornwall's Mining Heritage.* This offers a general introduction to existing trails as well as the new ones mentioned above. The publication also outlines the 2005-8 heritage project, mining history and facilities in the project area and many of its major heritage sites. It is not intended to offer detailed information or mapping, both of which are scheduled to be covered in future publications.

THE COAST-TO-COAST TRAIL

The wooden signs marking the Trail have in recent years nearly all been replaced by substantial granite blocks bearing the engine-house logo.

Many other improvements have been made to this route during the past few years, and work is still in progress. At the time of writing, for example, the A39 at Devoran is being converted into a dual carriageway, complete with a subway which will enable users of the Trail to cross in safety to and from Devoran; this should be available by 2007. The main changes already implemented affect the area where the Trail crosses the A30 at Scorrier: see the sketch map on page 27. As a result of the upgrading of existing paths to bridleway status and the creation of a new bridleway, both the southern and northern (Wheal Busy) routes are now open to cyclists and horseriders as well as walkers. See below for details.

Page 13 Certain small changes have been made to the numbers of the Western National bus services linking Portreath with Camborne and Redruth. See the current Cornwall Public Transport Timetable, available from Tourist Information Centres.

The one food shop Devoran used to have (line 4) has now closed.

Page 15, start of section 1 The crazy golf sign has gone, and the crazy golf course itself looked derelict in 2006. The concrete baulks mentioned a few lines later have, Rose Lewis (the former Mineral Tramways Officer) tells me, so affected the hydrography of the harbour that silting has become a major problem, especially at the landward end. The inner harbour slipway had a big drop below it to a granite bottom. Granite blocks were tipped there to try to resolve the silting problem, but the silt just collects on top now - so much so that fishermen lose two hours each end of the tide. The Harbour Association dredged the harbour about eight years ago, which helped somewhat, but the silt is rapidly returning.

Page 17 For "page 68" read "page 65".

Page 18, near bottom Portreath Arms: the anchor outside is said to be from the *Escurial,* which foundered off Portreath beach with all hands. Regarding the cannon, see the note below, concerning page 87.

Page 20, lines 30ff By one entrance to the first quarry are concrete bases on which quarry machinery was mounted (probably crushers). The rusty, tall iron chimney now lurks behind newish South West Water buildings.

Pages 25-6 The North Treskerby stamps-engine house at Wheal Rose has now been converted into a residence. The turkeys (foot of page 26) have gone now.

Page 27, line 11 and map As explained below (note about page 31), the southern route has been upgraded and is now open to cyclists and equestrians as well as walkers. The same applies to the northern route through Wheal Busy (note about pages 31-2).

Page 28, line 3 & bottom The general store (Spar shop)-cum-post office at Scorrier is now closed.

Page 31, top two paragraphs Here is one of the most important changes to the Coast-to-Coast Trail since the 2nd edition of this guide. A new bridleway has been created, running along the east side of the B3298 to link with the wide track which runs along the southern edge of Unity Wood. (The "Walkers only" label at this point on my page 27 map no longer applies.) Walkers might still prefer to use the path through Killifreth Wood, as described in the 1st edition.

Pages 31-2 What I called the northern route has now been christened the Wheal Busy Loop and is clearly indicated by Mineral Tramways granite posts. The whole route through the Wheal Busy site to Killifreth and beyond is now open to cyclists and horse-riders: they no longer need to use the road referred to in the second paragraph of page 32, but can turn left just after the bridge over the A30 and railway and follow the track through Boscawen and Kitbartly Farms to Wheal Busy.

Page 32, near bottom The Wheal Concord headgear is still in place, but the move to King Edward Mine may still happen if and when funds for the purpose become available.

Page 34, end of first paragraph Instead of turning right at the junction by the phone box, cross the road and go straight on, as indicated by a granite Mineral Tramways signpost on the left at the corner. Another such signpost directs you to turn right along a track, which takes you to the principal surface remains of Wheal Busy.

Pages 40-42 Shaft-capping in Unity Wood and consolidation work on both engine houses at Magor's Shaft were under way when this edition was being prepared.

Pages 42-3 The "Southern Route" as I have described it can still be walked, but there is now a further option, open to cyclists and horseriders too. For this, having come through Unity Wood turn left on the main track, then right where signed Little Beside Loop. After crossing the valley floor, the signed route follows the Portreath Tramroad trackbed where it approaches Factory Hill: watch for setts, mainly near the West Poldice Mine granite signpost. At the road in Little Beside you go left for a few yards, then right, beside the containers in the yard on your left, and beyond that you keep to the main track, which curves left beside a walled-round shaft. Cross the next road, passing beside the Wheal Unity Gate car park. The black arrows direct you round to the left, passing close to the Poldice arsenic works ruins before rejoining the main Coast-to-Coast Trail heading for Devoran.

Page 46, lines 10-13 Some removal of rubbish has been done in the Poldice Valley since 1997, but "The Sands" remain much as they were then. The whole valley is now officially a Site of Special Scientific Interest (SSSI). Much of the valley has been purchased by Carrick District Council with Cornwall County Council, who together have implemented a series of works to preserve the building remains, secure mineshafts and restrict access to the more contaminated areas of land at "The Sands" and the lambreth at the arsenic works.

Page 47, references to Wheal Henry The early engine house described is now known to have belonged to a mine named Killicor; Wheal Henry worked a sett a little further west, leaving dumps still clearly visible on the hillside there. A steep path from the valley floor up to the Killicor engine house has now been created, and vegetation around the building was cleared at the same time, but was rapidly re-establishing itself when I was last there (late 2005).

Page 53 (bottom)-54 The path on the right starts roughly opposite the far end of the Nangiles dump and is much narrower than the surfaced track. Despite my attempt to guide you to the portal of the Nangiles adit, I fear you are unlikely to find it because of thick vegetation.

Pages 54 & 56 Exposed setts of the Redruth & Chasewater Railway which till recently stuck out into the void near Point Mills at Bissoe have been protected by building up a bank beneath them. The concrete block buildings left by the hardcore plant have been preserved (though mostly buried now), but their immediate surroundings have been thoroughly tidied up to provide parking space and a picnic area in association with the Bissoe Tramways Cycle Hire enterprise. For details of cycle hire ring 01872-870341. There is now a café at the site with Internet facilities.

Page 57, line 4 Point Mills may still be "a rambling old cluster of buildings", but it has been given a thorough face-lift recently, with the help of major drainage works.

Page 58, lines 10-11 Closer inspection leads to the conclusion that this old chimney belonged to the foundry also shown on the map.

Page 58, lines 12-34 Here we have one of the most dramatic changes since 1997: a wide, well-surfaced multi-use track has now been established, wending its way through an almost park-like area of streams, ponds and low vegetation. It runs from the Bissoe arsenic works site via a new wooden bridge to meet the minor road a few yards north of Bissoe Bridge; the track passing the reed beds and filtration ponds set up by the NRA (now the Environment Agency) begins opposite.

Page 59, bottom This is an error. The road between Dunstan's Ford and the Perranwell-Carnon Downs road occupies the former railway trackbed.

Page 61, start of section 9 As this edition was in preparation, major road works were under way on this stretch of the A39. When these are complete (in 2007, if promises are kept) a subway beside the Carnon River will enable users of the Coast-to-Coast Trail to continue in safety into Devoran and along the Old Tram Road to Point, Penpol and beyond. Parking space on or beside the closed-off section of the original road is another likely benefit.

Page 61, photograph Whether the gate is a genuine relic of the railway is not certain. It looks very different from the level crossing gates shown in the photos on pages 139 and 196.

ROUND WALK 1a

Pages 63-4 Despite strong opposition, Smugglers' Cottage, one of Portreath's most historic buildings, has been demolished and replaced by a modern house. Exactly how old it was is uncertain, but Michael Tangye thinks it is likely to have been the harbour office in 1713. Further back still in time the site was probably occupied by fish cellars.

Page 65, end of section 6 There is now a wooden kissing-gate beside the farm gate.

End of section 8 The path beyond the viewpoint is now rather overgrown, and you may prefer to retrace your footsteps to the main path.

ROUND WALK 2

Page 71, end of section (A) The path now takes you past newish bungalows and over a bridge almost opposite the shops. All trace of the Porthtowan Inn has gone.

Page 73, line 2 The Commodore is now the Unicorn.

Page 74, top The long shadow of the nerve-gas operation at Nancekuke, where Sarin was produced during many of the Cold War years, was felt again in January 2000, when the local MP, Candy Atherton, met three former employees who believe their lives have been blighted by respiratory problems dating from those days. The local press also reported that two men claim to have suffered health problems since 1975, when they swam in sea water polluted by discharges from Nancekuke as far away as Trevone, near Padstow. Ms Atherton raised the matter in

Parliament, but was assured that nothing toxic had been buried on the site when the chemicals plant was dismantled, and that "no chemical warfare agents were ever disposed of to either the sea or the land at Nancekuke". Further "remediation" at Nancekuke has taken place during 2005. The big "radome sphere", designed to protect the radar installations, is a recent feature.

ROUND WALK 3

Page 80 At the time of going to print it is hoped that the course of the Incline can be included on two of the new Mineral Tramways trails: the Portreath Branchline Trail (following the course of the branch line which linked with the main Hayle Railway line near Brea village) and the Tehidy Trail (running beside the Red River as far as Coombe). A decision will depend on the findings of a detailed structural assessment report.

Page 83, last part of section 4 The directions should now read, "Here cross another grid and continue straight down the slope, with a fence on your left at first. After a kissing-gate, the path runs in a slight hollow, among trees and brambles. A second kissing-gate and one last grid and you are at the road ..."

Lines 3-4 in section 5 There is no blue arrow now. Follow the "Portreath Tramroad" sign, then go sharp-left at the big granite Mineral Tramways signpost.

ROUND WALK 4

Pages 85-6 Regarding Smugglers' Cottage, see the note about pages 63-4.

Page 87, lines 7-8 The cannon which stands outside the Portreath Arms (see page 18) is said to have been brought there from Battery House.

Line 23 In December 1998 it was reported that Illogan Parish Council favours a project to open up the disused Hayle Railway track as a footpath linking Portreath with the Cornish Engines site at Pool. Considerable difficulties, however, are presented by the fact that many local residents have incorporated sections of the old line in their gardens, and others have put in applications to do so. This has unfortunately led the MTHP to seek an alternative route for the Portreath Branchline Trail. (See also the note concerning page 80, above.)

Page 88 The former Tehidy Hospital buildings have been converted into apartments.

Pages 88-9, section 7 The directions for the more direct route should now read: "Immediately after you pass through two kissing-gates into more woodland, a sign directs you to the North Cliffs Circular Walk by following the wooden posts with a pink-painted groove cut into them. Turn right, therefore. The path brings you to a small clearing with a seat on the right. Take the next right turning. This winding path eventually takes you past another seat. At the crosspaths turn right again - though surprisingly there is no pink waymark post here to tell you so. Ignore the next path on the left. Where at least five paths meet and the large sign directs you to the left, still go straight on. Soon you leave the wood. After two stone cattle grids and a wooden stile you will reach the main coast road. The track down to Basset's Cove is a few yards away to your left."

ROUND WALKS 5 & 6

Parking for both walks There is a large Portreath Tramroad information board in the Mineral Tramways car park.

ROUND WALK 5

Page 91, line 4 Regarding the muddy path, see the note below about section 5, lines 4-5. You might need wellies to cross the stream.

Start of section 4 The Manor Parsley mill leat is in fact on the left side of the road; the stream is on the right, but crosses under the road just past the former mill, where the tailings leat joins it. It's worth walking a few steps along the signed footpath on the left there; after crossing the plank footbridge you will see a substantial adit portal, from which there is usually a flow of water. Two old mines worked this area, South Wheal Ellen and Stencoose and Mawla United Mine; both produced mainly copper but also small amounts of other minerals. Dines' accounts of these mines gives the impression that South Wheal Ellen is the more likely in this case, although this particular adit seems not to be mentioned.

Section 5, lines 4-5 The footbridge has gone (January 2006), but one or two unofficial-looking stepping stones enabled us to cross the stream more-or-less dryshod.

Page 92, end A slightly quicker way back to the car park would be to continue ahead across the road to Wheal Rose and Porthtowan and take the narrow path on the right a few yards before the road bridge over the A30.

ROUND WALK 6

Pages 95-6 An exploration of Wheal and West Peevor mines as they were in 2000 is described in detail in *Exploring Cornish Mines* Volume 5. Work is currently (2006) under way to conserve and make safe the remains of the three engine houses of Wheal Peevor, other mine structures and twelve shafts in and near the site. A network of trails is also being created for public access to this from the middle of 2007.

Page 97, end of section 4 "At the road continue ahead" is correct, but there is an error on the map (page 90): the dots indicating the route should be shown running along the road, with its left turn before reaching the crossroads.

ROUND WALK 7

Page 99, start of section 3 The Bible Christian chapel, built in 1905, had been nicely converted into a residence, "White Rose", in time for its centenary.

ROUND WALK 8

Page 103, line 8 "Wheal Unity Gate" is now indicated on the granite post where the short track meets the road, but the Poldice Valley Trust's sign above the information board has been stolen.

Page 104 Most of the wooden waymark posts with green arrows have now been replaced with granite signposts.

Page 105-6, section 2 If you delay the right turn until you reach the line of granite posts at the far end of Bissa Pool, after turning right again you will pass on your left a substantial retaining masonry wall and plenty of other evidence of mining operations here, most if not all dating from the Berrida operation. A sharp-left turn brings you to several massive structures, and the bases of Californian stamps are clear to see on the ridge above.

Page 108, lines 3-4 of section 5 Both these signs had gone by 2006.

Section 6, lines 3-4 Triplets Car Spares is now the Truro Auction Centre.

End of Section 6 & start of 7 In fact you now have to turn right and then left to reach the road; there turn left and cross where directed by a granite Mineral Tramways signpost. The Zimapan sign has gone.

Page 109, lines 10-11 The way to go is indicated "Portreath, Walkers only". One fairly lengthy section of this path tends to be overgrown with brambles, nettles, etc, especially in summer, so long trousers rather than shorts are recommended, plus a stout stick and secateurs if possible.

Line 17 The wooden gate above the stile has gone now.

Lines 21-4 The "low arch" is now identified as "Trestrail Adit Shaft", part of Wheal Unity Wood. (Trestrail Shaft itself is marked by another post on the grassy patch to the right.) It would seem, then, that there is no visible evidence of the Wheal Unity Leat at this end of it - apart from the pond in this valley. The leat was severed by the A30 dual carriageway in 1976, but it remains under the road passing through Zimapan and it is this remnant that fills the pond via highway drainage.

Page 112, top The "narrow gap" is now equipped with a small kissing-gate.

Section 8, line 3 The access to Williams' Shaft is at the point where this track meets the wider one recently developed as part of the Coast-to-Coast Trail.

Section 9, line 4 The words "as it bears right" could be misleading. For the most direct route, don't follow the "Little Beside Loop" but continue ahead, signed "Devoran". For information on the Little Beside Loop, see the note about pages 42-3, above.

Foot of page Black arrows on granite posts guide you back to the car park.

ROUND WALK 9

Pages 129-30, section 1 As already mentioned, the wooden Wheal Unity Gate sign has gone. The brick top of the arsenic works chimney has been rebuilt, so it no longer looks "ruined". Instead of following the direction to "fork right again" (line 5), I recommend going straight on, heading towards the chimney and passing close to it; then at the T-junction turn right. The reason for this is that the last part of the "rough path" mentioned on page 130, line 5, was overgrown with brambles and gorse when my wife and I last fought our way through it (March 2006). There is very little left of interest visible now at the Trussal's Engine Shaft site.

Page 130, near bottom Plans to begin large-scale dumping in the Wheal Maid Valley, which have provoked strong opposition from local residents and others, appear to have been shelved, at least for the time being. In September 1999 it was announced that Carnon Enterprises Ltd had accepted Gwennap Parish Council's offer to purchase the 40-50-acre site for £1, though there was still "paperwork to be done". The hope is that now the Council can "preserve the heritage of the area" and obtain grant funding to help with restoration work. A leaflet in the Mining Villages series, "Gwennap - Copper Kingdom", published in 2004, provides more information on this area.

Page 130, bottom The lower path on the left side of the dam is the better way to go, avoiding a very steep descent at the far end.

Page 131, bottom The Harmony Cottage sign and the blue waymark arrow were no longer to be seen in 2006.

Page 132, section 3 A surfaced track had been created at a low level on the south side of the former tailings lagoon. Part of the Sustrans cycleway, it either occupies or runs beside the trackbed of the Redruth & Chasewater Railway as shown in the photos on pages 1 and 131, and it continues all the way to the road south of Crofthandy (point 4 of Walk 9: see the map on page 102). It belongs to Gwennap Parish Council and is a permissive right-of-way only: the Council has the right to close it if necessary, but meanwhile it provides the easiest route through the valley, especially for cyclists and horse-riders. The route through the Consols site as described on pages 132-5 can still be used by walkers and gives a better view of the mining remains.

Page 134-5 Since 1997, the area surrounding Taylor's Shaft and the clock tower at Consols has been thoroughly "tidied up" by Cornwall County Council, who have bought the land (but not the mine buildings) from South Crofty plc: surfaced paths have been created, shafts have been capped and walled round, the buildings too have been walled or fenced round, and other walls and gates have been set up to prevent access by four-wheeled vehicles. My note written in 2000 stated, "all the fencing is temporary - there to protect revegetation schemes involving the planting of heather", but six years later the fences are still there. It is likely that more fencing or ditching will be required to counter illegal incursions to the area by scramble bikes. The portal of the Wheal Maid Decline Shaft is now obscured - buried, it seems.

Pages 135 (bottom) - 136 The footpath following the course of the mineral railway towards Carharrack, passing beside the remains of the Great Yard, is clearly indicated on the latest OS map as a right of way, but is currently (2006) blocked off at the point, about 100 yards from the start, where a fence and barbed wire have been placed across it. A dog's-leg there now takes you to a bridleway at a lower level, which soon curves right to meet a road. Turning left along that will bring you to the junction referred to in the bold-print direction on page 137. The official footpath clearly needs reinstating. I understand that the matter has been raised with Cornwall County Council's Countryside Access Section and Gwennap Parish Council. The route of the proposed Redruth & Chasewater Railway Trail includes this path, which will be redesignated as a bridleway.

Page 142, point 7, lines 2-5 The broken sign has gone, and we didn't see Northwethel; there is a newish waymark post at the corner where walkers turn right, past a house simply called The Cottage.

Page 143 Thanks to the continued efforts of local people and the arrival of the necessary funding, good progress has been made with the stabilisation of St Day old church.

Page 145, lines 27ff Apart from the work on St Day church, the European grant aid has been used for several projects, including improvements to St Day square and the creation of "village trail" leaflets for both St Day and Carharrack. The St Day trail plan involved the fixing of plaques to fourteen properties.

Page 147, bottom Portreath Tramroad setts cross the path here.

ROUND WALK 10

Page 151-3, section 2 This part of the Redruth & Chasewater Railway trackbed, from Twelveheads to Hale Mills, has now been cleared and surfaced with fine, sand-like gravel. Plenty of granite setts can still be seen in the section beyond Woolf's Shaft, but many were taken up from some sections of the track by the contractors, and found their way to places as far afield as Redruth and Camborne. The outcry this provoked has led to the return of the setts to Gwennap Parish; early in 2000 they were stacked in a field at Goongumpas.

Page 153, lines 9-10 Most of this black piping has now been removed.

Lines 26-7 The directions here should read:

But for the walk route turn left, towards the dam wall, then after about 35m sharp-right up a wide track, which soon bends left and brings you level with the top of the dam wall. There take the narrow, stony path sharp-right.

Near foot of page Regarding "Wheal Henry", see the note on page 47, above.

Page 154, lines 8-9 The "assorted rubbish" has all been cleared away, but fencing now prevents access to the ruined buildings.

ROUND WALK 11

Page 158, section 1 lines 8-10 The bund and the sign have gone.

Page 159 No part of the second waterwheel at Hicks' Mill seems to remain now, but its former position is still obvious.

Page 160, bottom The powder house is in the first field on the left beyond the entrance to Wheal Clifford Farm. Being round, such buildings had no internal corners where dangerous gunpowder dust might lurk.

Page 161, start of section 5 The track in fact runs gently **up**hill at first.

Section 6 Taylor's Shaft is made easier to find by the fact that two parts of a large Clwyd cap have been placed over the rusty iron grid. Neither cap nor grid inspires much confidence as a means of making the shaft safe. Notice, adjoining the derelict concrete-block building nearby, a fairly large cobbled area. This is likely to have been a "spalling floor", a common feature of old copper and tin mines, where balmaidens and boys were employed to break up and sort the lumps of ore. Lynne Mayers' *Balmaidens* gives clear explanations of the tough work involved, almost always done in the open air until late in the 19th century. See also *Tramway Trails* Volume 1, page 37, and colour photograph 15 in the same book.

Page 163, top The "interpretive board" at Eldon's had gone by 2006.

Section 7, line 7 The track to the stamps-engine house now runs through what newish Cornwall County Council notice boards describe as "community woodland".

Page 164 The Mount Wellington headgear was taken down in October 2005. Its loss has been deplored by many local people as well as prominent mining historians. David Shrigley of DRS Demolition, owner of the site, was reported as saying that trespassers were regularly entering it and climbing on the equipment. "If anyone got hurt it would come back to me," he said. The plan now is to "regenerate the site for industrial use".

ROUND WALK 12

Page 169 The treatment of mine water at Wheal Jane is now by an improved method which obviates or reduces the need to add further metalliferous contaminants to the tailings reservoir. The demise of South Crofty mine is another factor which should help prolong the useful life of the reservoir.

Pages 169-70 The Tregellas Foundation's plans for Baldhu Church came to nothing; the tapestry is now attractively displayed in the covered arcade beside the Cornwall Centre in Redruth. In June 2003 a plan was announced to convert the church into a five-bedroom house; this too failed to materialise. In December 2005 the local press reported that planning permission had been granted for conversion into two houses, with work starting in March 2006. The tower is to remain, and the public will retain access to the graveyard.

ROUND WALK 13

Pages 176-7 A more detailed and accurate account of the history of Tullimaar is given in the 1999 and 2000 issues of the Restronguet Creek Society's newsletter - see page xvi for details about the newsletter.

Page 182 The following paragraph was my outline of the situation regarding the Perran Foundry site in 2000.

'In July 1999 the purchase of Perran Foundry by a company called Perran Foundry Limited was greeted in the local press with enthusiasm: "the county's sole surviving foundry complex is to be brought back to life in an £8 million project creating 100 new jobs," declared the *West Briton,* reporting on a euphoric public meeting held on 14th July. Work on stabilising and restoring the old buildings ("Phase 1") was due to begin in the autumn, and the new complex ("Phase 2") was scheduled to open at Easter 2002, including a restaurant, "leisure and retail facilities", and a Heritage Visitor Centre managed by the Trevithick Trust. Towards the end of the news item, however, occurs the ominous phrase, "subject to the allocation of grants". Only a month later, the Newsletter of the Friends of Perran Foundry painted a far less rosy picture. "One thing is very clear," stated Ian Searle, Hon. Secretary of the Friends: "it is very difficult indeed to discover what the state of play is at any one time." At the time of writing, February 2000, however, things are beginning to look more hopeful again, with a fair chance of funding for Phase 1 from English Heritage and the National Lottery Heritage Fund, though the start of any such work is likely to be delayed by several months so that a full archaeological survey of the interior of the buildings can take place. Oddly enough, the prospects for Phase 2 look even more positive, because there is a good chance of obtaining "Objective One" funding for that.'

Six years later, following a period of neglect during which the Trevithick Trust has been wound up and the foundry buildings have deteriorated almost to the point where demolition looks like the only option, once more hope has been revived. Early in 2006 North Hill Estates Ltd, owners of the site, applied to Carrick District Council for permission to "restore and reconstruct the existing derelict buildings" and to build over 120 homes plus work units and a new wharf, with floating walkways, shops, a gym and car park, at an estimated cost of £14 million. The Friends expressed strong reservations about the scheme, pointing out in particular that many of the proposed homes would be built on the flood plain; and English Heritage recommended refusal of planning permission on the grounds that the scheme did not adequately reflect the history of the site. In the event the developer pre-empted CDC's decision by withdrawing the application in order to redesign the scheme in such a way as to meet these objections. As far as I know at the time of writing (June 2006) the revised application has not yet been submitted.

Page 183, lines 8-9 The shell of Goonvrea has in fact been demolished.

Page 187, near bottom The site of the former blowing house at Mellingey appears in fact to have been about 100m SW of the point I originally suggested.

Page 187, last 2 lines One of Perranwell's plans to mark the new millennium was the creation of a footpath linking the station with the centre of the village. After long delays it has materialised, running along beside the road on the left for part of the way.

ROUND WALK 14

Page 193 In September 1998 the Devoran Quay Preservation Society completed the purchase of the ore hutches apart from those already belonging to Lower Quay Cottage. Since then, stabilisation work on them has been carried out.

Page 194 A photograph of the model of part of Devoran Quay, together with a map and brief explanatory article, can be found in the 1997 issue of the Restronguet Creek Society newsletter - see page xvi for details about the newsletter

Page 196, end of section 5 Devoran School is to move to new buildings closer to the A39. The question of future uses for the existing buildings is under discussion at the time of writing.

ROUND WALK 15

Page 197 There is no longer a shop in Feock village. Directions for driving into Devoran will need revising when the A39 Carnon Gate road improvements (including a new roundabout) are complete, in 2007.

Page 199, line 11 A misprint here: the figure should be £50,000.
Page 200, bottom A more likely explanation of "Black Lane" may be that it was originally surfaced with clinker from the smelting works, most of which - as mentioned later - seems to have been dumped on the foreshore opposite, still known as "Clinker Beach".
Page 202, top Postcards featuring a colour reproduction of the 1857 painting have been, and may still be, available in some local shops.
Page 203, top A few yards beyond the stepping stones is an attractive board giving information about the tide mill and other features of this area. Whether the mill wheel was mounted in the way described is uncertain: such an arrangement, referred to by D.E.Benney in *Cornish Watermills* as "the Norse or Greek mill", was very rare in Cornwall, and tide mill waterwheels were normally undershot.
Page 204, section 6 The road to Restronguet Point was once part of the main route between Truro and Penryn/Falmouth. At least as far back as the 15th century a rowing-boat ferry service linked the Point with the Passage House Inn (now the Pandora); in early times it carried wheeled vehicles and horses, but latterly only foot passengers. It closed about 50 years ago.

COMPLETING THE LINK

Pages 218 (map) and 219, lines 7-8 The path described on the map as blocked is now clear and properly signposted.

APPENDIX 2: CYCLING THE TRAMWAY TRAILS

Page 227 <u>Portreath to Mawla</u>: In practice both cyclists and horses regularly use the tramroad. The section from Portreath to the road leading to RAF Portreath is owned by the Parish Council, who have said horses may use it because the road is so dangerous.

<u>East face of Carn Marth</u>: This can now be placed in the "B" category, because the track has been resurfaced.

Page 228 <u>Tregajorran to the top of Carn Entral</u>: now B. A new section of well-surfaced track leading to the railway bridge near Old Cook's Kitchen cuts out the worst of the road between the Mineral Tramways Discovery Centre and Brea Leats. Brea Leats itself has been resurfaced and widened; and the steep track up to Carn Entral has been resurfaced and cleared.

<u>Newton Moor to Treskillard</u>: now A. A causeway now crosses the boggiest section of Newton Moor, and the track down to it has been drained and resurfaced all the way to Treskillard.

Pages 230-232 These Appendices should be numbered 4 and 5.

FURTHER READING

Page 232 Recently published relevant books include:

Acton, Bob: *Around Perranporth, St Agnes & Portreath* (Landfall Publications, 2005)

Brown, Kenneth & Acton, Bob: *Exploring Cornish Mines* (Landfall Publications, 5 volumes, 1994-2001) Volumes 1, 2 and 5 are particularly relevant to the area covered in this book.

Buckley, Allen: *The Great County Adit* (Penhellick Publications, 2000)

Buckley, Allen: *The Story of Mining in Cornwall* (Cornwall Editions, 2005)

Bullen, L.J.: *Mining in Cornwall,* Volume 4 (Tempus, 2001)

Carharrack Old Cornwall Society: *The Book of Carharrack* (Halsgrove, 2003)

Mayers, Lynne: *Balmaidens* (The Hypatia Trust, Penzance, 2004)

Mills, Joseph & Annear, Paul: *The Book of St Day* (Halsgrove, 2003)

Schwartz, Sharron & Parker, Roger: *Lanner, A Cornish Mining Parish* (Halsgrove, 1998)

Stanier, Peter: *Mines of Cornwall and Devon, An Historic Photographic Record* (Twelveheads Press, 1998)

Trounson, J.H. & Bullen, L.J.: *Mining in Cornwall,* Volume 2 (Tempus, 1999)

Van der Eyken, Willem: *Chacewater, The story of a Cornish mining village* (Chacewater Projects, 1999)

Five attractive and informative leaflets in a series named "The Mining Villages" are now available, dealing with Lanner, St Day, Carharrack, Stithians and Gwennap.

Copies of most issues of the Restronguet Creek Society annual newsletter can be consulted at the Cornwall Centre, Alma Square, Redruth - or telephone me (Bob Acton) on 01872 862581.

PHOTOGRAPH OPPOSITE

Granite setts which mark the course of the Redruth & Chasewater Railway in the Wheal Maid Valley, just below the ancient engine houses and clock tower of the great copper mine known as Consols.
(Photograph by Simon Vere Jones, 1996)

First published 1997

LANDFALL PUBLICATIONS
Landfall, Penpol, Devoran, Truro, Cornwall TR3 6NW
Telephone: 01872 862581

A CIP catalogue record for this book is available from the British Library.
ISBN 1 873443 28 5

DEDICATION

To Rose, Rob and all at Groundwork Kerrier without whom none of this would have been possible.

ACKNOWLEDGEMENTS

I am most grateful to the following people for their help: Fred Bawden, Paddy Bradley, Kenneth Brown, Allen Buckley, Denis Ebsworth, Rob Gibson, Peter Gilson, D. Endean Ivall, Rose Lewis, Geof Purcell, Anthony Hitchens Unwin, Mrs G.Woodhouse and the staff of the Cornish Studies Library, Redruth. Special thanks, as ever, to Simon Vere Jones, who again made many special journeys from South East England to Cornwall to take photographs for this book. If I have inadvertently omitted anyone else, I ask forgiveness. I am also, of course, greatly indebted to the many writers who have already published books, articles and photographs related to the places covered on these walks.

IMPORTANT NOTE

Whilst every effort has been made to ensure the accuracy of the directions and other information contained in this guide, no responsibility can be taken by the author for any errors leading to action being taken against users or readers of the book, or to disappointment, loss or injury.

PHOTOGRAPHS

The archive photographs in this book are reproduced by courtesy of the Royal Institution of Cornwall, unless otherwise stated. Most of the other photographs (identified by the initials SVJ) were taken in 1996 by Simon Vere Jones. The remaining photographs are by Bob Acton unless otherwise identified.

Typesetting, maps and sketches by Bob Acton except where indicated.

Printed by the Troutbeck Press
and bound by R. Booth Ltd., Antron Hill, Mabe, Penryn, Cornwall.

Bob Acton

EXPLORING CORNWALL'S TRAMWAY TRAILS

Ancient and Modern: one of Cornwall's oldest engine-house ruins, at Taylor's Shaft, Great Consolidated Mines; and in the valley, the dams built to create tailings lagoons in recent years by Mount Wellington Mine (SVJ)

VOLUME 2

THE COAST-TO-COAST TRAIL

Portreath to Devoran - & beyond

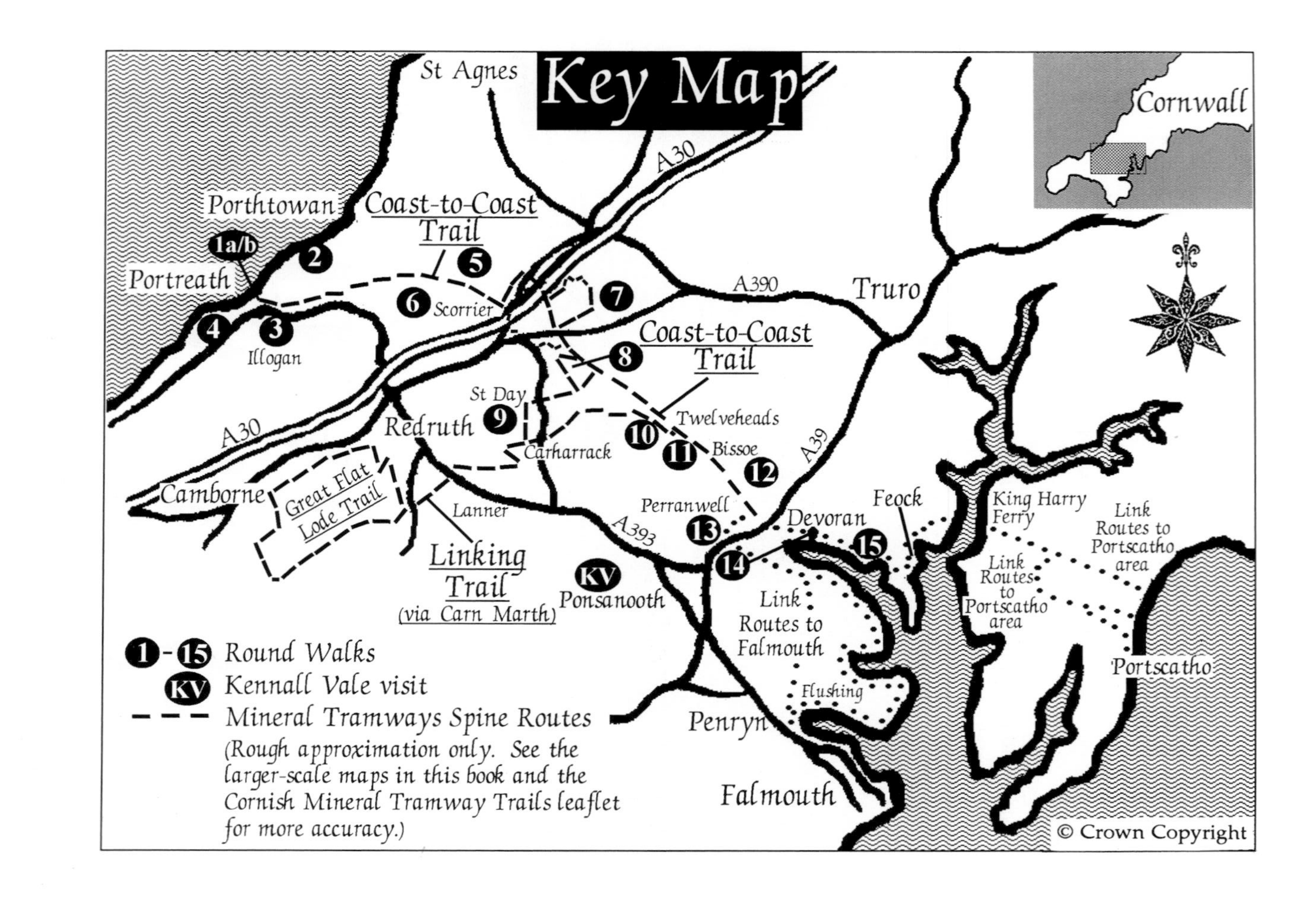
Key Map
Cornwall
St Agnes
A30
Porthtowan
Coast-to-Coast Trail
1a/b
2
5
Portreath
6
Scorrier
7
4
3
Illogan
A390
Truro
Coast-to-Coast Trail
8
St Day
9
Twelveheads
A30
Redruth
10
11
Bissoe
A39
12
Carharrack
Camborne
Great Flat Lode Trail
Lanner
Perranwell
13
Devoran
Feock
King Harry Ferry
Link Routes to Portscatho area
15
14
A393
Linking Trail
(via Carn Marth)
KV
Ponsanooth
Link Routes to Falmouth
Link Routes to Portscatho area
Portscatho
Flushing
Penryn
Falmouth
1 - 15 Round Walks
KV Kennall Vale visit
Mineral Tramways Spine Routes
(Rough approximation only. See the larger-scale maps in this book and the Cornish Mineral Tramway Trails leaflet for more accuracy.)
© Crown Copyright

CONTENTS

The North Treskerby stamps-engine house at Wheal Rose, as glimpsed from the Coast-to-Coast Trail (SVJ)

FOREWORD

Over 40 years ago I came to Cornwall as a guest of the Treloar family of St Agnes, whose daughter had been at teacher training college in London with my mother. At such an early age I was inspired by Mr Treloar's tales of his work as a mine carpenter around St Agnes, Castle an Dinas and other sites. My childhood in Lancashire was also punctuated with inspirations from Cornwall whether they be by Methodist preachers or touring politicians. Over these years, despite having worked in the North East of England and then for 20 years in Shropshire, I have been constantly pulled back to Cornwall for holidays inspired by its landscape, its industrial archaeology and my own personal interest in the Lizard serpentine industry. It never occurred to me at any time that I would end up my career working in Cornwall to establish the Trevithick Trust and to ensure that the Cornish mining landscape became a World Heritage Site. Peter Mansfield of the National Trust, Jimmy Dann of Kerrier District Council and Nick Johnson the County Archaeologist all conspired to make sure that I came to Cornwall to carry out this task. We all stand on the shoulders of giants, and that is why I pay respect to Groundwork Kerrier and the Mineral Tramways Project who have done so much to create the environment in which this book and its companion volume fulfil a need.

The flame lit by Mineral Tramways is now being taken forward by means of a major marketing exercise which will ensure that their work, together with the activities of the Trevithick Trust, will create major visitor attractions in West Cornwall, a testimony to those who have laboured underground and at grass for many centuries.

Stuart B. Smith, Chief Executive, Trevithick Trust

Workmen and boy photographed (at Devoran?) in or soon after 1915, when the rails and "chairs" of the Redruth & Chasewater Railway were being taken up

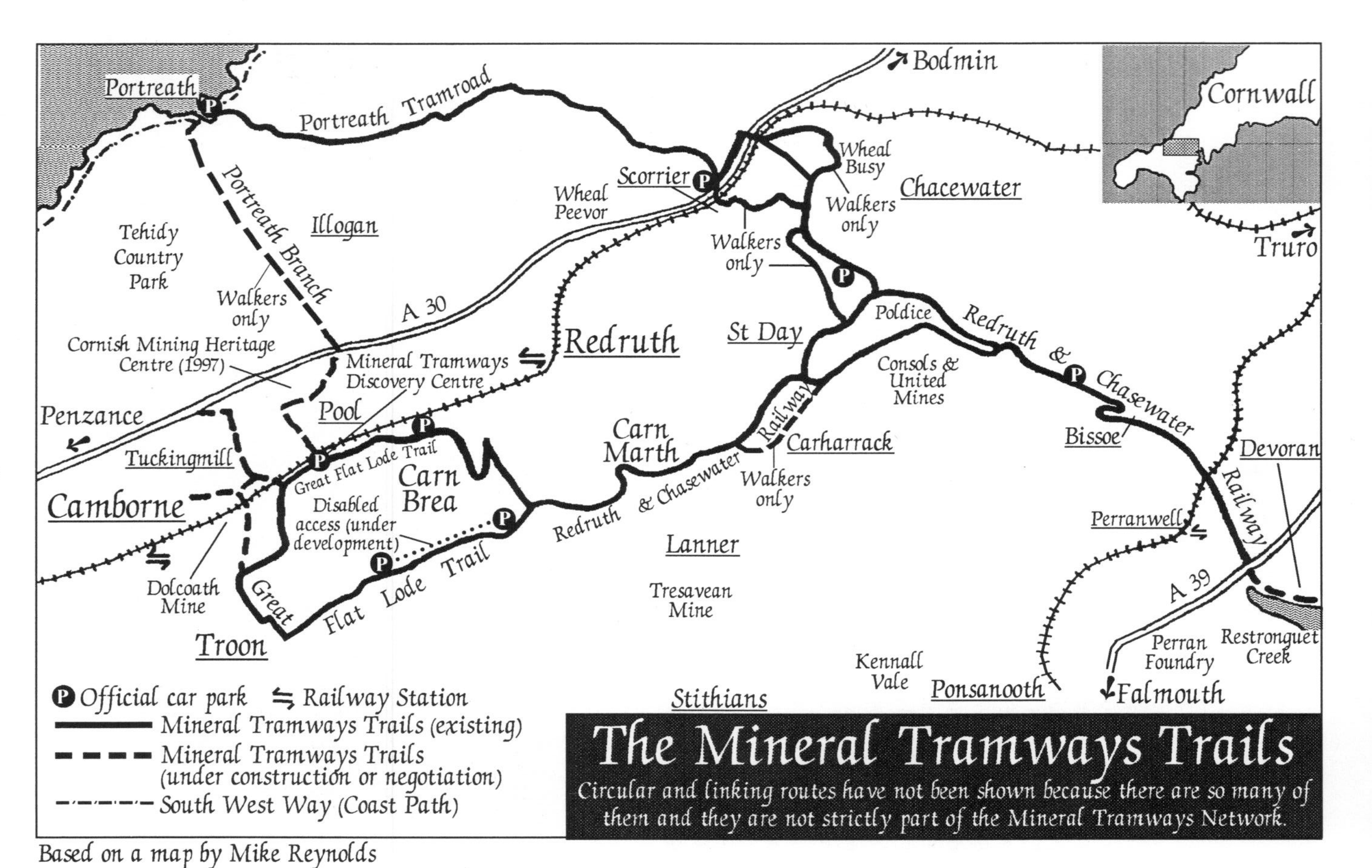

Based on a map by Mike Reynolds

INTRODUCTION

The network of trails with which Cornwall's Mineral Tramways Project is concerned is complex, but the two most readily identifiable elements that make up the "Spine Route" are a circular trail around Carn Brea, known as *The Great Flat Lode Trail*, and a linear trail between Portreath and Devoran. The former was the focus of Volume 1 of this guide; the latter is the subject of Volume 2, along with a choice of routes linking the two. The territory covered by this second volume is much larger, and there is a correspondingly much larger number of Round Walks and other routes to be described; in addition, I have included a good selection of reproductions of early OS maps in this book. In the interests of preventing the book - and its cover price! - from swelling to gargantuan proportions, I have not included a full Glossary or Bibliography this time, and have omitted the lists of Other Places to Visit and Useful Organisations (Appendices 5 & 6 in Volume 1). (Sorry, but you definitely ought to have both books!)

There is no fold-out map at the back this time, mainly because a linear route such as the Coast-to-Coast Trail refuses to fit into a map of convenient shape and size. Instead, I have included six small maps in the body of the Coast-to-Coast Trail section.

It is intended that the Mineral Tramways Spine Routes will, when all negotiations are complete, be of at least bridleway status, so that cyclists and horse-riders (plus wheelchair users on some sections) as well as walkers will be able to use them. Please be courteous to other users, remembering that all have an equal right to be there and that some are more agile than others. Horses, for example, can be difficult to manoeuvre, and are easily startled. Cyclists are asked to give a warning of their approach. (Appendix 2 is addressed to those who want to cycle the Mineral Tramway Trails, and gives information about the Great Flat Lode route as well as the sections covered in this volume.) The rich choice of alternative ways and circular walks also on offer in these books all include sections of footpath available only to walkers.

Recent developments affecting the Mineral Tramways Project

Most readers will no doubt be aware that, not long after the publication of Volume 1 of this guide, the decision was taken to dissolve Groundwork Kerrier, the organisation which has from the beginning managed the Mineral Tramways Project. As I write (February 1997), many of the Trust's officers have already been made redundant, and the rest will have gone by the time this book is published. I have my own views on the reasons for this move and the likely consequences of it, but this is no place to air them. It is, however, necessary for me to spell out, as far as is possible at this early stage, in what ways the Mineral Tramways Project itself is likely to be affected.

First let me stress that I have it on good authority that the Project is "safe", at least in the long term, though it is possible that a fallow period of several months may follow the demise of Groundwork Kerrier whilst the question of exactly who will assume the management of it is being sorted out. If that does occur, it is almost inevitable that the paths network and the historic mine buildings will deteriorate, resulting in extra expense when active management is resumed. (This despite the efforts currently being made by the few remaining staff to complete such tasks as the erection of routeway signs and the negotiation of rights of way, contracts for repair works, and so on.)

It also seems probable that Old Cowlin's Mill will continue as the Mineral Tramways Discovery Centre. Time Cycles, however, (advertised inside the front cover of Volume 1) has already closed down - one of many educational/leisure services formerly provided by Groundwork which may prove difficult to replace.

Using this book

This aims to be a book which is interesting and informative to read, but essentially it is intended as a practical guide, to be taken out into the countryside and towns and *used*. The introductory sections and appendices have been printed in smaller type than the directions to help make the book reasonably compact and portable, in the expectation that they will be read at home with the aid of spectacles if necessary!

Before setting off on one of the walks or rides, please read the introductory remarks about it, which will give you some hints about such things as how tough or easy the going is, and whether you will be able to find refreshments *en route*. In some cases, too, you could increase the pleasure of the experience by making prior arrangements, such as telephoning for permission to visit certain sites.

Directions are printed in **bold type**, and *italics* are used for the main items of information about points of interest. In the directions, the paragraph numbers (white figures in black circles) correspond to the numbered points in the relevant sketch map.

The directions given are detailed, and along with the maps in the book should be adequate to enable you to follow the routes. Mineral Tramways routes (but not the routes which join on to them) are or will be fully waymarked. Routes change, and signs can be changed to match, so you should always follow the waymarks rather than books or maps, which take longer to catch up with such changes. Nevertheless, I strongly recommend you to take with you the relevant Ordnance Survey map, preferably one of the 1:25000 "Pathfinder" Series. The ones you will need for routes in this volume are Nos 1359 (Camborne North), 1360 (Truro) and 1366 (Falmouth & St Mawes).

In a book designed to be portable it is impossible to give as much information about points of interest as some readers will wish. In an attempt to overcome this problem, a list of Further Reading has been provided in Volume 1, with a supplement on page 232 of this volume. Where books in this list are mentioned in the text, to save space their titles are reduced to a few initial letters; for example, ECM1 refers to *Exploring Cornish Mines* Volume 1.

Since the focus of interest when exploring this area is inevitably Cornish mining and associated industries, certain technical terms have to be used in the explanations. To avoid having to define them each time they crop up, a Glossary of Mining & Engineering Terms is included in Volume 1, again with a supplementary Glossary in this volume.

Rights of Way & Access to sites of disused mines

To the best of my knowledge the routes described in this book adhere to rights of way (either long-established official footpaths / bridleways / byways / roads or new rights of way recently agreed by landowners), with certain exceptions to which attention is drawn at the relevant point in the directions. Some of these exceptions are permissive paths, usually on land owned or administered by public bodies such as Carrick District Council. Others are diversions (usually short) from the strict route of a public footpath, made necessary by some kind of barrier such as a missing stile or footbridge. Some of these diversions become official and permanent, and in other cases the original path gets reinstated: please look out for any new signs in such places. Finally, in one or two walks I have made use of paths or tracks which are not on the definitive rights of way map but which have been used by the public over many years. My inclusion of such paths or tracks in the routes is not, of course, an invitation to trespass.

The same applies to many of the sites on which stand the ruins of engine houses and other mining remains. Please bear in mind too that such places are potentially dangerous. Always treat them with the utmost caution. NEVER attempt to enter underground workings except in the company of an official, experienced guide. Don't climb on the buildings, and respect the few safety barriers that have been erected.

Using Public Transport

Information about bus and other services available is given in the introductory comments to the Coast-to-Coast Trail and the Round Walks.

The Portreath Tramroad Leaflet

A well-illustrated leaflet incorporating an aerial photograph of the entire route of the Tramroad is currently available free of charge from the Mineral Tramways Discovery Centre at Penhallick, Pool, Redruth. It includes very brief outlines of eight round walks, and the first eight Round Walks in this book (with the exception of Walk 1a), intentionally adhere to the same routes, with a few minor variations.

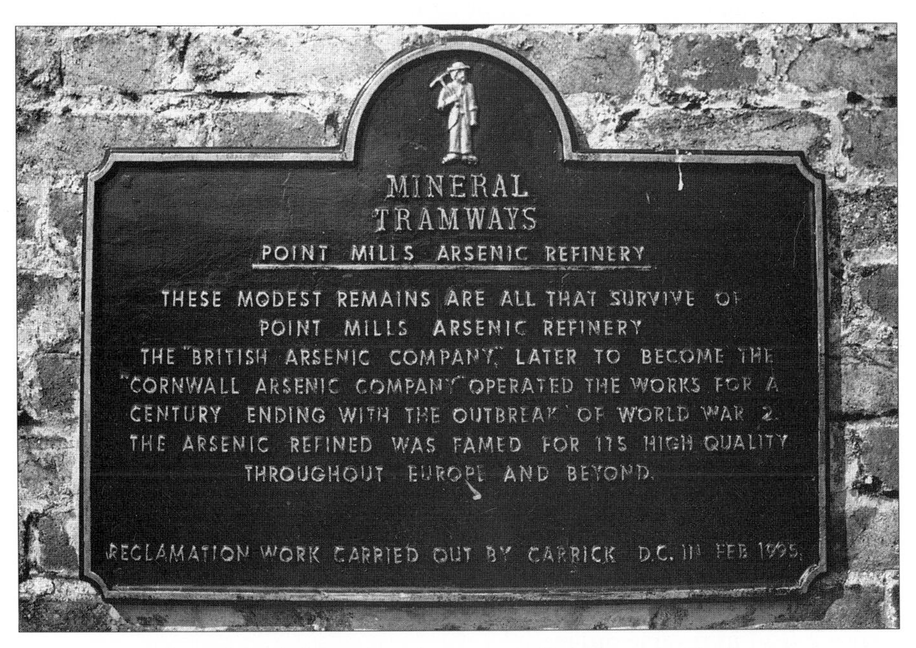

One of the information plaques provided along the Trails by the Mineral Tramways Project. (See pages 57-8.) (SVJ)

THE COAST-TO-COAST TRAIL

About 15 miles (24km): roughly 6 hours' steady walking.

I have adopted the name "Coast-to-Coast Trail" because it's rather less of a mouthful, and fits more easily on to a book cover, than "The Portreath Tramroad and Redruth & Chasewater Railway Trail". In one sense it's more accurate, too, because a good deal of the route does not in fact follow the tramway or railway trackbeds. On the other hand, readers may complain that the southern end of the Trail at Devoran - and even Point Quay, if you continue that far - is hardly "coast". I could reply that a tidal creek is as close to being coast as makes no difference; but I have to admit that the Trail does stop frustratingly short of linking the North and South Cornwall Coastal Footpaths. Perhaps this will not always be so; in the meantime I shall have to content myself with offering several strategies for completing the link, either on foot or by using bus, train and/or ferry.

Some of the recommended alternative routes and diversions to points of special interest consist of or include footpaths, but the official Trail is designed to be suitable for cyclists and horse-riders as well as walkers. Where I refer to "walking", therefore, this should normally be understood as shorthand for "walking, cycling or riding". (At the time of writing, however, a few sections of the Trail are only of footpath status. See Appendix 2 for details.)

I have described the route in the northwest-to-southeast direction, for two main reasons: (1) the Portreath Tramroad was the earlier of the two railway systems, so it seems logical - chronological, anyway! - to walk that first; (2) nearly all guides to the South West Way (coastal footpath) assume it will be walked in an anticlockwise direction, and that therefore those "doing" it reach Portreath long before Falmouth. I am hoping that some of them will decide to make this a short cut, at the same finding out just how much more there is to Cornwall than the coast. By the time this book is published, the whole of the Mineral Tramways Spine Route should be fully signposted (unless the demise of Groundwork Kerrier delays or even halts the process), so going the opposite way should present no difficulties, and the explanatory notes and background information should make reasonable sense if read in reverse order.

Unlike the Saints' Way, the Coast-to-Coast Trail is short enough for most reasonably fit walkers to manage in one day. Again, since much of it follows former railway lines, most of the gradients are very gentle. A good choice of refreshments is available at several places, notably Scorrier, roughly the half-way point, and for those who prefer to divide the walk/ride into two fairly equal chunks, Scorrier also offers accommodation (the Crossroads Hotel, 01209 820551), as well as being linked by bus (Western National service 43A - not Sundays) to Redruth and Camborne. Portreath, being a holiday centre, naturally has several pubs and shops and plenty of accommodation; Devoran has just one food shop, with rather brief opening hours, and also just one pub, the Old Quay Inn, which has food on offer and a few rooms to let. Enquiries: phone 01872 863142.

Walkers wanting to "do" the Coast-to-Coast Trail and return to their start-point by public transport will need to do some careful planning. The likely route by bus would be Devoran - Truro - Redruth - Portreath (or vice-versa); for rail services you would need to use Perranwell Station, not far from the Devoran end of the Trail: directions are included as part of Round Walk 13. From there you could travel by train to Redruth via Truro, completing the journey by bus.

* * * * *

So much for the practicalities. It remains for me to try to give you some idea of what makes this such an enjoyable and fascinating walk/ride.

Can there be many other walks of such modest length which offer such contrasts as we have here? Between the high, bare cliffs of Portreath and the wooded slopes of the gentle hills around Devoran ... Between the pretty, flower-filled woods around Scorrier and Killifreth and the open heath around Wheal Busy, scarcely a mile away ... Between the cosy little green valley which is the setting for the attractive cottages of Todpool and the "moon landscape" of the same valley no more than a few yards to the south and east, which has a weird beauty of its own ... More important than any of that for those who, like myself, delight in exploring local history through walking, there is a special pleasure in following old routes linking long-disused mines with the ports that once served them. The pleasure is partly one of discovery, of finding the little clues that can build into a coherent picture of a way of life almost unimaginably different from our own. Part of my aim in writing this guide is to help you notice such clues and piece them together, but our knowledge and understanding of the great days of Cornish mining is and will probably always be patchy and unreliable. Hundreds more clues to the truth must still be awaiting discovery, not only in dusty attics and museum archives but in the landscape where it all happened.

Directions are given from the main car park overlooking the beach at Portreath. Bus services 43 and 44 from Camborne and 46 from Redruth run to Portreath (Monday to Saturday only). Check current timetables.

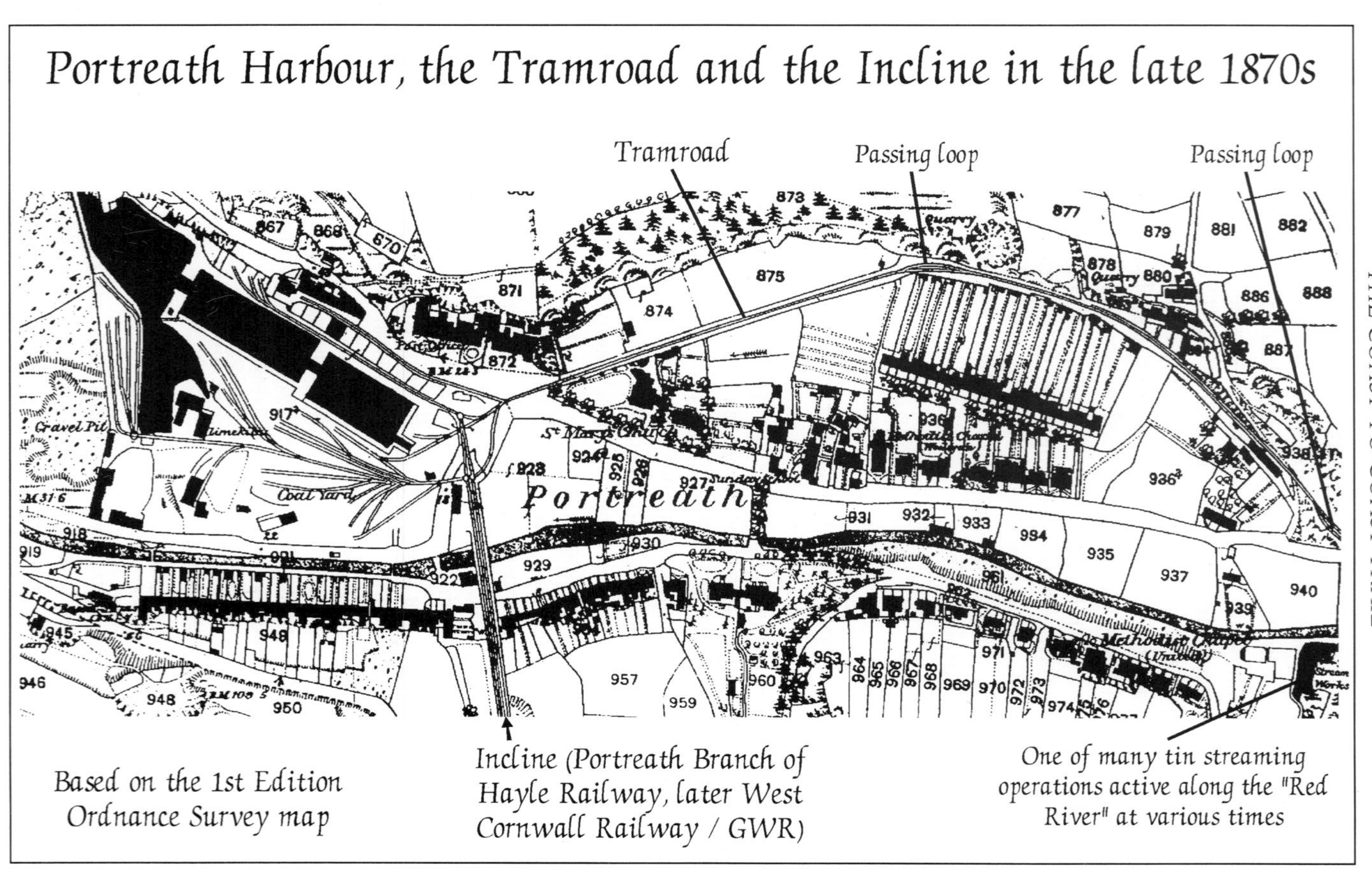
Portreath Harbour, the Tramroad and the Incline in the late 1870s
Tramroad
Passing loop
Passing loop
Portreath
Coal Yard
Gravel Pit
St Mary's Church
Methodist Chapel
Incline (Portreath Branch of Hayle Railway, later West Cornwall Railway / GWR)
One of many tin streaming operations active along the "Red River" at various times
Based on the 1st Edition Ordnance Survey map

PORTREATH

The name "Portreath" means "sandy bay" or "sandy harbour". For many years it was known as Basset's (or Bassett's) Cove, from the family that owned most of it and played a leading part in financing the building of the harbour. Traces of a harbour on the western side of the cove have been found; it is known that the building near Amy's Point of "a mould or strong key" 150 feet long and 35 or 40 feet high was contracted for in 1713, but some of the remains there may date back to the sixteenth century. The present harbour was built between 1760 and 1860.

Portreath was described in 1827 as perhaps Cornwall's most important port. Welsh coal and timber were imported here, and the products of the tin and copper mines exported; in particular, copper ore was sent to South Wales for smelting. As explained in a later note, between 1809 and 1818 the Portreath Tramroad was built to serve the mines on the cliffs to the east and the important copper mines around Scorrier, such as Great North Downs and Poldice. By the 1830s there were already ominous signs of a falling-off in trade, partly because the new Redruth & Chasewater Railway was now taking much of the ore south to be shipped from Devoran (see Round Walk 14). When a branch of the Hayle Railway was extended to Portreath a new lease of life was given to the port (see the note on the Incline in Round Walk 3), but the decline of the copper mines served by the Tramroad and the conversion of the Redruth & Chasewater Railway to steam traction during the 1850s hit Portreath hard. For the ships carrying ore and coal to use Portreath's south coast rivals like Devoran and Penryn involved a long and very dangerous journey, but on the other hand Portreath's harbour, like those at Newquay and St Agnes, was too exposed to be used safely in rough weather. Many attempts were made to protect ships in Portreath harbour from heavy seas surging in, and some were fairly successful, but it remains very dangerous to enter. Nevertheless, from the 1850s till the 1920s the port was used by the fleet of small steam colliers or "cawl" boats owned by the Bain family, as described by Clive Carter in the first issue of "Archive" magazine. (See Further Reading, page 232.) According to Michael Tangye no large vessel has put in since 1960.

Shipbuilding flourished here in the 1860s and 70s, and so did seine fishing until the disappearance of the pilchard shoals early this century.

❶ **From the car park take the pedestrian exit on the east side, where steps go down beneath the signs "Crazy Golf" and "Waterfront Inn".** *At the bottom you reach part of the so-called New Dock, a slipway built in the 1860s for the launching of newly-built ships; now it is a small sandy beach. Concrete baulks have been used to build a wall that protects the beach and the new houses nearby in stormy weather.* **Walk straight ahead beside a row of modern houses and then left past the entrance to the Waterfront Inn.**

A permanent exhibition, "Portreath and its Tramroads", has been mounted by the Mineral Tramways Project at this pub. Fascinating old photographs, together

Portreath in 1860 (Courtesy Michael Tangye)
Notice the storage bays on the cliff top on the far side of the harbour with chutes to the copper ore hutches below them. Closest to camera is the double limekiln, with the large "fish palace" or cellars beyond.

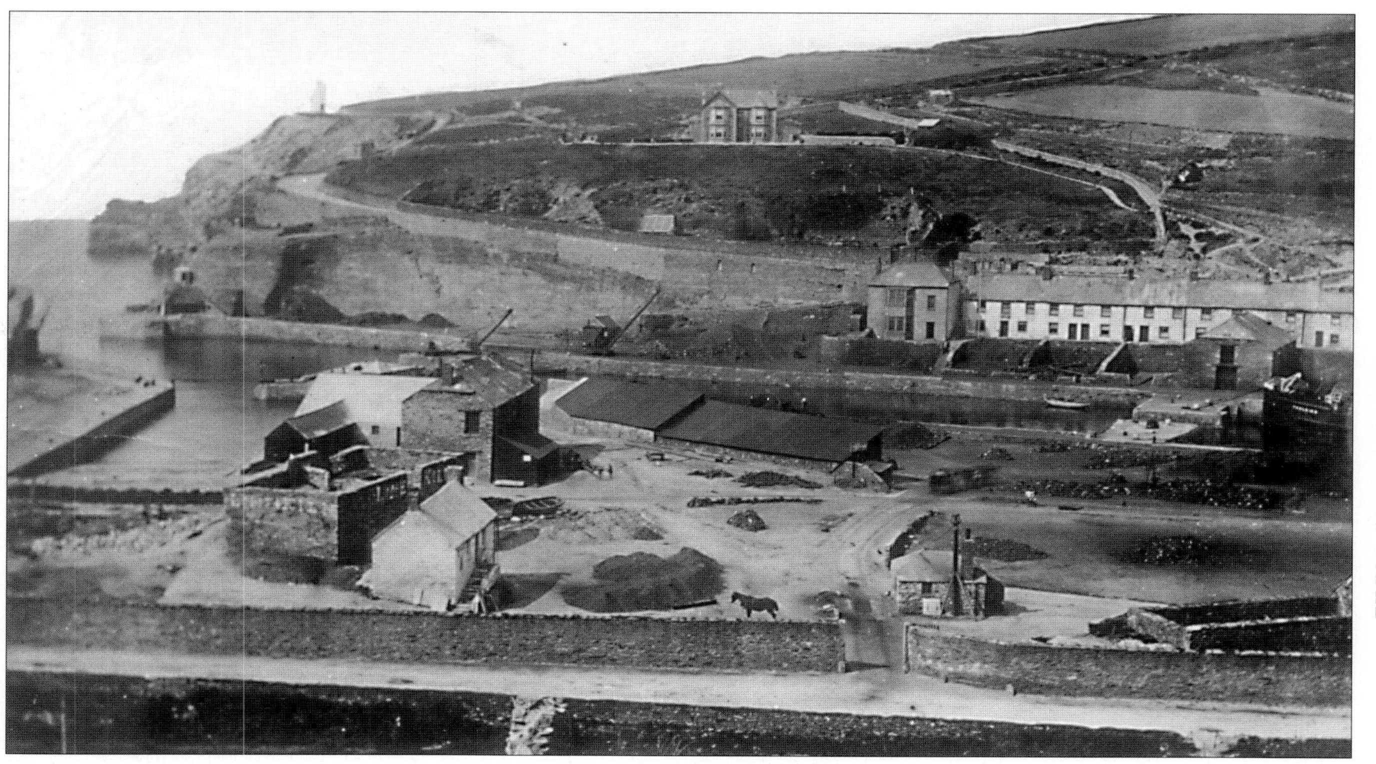

The same scene 30 years later (Courtesy Paddy Bradley).
The cliff has been cut back, destroying the bays and hutches, and the seaward side of the fish palace has made way for shipbuilding - hence the creation of the large slipway or "New Dock" (Compare the photograph on page 65.)

with other pictures, maps, written explanations and artefacts, are displayed on the walls of several rooms. If the pub is open, before taking a close look at the harbour it would be worthwhile to go in and study the parts of the exhibition that deal with it. The pub stands on the site of the old "Fish Palace", where pilchards were salted, pressed and packed; it was a large building with an open central courtyard, not unlike the fish cellars still to be seen at Port Isaac. Part of the cellars at Portreath was adapted for shipbuilding at the time the slipway was made. The west wall of the present building derives from the original building, and features ship timber and a treenail, a wooden pin used to fasten the planks of a ship to the timbers. The word is usually pronounced "trennle" or "trunnle".

From beside the pub you have a good view of the outer harbour basin. At the seaward end you can see one of the vertical slots that held the ends of timber baulks which used to be lifted by crane and placed across the entrance to protect docked vessels from heavy seas. The Roman numerals cut into the masonry on the near side of the entrance indicate the water depth in feet. The terminus of the Tramroad was on the far side; the plateway itself ended at the wall surrounding the harbour, but within the harbour there was a rail network belonging to the harbour company.

The area you are walking through was formerly occupied by sheds, workshops, a double lime kiln which survived till 1967, and the various sidings of the railway, plus large heaps of coal and limestone. The "hutches" provided as bins for copper ore were on the far side of the harbour. Much of the cliff behind the wharf on that side has been removed over the years, and it is hard to discern any traces of the chutes by which ore was delivered from the road above, Lighthouse Hill, with the possible exception of the two openings referred to in the comments on the photographs on pages 16 and 17.

Continuing inland, after passing a few more houses turn left to walk beside the inner harbour basin.

Turn left at the main road, which now curves right as it passes a group of shops on the right and the Portreath Arms on the left. (This part of Portreath is known as The Square.) Immediately beyond the pub, take the side road to the left, Sunnyvale Road, which follows the course of the old tramroad, as indicated on a wooden post at the start of it: the first of many such you will see on this route.

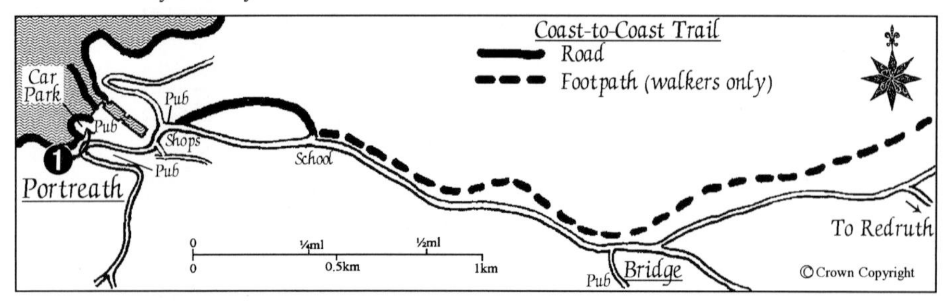

The Portreath Tramroad was the first railway to be laid above ground in Cornwall. (The first recorded use of a railway in Cornwall was in a tin mine, Happy-Union streamwork, near Pentewan on the south coast: "a very well organised underground tramroad" was seen there in 1783 by Rudolph Eric Raspe, author of the "Baron Munchausen" tales.) Work on laying the track began at Portreath in 1809, and the complete six-mile line was in use by 1819. Until then, most of the minerals had been transported over unmade roads by trains of mules and horses with panniers; a scheme to construct a canal from Portreath to the North Downs mines and Poldice was investigated in 1798, but nothing came of it. It was the great expansion of copper mining that promoted railways, because huge tonnages of copper ore had to be transported to South Wales for smelting, since Cornwall has no coal of its own, and copper smelting required much more coal than tin smelting. In addition, the mines were beginning to import larger and larger quantities of coal as the use of steam-engines increased. The Williams family, one of whose homes was and still is Scorrier House, hidden among the woods just south of the A30, were part-owners of several mines, notably North Downs and Poldice, and in partnership with the Foxes of Falmouth they had the railway built to serve these mines. The line at first served the North Downs mines, its original southern terminus being just north of Scorrier; soon a short branch south-westwards to Treskerby Mine was added, and by 1818 the main line had been extended a further two miles south-east to Crofthandy, where a storage yard was built. In 1819 two further short branch lines were planned, extending to United Mines and Wheal Maid, but there appear to be no physical remains of these, and it seems unlikely that they were ever laid.

The gauge was about three feet, and horses drew the wagons, which did not have flanged wheels but ran on flanged rails (shaped like an L in cross-section) - in other words, this was strictly a "plateway". The three-feet-long cast-iron rails were attached to two lines of granite blocks, known as setts, by means of iron spikes driven into wooden plugs. There were no wooden sleepers between the rails, as on modern railways, because there was no need for them: maintenance of an exact gauge was not important for horse-drawn wagons. Sleepers would have had to be buried, making them very

liable to rot, because they would otherwise have impeded the horses or been worn away by their hooves. Sleepered track appears to have been used for the first time no earlier than about 1825, in the north of England.

By 1855 the tramway had begun to fall into disrepair, partly because of the problems in using Portreath harbour. Long before then, most of the ore was being carried south to Devoran by the Redruth and Chasewater Railway. The exact date when the Portreath line closed is uncertain; it has been suggested that it coincided with the final closure of Poldice in 1873, but in 1885 the "West Briton" reported that it "is still used occasionally for the conveyance of coal and other good, but it is going into decay."

The Tramroad never transported paying passengers, but, amazingly, a carriage or wagon built or adapted to carry four Directors has survived. It belongs to the Trevithick Society but following restoration in Bristol during 1992 it has gone on permanent display at the Royal Cornwall Museum in Truro. According to John Stengelhofen in "Cornwall's Railway Heritage" (Twelveheads Press), this is "probably the oldest railway passenger vehicle in the world."

For a detailed account of the history of the Portreath Tramroad, see ECMH2.

Beyond a small park, Greenfield Gardens, is the back view of a row of old cottages, each with its long, narrow garden, the produce from which would have been a vital part of the domestic economy once; now most of the gardens are neglected or have been taken over by sheds, garages and parking spaces - for boats as well as cars.

Sunnyvale Road eventually rejoins the main road opposite the village school, but a few yards before that take the footpath on the left, still following the tramroad track. The line ran just above the road for quite a long stretch, and evidently a good deal of excavation into the hillside had to be done. It now makes a delightful walk (see colour photo 2) - a kind of rural cocoon just feet away from the busy road, and in May a mass of bluebells, campion and onion-scented three-cornered leeks or snowbells (*Allium triquetrum* - often just called "white bluebells"!). Along the way are a few small, dripping quarries, and in the first, where there is a public seat, is a tall iron chimney, now rusty but still showing the decorative detail typical of the Victorian age. The sound of rushing water below (and, I'm told, occasionally the smell) hints that this is a sewage outfall from Redruth to the sea, but it also probably marks the route by which the "Red River" was diverted away from Portreath beach during the 1930s. (See Round Walk 1a, page 66.) Some 60m beyond that, notice the small group of exposed setts. Several of the setts still feature the remains of the iron spikes that held down the plates.

The path tends to get muddy in places during typical Cornish weather, especially where a small stream crosses it. **A road crosses, leading to RAF Portreath, the MOD establishment at Nancekuke** (details in Walk 2), **but**

Exposed setts of the Portreath Tramroad at Cambrose (SVJ)

the tramroad path continues as before, becoming particularly attractive as it approaches the small village of Bridge, previously called Tresillian Bridge; a side path on the right there leads down to the Bridge Inn. (This is the link with Round Walk 3.) **Continue past the cottage called Hillside, then keep right, ignoring the uphill track.** Now the tramway diverges further from the road, and after a small industrial estate the surroundings become increasingly rural. Once out in the open you have a good view, the most prominent features being, from right to left, Illogan church tower; Carn Brea - the hill easily recognisable by the Basset monument and castle on its summit; Redruth sprawling over a lower hill; and the group of three engine houses belonging to Wheal Peevor. At about this point you will find probably the best-preserved group of granite setts on the entire Coast-to-Coast Trail; here we have one of the passing loops which were constructed every half-mile along the tramroad.

The next small settlement is Cambrose (the name probably means "curved thicket or copse"). **Continue ahead there, bearing left just beyond the small row of cottages, and this brings you to a minor road, with Carn View Cottage opposite.**

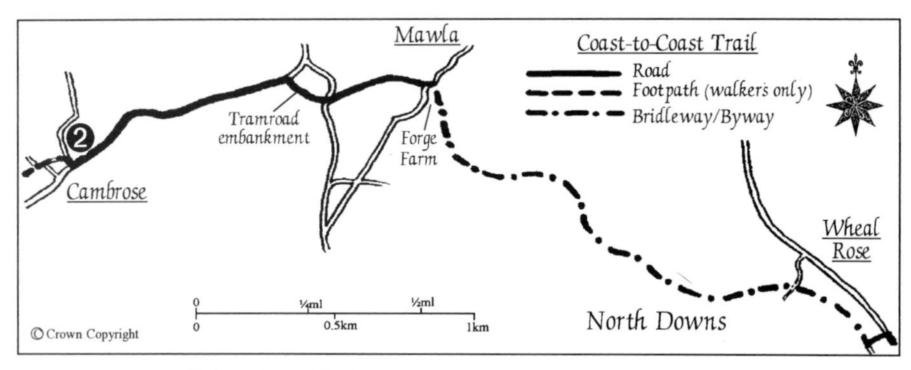

❷ At this point, turn left, uphill, to continue Round Walk 2.

To continue the Trail, turn right on the minor road, then left on the wider one below. Traffic tends to be quite fast on this stretch, so it's best to cross to the far side and walk along the verge. The road here occupies the trackbed of the tramroad at first, except where two "laybys" on the left mark the course of the "tram". **Take the first right turning - another minor road, indicated by a Portreath Tramroad sign.** Now again you are following the course of the tramroad, and here we have the one major engineering feature of the line, a substantial embankment carrying it across a little valley. An oval plaque outlining the history of this place has been fixed to one of the parapets as part of the Mineral Tramways Project. **At the first junction, cross and continue ahead.**

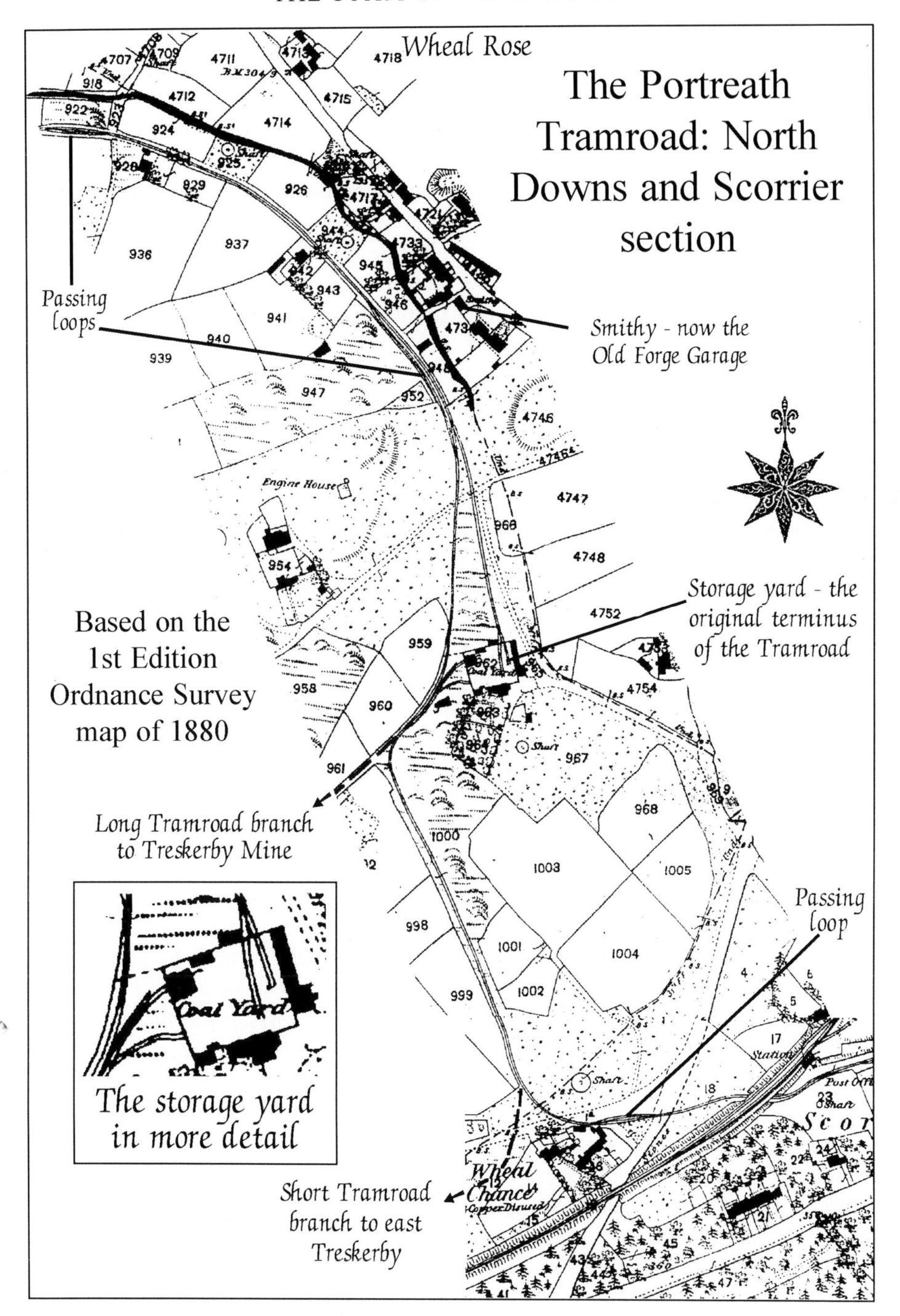
The Portreath Tramroad: North Downs and Scorrier section
Wheal Rose
Passing loops
Smithy - now the Old Forge Garage
Storage yard - the original terminus of the Tramroad
Based on the 1st Edition Ordnance Survey map of 1880
Long Tramroad branch to Treskerby Mine
Passing loop
The storage yard in more detail
Coal Yard
Short Tramroad branch to east Treskerby
Engine House
Wheal Chance
Station
Post Office

The second junction is at the hamlet of Mawla; the name possibly means "bare place", but if so, Mawla must have changed a lot since the name was given.

Here turn left along the road through Mawla for Round Walk 5 - or right for the extended version of Round Walk 6.

For the Trail, continue ahead. Here the tramroad track becomes a bridleway, rather rough but otherwise easy going. A few years ago, the first section, beside the buildings of Forge (= "dwelling") Farm, was so muddy as to be almost unwalkable for anyone not equipped with thigh-boots; great improvements have been made, but it may still be rather sticky in wet periods. This was the site of one of the "watering ponds" provided for the tramroad horses. Watch for the occasional granite sett as you go.

Ignore the signed bridleways to left and right; later you come to a gate across the track, with a signed footpath to the right and another bridleway to the left. The footpath is part of the shorter version of Round Walk 6; the bridleway may eventually be the start of a route to the well-preserved pumping-engine house at Doctor's Shaft, North Treskerby Mine, but at the time of writing rights of way for the full route had not been negotiated.

To continue along the main Trail, carry straight on along the old Tramroad. Soon you have a good view to your left of the North Treskerby stamps-engine house (commonly misnamed Wheal Rose). Also visible now are two other engine houses: the one on the skyline, with an unusually tall chimney, is at Hawke's Shaft, Killifreth Mine, and the less prominent one almost straight ahead, with a second stack close by, belonged to Hallenbeagle Mine. Notice also the good examples of old mine "burrows" (waste tips) quite close to the Trail, on the right.

Such burrows are becoming increasingly rare, for several reasons: many were taken away for reprocessing, to extract valuable minerals; others have provided roadstone or other building materials; some have been the victims of shaft-capping and landscaping schemes. Many of the burrows and other mining features of this district were obliterated when the A30 bypass road was constructed, creating pasture from land that was derelict. The importance of preserving those burrows that do remain, however, is increasingly recognised, not only by mineral collectors but also by mining historians, naturalists and all who value Cornwall's unique landscape.

These particular examples, along with several old shafts close to the Trail in this area, are relics of Great North Downs, one of the very few copper mines which rivalled Consols and United in importance during the early part of the 19th century. The principal old mines which amalgamated to form Great North Downs, such as Wheal Messer and Wheal Briggan, were roughly in a line between North Treskerby and the prominent group of three engine houses at Wheal Peevor, of

North Treskerby stamps-engine house at Wheal Rose (SVJ)

which we had a distant view earlier. Here the ground is riddled with dozens of shafts, and this is the area chosen by D.B.Barton to illustrate "the landscape of copper mining" in <u>*CMC*</u>*: see the aerial photograph on page 82. (The caption, however, is wrong: the view is looking westwards from North Treskerby, with Wheal Peevor and West Peevor engine houses in the distance.) Until 1828 these mines were mostly profitable, but then they - or at least some of them - fell out of use until a new company reopened them in 1861 under the name of Great North Downs. The venture was not a financial success, largely because of drainage problems, but work was still continuing at least until 1897. (The North Downs mines, Wheal Rose [see below] and Wheal Peevor were all linked to the great County Adit, so that water from them came to surface almost four miles away near Twelveheads in the Carnon Valley, visited later.)*

A small diversion from the tramway track will enable you to take a close look at the North Treskerby stamps-engine house. For this, take the signed Public Bridleway on the left just after passing the Wheal Rose Nursery. At the road turn left again for the engine house.

This building was never, in fact, occupied by an engine, owing to financial problems faced by the mine. It now has planning permission to convert to a dwelling. The whim-engine house that once stood nearby has gone without obvious trace.

The mine from which the settlement here takes its name, Wheal Rose, lay just to the south of North Treskerby; little if anything remains on surface now, as a result of road works and later industrial development. It was a fairly small-scale copper-mining operation whose recorded production was between 1826 and 1872. J.H.Collins, however, writing in 1912, says that it was reported as "highly profitable" as early as 1739, and Thomas Tonkin's manuscript of 1736 refers to "Wheal Rose, wherein Mr Newcomen's Fire Engine, an improvement on Mr Savery's, has been erected to draw out the water." This was one of the earliest Newcomen engines in Cornwall. By 1864, when as previously mentioned it was a part of Great North Downs Mines, the workings were "90 fathoms below adit", that is, 540 feet below the level of the County Adit. At that stage it employed 340 people. By 1870, the deepest shaft was about a thousand feet down.

Now retrace your steps to the point where you left the Tramroad track and continue as before.

Cross the minor road where there is a model of a Cornish mine in the garden of a bungalow on the left. **You now pass beside a long breeze-block shed from which a cacophony of gobbles usually emanates: it belongs to British United Turkeys. Next comes the main entrance to Rodda's creamery.** The coal yard which was the original southern terminus of the Tramroad was situated close to this point, but no trace of it appears to have survived. **Continue along the road as it curves left, passing the small Mineral Tramways car park (the start-end point for Round Walks 5 & 6). Here walkers can take a short cut by using the path from the car park up to the A30 slip road; on reaching that turn either left for the northern route or right for the southern, as explained below. Otherwise carry on along the road, turning right at the T-junction.**

❸ Here you have to choose between alternative routes to Devoran, as shown by the fact that the Mineral Tramways sign points both left (north-east), past Dale's car showrooms, and straight on (south) towards the Crossroads Hotel, Scorrier, via the nearest bridge over the A30. As the sign indicates, the southern route is for walkers only.

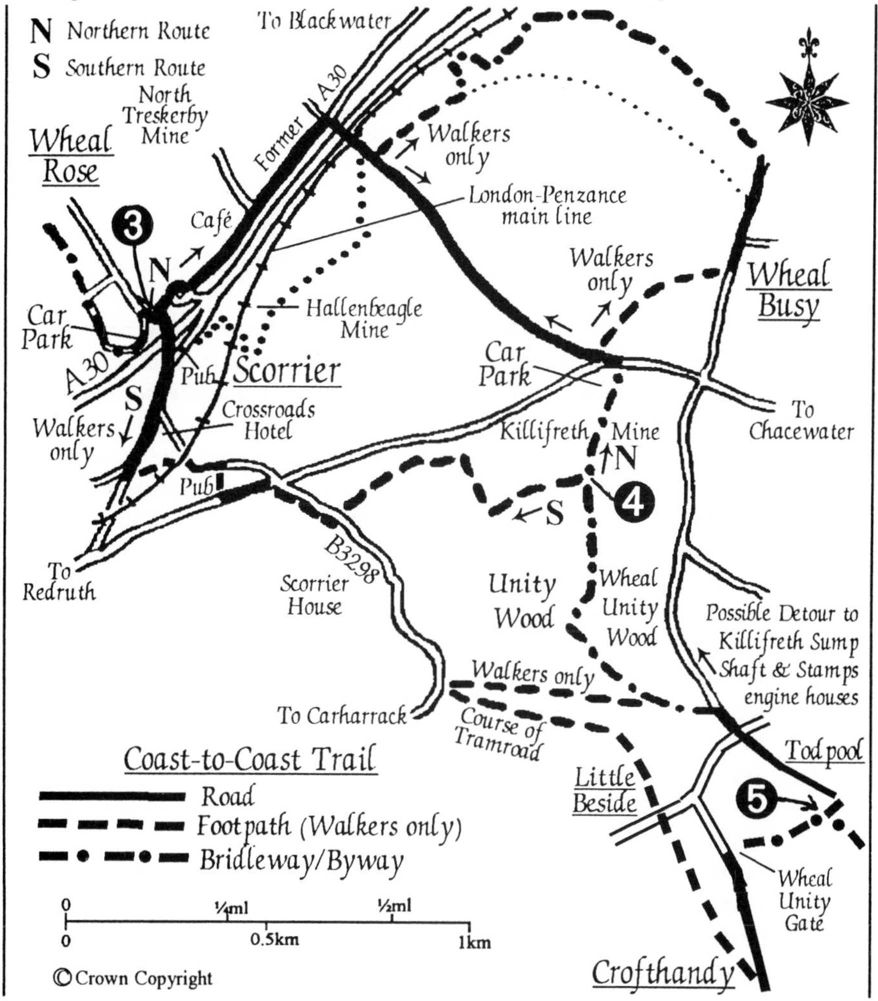

Whichever route you decide on, you may want to start by crossing the bridge if you are in need of refreshments, because Scorrier offers a good choice: two pubs, a restaurant and a general store, all within a few minutes' walk. (In the other direction, though, you would soon come to Smokey Joe's Café.)

The main factors for walkers to consider in making their choice are:
(a) If mines are your main interest, head north-east, because this gives you the opportunity to visit one of the most important and interesting of Cornish mine sites, Wheal Busy. (This is also featured on Round Walk 7, though.)
(b) The route via Scorrier shows more of the Tramroad and passes through attractive woodland, whereas the fairly lengthy stretch beside the former A30 is an unappealing feature of the alternative way - although of course the new road carries most of the traffic.

I'll start by describing the more southerly route, for walkers only, via Scorrier. If you have decided on the other direction, read on from the heading "NORTHERN ROUTE".

SOUTHERN ROUTE

Cross the bridge over the new A30. Immediately on your left here is the first of the pubs, the Plume of Feathers.

For a short detour to take a close look at the surface remains of Hallenbeagle Mine, turn left past the Plume of Feathers. On reaching the No Entry signs, fork right along a narrow country road which heads straight towards the mine buildings. At the T-junction turn right and cross the railway with due care and attention. (See colour photo 5 - when you're safely across!) The footpath continues to the right, then curves left past the entrance to a long-defunct concrete works. Turn left along the wider lane, which soon brings you to the best point for reaching the two ruined engine houses.

Like all the other mines around here, Hallenbeagle was a copper mine. J.H.Collins says it produced 30,580 tons between 1835 and 1846, and was still employing 126 people in 1865, when the main building housed a 70-inch pumping engine and there was a 22-inch engine for the whim (winding). By 1870 the workforce was down to ten. The expanse of concrete yards and the crude concrete buildings date from our own century, and are not related to mining. A steam-driven sawmill stood somewhere in this area in the 1940s.

Return the same way to resume the Trail route.

After crossing the bridge over the A30 turn right, passing both the Spar shop and the Crossroads Hotel on your left. Immediately beyond the Cornish Estate Car & Diesel Centre, take the path on the left. (The CEC&DC may change its name or disappear, but I trust that the Portreath

Hallenbeagle Mine (SVJ)

Tramroad sign, with its blue [bridleway] arrow pointing the way for you, will survive.) This path follows the old Tramroad, passing under the bridge built about 1852 by the West Cornwall Railway, as explained on the oval plaque.

The bridge at Scorrier, carrying the main line over the Tramroad track (SVJ)

At the road, continue ahead, then take the first right turning, a narrow road running beside the second pub, the Fox & Hounds. At the T-junction turn left on to the busy A3047, and then at the crossroads turn right. This is the B3298, almost equally busy, but you can walk along the Tramroad trackbed, which resembles a little rural lane running on the right-hand side of the road. On the right is the wooded park surrounding Scorrier House, still one of the homes of the descendants of John Williams, who played a leading part in the creation of the Tramroad.

Unfortunately it is not possible to continue much further along this part of the trackbed, because it soon runs through the private estate. When you come to the Killifreth signpost, therefore, climb the wooden steps, cross the road with care and take the path through the woods. After some 15m the path crosses a leat or drainage channel. The pipe it runs through at this point is worth a close look: it bears all the hallmarks of a section of a rising main from a mine's engine shaft. (Colour photograph 14.) **The path (colour photo 8) winds its way among old shafts protected with "Clwyd caps".** *These galvanised welded-steel cages - one of which is shown in colour photo 12 - have been shown to offer less security than had been expected, and their use is now being superseded.*

Pass through the rusty gate. Now the path runs near the right edge of the wood at first, then swings over to the left edge. At the choice of ways go right. Here you have to climb over or duck through a fence of three metal bars. The path continues along the left side of the wood, with the fine engine house at Hawke's Shaft, Killifreth Mine, in clear view. **Steps lead down to a wide track; turn left on that, and walk on till you reach a stile. This is where the two routes of the Coast-to-Coast Trail converge; after crossing the stile turn left for a short and very worthwhile diversion to the engine house, briefly described on page 38, or right to continue towards Devoran. Pick up the directions at point 4.**

NORTHERN ROUTE

Turn left along the slip road, following the signs Blackwater and A30 Bodmin, past Dale's, and continue along the tarmacked sidewalk beside the old A30. You get a good view of engine houses on both sides: that at Doctor's Shaft, North Treskerby Mine to the left, and the two - or rather, one-and-a-bit, at Hallenbeagle Mine to the right. Soon you pass Smokey Joe's Café, open from 7 am to at least 8 pm every day except Sunday, when it opens at 10 am; you can get anything from a cup of coffee to a full-scale meal. **Continue beside the road till you reach Mitchell & Webber, where a black waymark arrow directs you to cross the road bridge on your right, which spans both the new A30 and the main London-Penzance railway.**

> **For a short detour to visit Hallenbeagle Mine (walkers only), take the surfaced but fairly rough lane on the right a few metres beyond the bridge.** After rather less than 500m you will reach the remains of the two engine houses, a famous landmark because of their closeness to the main road and line. *(See above - page 28 - for a brief note about the mine.)*
>
> **From the engine houses, return the way you came, turning right at the T-junction.**

Those on foot now have the option of visiting the main site of Wheal Busy. Directions for this route are given following the next three paragraphs.

Horse-riders and cyclists have to continue south-east along this pleasant, quiet country road, which gives good views to the right towards Scorrier Woods, with the three engine houses of Wheal Peevor on the skyline and a glimpse of the monument on Carn Brea. After about half a mile you will pass, on your right, what remains of the pumping-engine house at Black Dog Shaft, Wheal Busy. *Little, in fact, does remain apart from the rather impressive bob wall, because the engine house was the victim of a demolition exercise by the US troops stationed in this area during the run-up to D-Day. The date stone refers to the year 1872, when an abortive attempt was made to rework Wheal Busy: a 76-inch engine was bought for installation in this engine house, but in fact it merely lay on the ground beside it until eventually it was scrapped. A 70-inch engine had been set to work pumping from this shaft in 1858; whether the engine house was completely rebuilt in 1872 is not known.*

Continue to the main Chacewater-Redruth road; there turn left for a few yards till you see a lane on the other side, at the start of which a stone plaque and a signpost announce Killifreth Engine House. Cross with great care - the traffic tends to be speedy - and go along the lane.

Now pick up the directions at line 9 on page 37.

Alternative route via Wheal Busy (walkers only at the time of writing, but multi-use status may be negotiated): Take the wide track or lane on the left which begins some 20m beyond the one on the right leading to Hallenbeagle. Notice, as you go, the old mine burrows and shafts beside the track, mainly on the right, and also the view. Almost straight ahead on the skyline is Mithian Church, built in 1846 at Three Burrows, a very long way from Mithian village. Further left is the derelict headgear of Wheal Concord.

In 1980 a company named Wheal Concord Ltd. was formed to explore for tin on the site of an old mine called Wheal Concord, west of Blackwater. By 1982, 21,000 tonnes had been raised by the workforce of forty. Because of problems over processing the operation ceased in 1982, but the workings were kept in viable condition, and in 1984 "development and exploration" was begun again by a different company. The sudden fall in tin prices in 1985 brought the operation to an end; the wooden headgear was still in place at the time of writing, but plans exist to remove it to King Edward Mine to be erected at Engine Shaft. (See Volume 1 of this guide, and "Exploring Cornish Mines" Volume 2.) The modern "Count House" at Blackwater became a restaurant but is now closed again.

Further left again you can see St Agnes Beacon.

The bob wall at Black Dog Shaft, Wheal Busy (SVJ)

The lane is well surfaced as far as Boscawen Farm; when you reach the farmyard entrance *(notice the farm buildings, by the way, which originated as the headquarters complex of Boscawen Mine, including the count house)*, **take the track on the left, which heads at first for the railway but soon makes a wide curve to the right**, passing among mine burrows. Following a left bend there are more burrows, topped with Clwyd caps over shaft mouths. *This area was worked by Boscawen Mine, a copper producer at various periods between the 1790s and the 1860s. During some of that time it was linked with other nearby mines, including Hallenbeagle and Wheal Busy. Boscawen, of course, is the family name of the landowner, Lord Falmouth.* Now you have a closer view of Wheal Concord, with Blackwater village also prominent. The old A30 passes through it, but much more noticeable from here, to the ears as well as the eyes, is the road's modern successor. **Keep to the main track ahead, which soon takes you past the Wheal Busy Bible Christian Chapel (1863). At the road, where the phone box is, turn right, passing Leigham Farmhouse and Duckworths Car Spares.**

For a very short detour, take the first turning on the left to inspect two of the most important surviving buildings of Wheal Busy, the smithy building and the engine house at Engine Shaft.

Wheal Busy - known in its early days as Chacewater or Chasewater Mine - is one of the oldest visited on walks in this book; just how old is uncertain, but we know it was active as a tin mine in the 16th century, and was producing copper in 1724. In 1823 two neighbouring mines, Eastern Works and Metal Work, amalgamated with Wheal Busy, and the name Wheal Busy was then applied to the group as a whole. Its prosperity as a copper mine was greatest from about 1815-70; from about 1857 the production of tin again became important. A severe fall in prices on the metal markets caused the mine to be abandoned in 1873, only months after a huge sum had been spent re-equipping it. During the last few years of the 19th century, and again from 1907 off-and-on till 1924, the sett was worked mainly for arsenic.

The mine played a leading role in the history of the Cornish beam engine: Joseph Hornblower erected a very early Newcomen atmospheric engine here in about 1725; John Smeaton erected a 75-inch "improved" atmospheric engine at Wheal Busy in 1775; and in 1777 it became the first Cornish mine to install an engine designed by James Watt. In 1856 an impressive house was built for an 85-inch pumping engine; in 1872 it was modified to take an even larger engine (90-inch); finally in 1909 a new 85-inch engine was put into it. New to Wheal Busy, that is. In fact, like so many of the great beam engines, it had been moved from place to place. This one, built by the Perran Foundry in about 1852, had previously worked near Par, and then at a coal mine in South Wales. At Wheal Busy it was put to work intermittently until 1924,

Wheal Busy, Engine Shaft (SVJ)

then lay idle for 28 years before being broken up for scrap. Photograph 76 in MC2 gives, among other things, a vivid impression of just how large an 85-inch-diameter cylinder was. The shed attached to the engine house was built to house three Lancashire boilers. The nearby old building was the smithy, fitting shop, miners' dry and shaftman's office; notice the impressive cast-iron lintels, made at Perran Foundry in 1872 when the abortive expansion and refurbishment of the workings took place; but the main part of the building itself is much older.

The huge burrows and surrounding land are seen by their owner, Lord Falmouth, as ripe for "development", and early in 1989 ambitious plans were published for a new town here, complete with international airport. The proposals were, to put it mildly, given a mixed reception. The Wheal Busy Area Residents' Association conducted a spirited campaign against them, and in 1990 a study commissioned by Carrick District and Cornwall County Councils rejected the airport scheme. In 1994 a new set of proposals was announced for a £3m golf and leisure complex with 80 holiday lodges, 10 timeshare homes, staff houses and service buildings. Whether this will materialise remains to be seen. Clearly the historic Wheal Busy site has been under severe threat, but I am told that the Tregothnan Estate has in recent times shown increasing concern to preserve what is important there.

A brief account of the flora and fauna of the Wheal Busy site is included in Appendix 1. For more detail about the mine, together with a suggested tour of the surface remains, see Walk 2 in ECM2.

Return to the road, either the same way or by using the public footpath on the south side of the smithy building.

A further short diversion along the road to take a close look at the Wheal Busy arsenic stack, labyrinth and calciner is recommended. The "lambreth" or labyrinth flue links the tall stack with a Brunton calciner, parts of the mechanism of which can still be seen. These features date from the period immediately following the re-opening of Wheal Busy in 1907. As you return past the stack, notice on your right the remains of the mine's 20th-century mill. This included a battery of Californian stamps, which were fixed to the row of vertical timber piles.

To continue the walk, take the wide track which starts opposite the point where the public footpath running south of the smithy building joins the road - that is, the first left turning as you return from the arsenic stack. A little way along this track, continue ahead, following the yellow waymarker, and then as you near the bungalow ahead take the short track on the left to the main road (but see the note* below).

Brunton calciner at Wheal Busy. Smithy and Engine Shaft in the distance. (SVJ)

Cross the road with great care and go along the lane almost opposite, signed to "Killifreth Engine House".

***Strictly speaking, the short track just mentioned is not a right of way; I'd be amazed if anyone ever challenged your right to use it, but to avoid any risk of that, continue ahead till you reach another road. This way has the advantage of taking you quite close to the ruins of the Black Dog Shaft engine house. (See page 32.) Turn left on the road, then left again at the main road and cross to the lane mentioned above.**

Continue past the car park (the start / end point for Round Walk 7) and the gate.

Ahead of you now is the pumping-engine house at Hawke's Shaft, with its extra-tall stack, and away to the left are two other substantially complete engine houses that belonged to Killifreth Mine: another pumping-engine house at Old Sump Shaft and the stamps-engine house beyond, with arsenic stack to the right. (These are not on the Coast-to-Coast Trail route, but if you wish to take a close look at them you can easily do so from the minor road running south towards Todpool, as shown on the map. A possible diversion to visit them is suggested on page 40. Full details are given in ECM2.) Also to the left, but hard to pick out even though it is quite close, is the ivy-covered surviving wing wall of the mine's whim-engine house. Like the building at Black Dog Shaft, Wheal Busy, this was the victim of a demolition exercise by American troops shortly before D-Day. (The bob wall of the Black Dog Shaft engine house is also visible from here, over to the right; from here it looks rather like a pair of horns. As I have mentioned, some information about it is given on page 32.)

Walk on towards Hawke's Shaft, passing as you go a semi-ruined concrete farm building on the left, which started life as the count house and office of the mine's last manager.

Killifreth Mine produced copper between 1826 and 1860 and tin after 1864. The engine house at Richards' Shaft, later named Hawke's Shaft, was built in 1891 for an 80-inch engine. A lot of tin remained to be worked in 1896 when a dispute between owners and shareholders arose over plans to raise capital for new machinery; this, along with the breaking of the bob of this engine, led to closure in 1897, and the engine was scrapped. For a time after this the mine was used by the Truro Mining School. It reopened in 1912, and the following year an 85-inch engine was installed in the same house. Four boilers were required to serve it plus the air compressor and horizontal whim engine whose concrete loadings stand just west of the engine house, and in order to create enough draught for the boilers the brick-built upper section of the stack was doubled in height. Notice the balance pit beside the shaft, whose concrete cap incorporates an early form of "bat castle".

Arsenic was produced in the mine's latter years: the Killifreth company acquired the Wheal Busy sett for this purpose in 1923. Killifreth finally closed in February 1928, although there is still reported to be plenty of tin underground.

In 1987-8, restoration of the Hawke's Shaft engine house was carried out as part of Carrick's Operation Engine House in conjunction with the MSC's Community Programme. St Day bricks were obtained from the arsenic works at Bissoe, visited later on the Trail. Following the successful completion of the Hawke's Shaft restoration, the same team went on to restore the engine house at Old Sump Shaft; hopes of adding the stamps engine house to the list were dashed by the unwillingness of the owner to allow the work to be done.

Continue along the path that zigzags around the engine house and the base of the horizontal whim. A little further on, the stile on the right is the point at which what I have called the Southern Route converges with the Northern one.

❹ The path heads due south. Just left of straight ahead are the two engine houses at Magor's Shaft, Wheal Unity Wood, and cutting the skyline in the same direction are the most obvious remaining buildings of one of the world's greatest copper mines - really a grouping of older mines, hence its name, Consolidated Mines, usually shortened to Consols (visited on Round Walks 9 and/or 10). You can see the ruins of engine houses and also the base of the clock tower, wrongly shown on some OS maps as a chimney.

A metal farm gate admits you to Unity Wood.

The pumping-engine house at Hawke's Shaft, Killifreth Mine (SVJ)

This consists mainly of sessile oak coppice, some of which is thought to be ancient woodland, with a well developed ground flora. It was originally called Killifreth ("speckled grove") or Killefreth Wood. Its present name derives from the fact that an important mine called Wheal Unity, whose underground workings were further south near Todpool, had its dressing floors in the valley immediately below the wood. Everywhere in the wood there is evidence of mining activity, with numerous shafts, openwork pits and trenches ("coffin works"), leats and plats. What makes it very unusual if not unique in Cornwall is that the wood was here long before the mining began, rather than having grown up around abandoned workings. The earliest substantial workings in the wood are believed to date from the 15th century, and the most recent from the 1920s.

The small shed on the right was the foreman's office during the last period of working, when this northern section of the wood was part of the Killifreth Mine sett; on the left is the base of a steam hoist which hauled from the nearby Skip Shaft at that time. Most of the other shafts you will see were created by Wheal Unity Wood during the 19th century, although some may be relics of Wheal Union, which worked the upper part of the wood during the last two decades of the 18th century.

Keep to the main path ahead, passing close to many gaping shafts with Clwyd caps perching atop. (See colour photograph 12.) **Where the path divides, go left, following the blue arrow on the wooden signpost.** (Note: the right-hand path leads, by fairly tortuous means, to some particularly interesting mining remains, notably Williams' Shaft of Wheal Unity Wood. For details see ECM2 p68-71. An easier route to Williams' Shaft is described in Round Walk 8.)

At the next junction, where you emerge into a clearing and there is a walled shaft ahead (Oate's Shaft), turn left. Keep to the widest track, and continue downhill, with the two engine houses quite close now, to your left.

On reaching the main track at the bottom walkers again have a choice of northern and southern sections of the Mineral Tramways spine route. But first I suggest the following diversion.

> **By turning left, then immediately left again, on a narrower, uphill path, you can make a short diversion to inspect the nearby engine houses, and then if you wish extend the diversion in order to visit the Old Sump Shaft and stamps engine houses of Killifreth Mine.** The first and larger of the engine houses close by stands beside Magor's Shaft and was built in 1872 to house a 70-inch pumping engine. Much of the balance-bob mounting has survived, as have some long iron stays projecting from the building. These were to support the headframe over the shaft. The smaller building was built at the same time and contained a 20-inch engine which drove stamps

The two engine houses at Magor's Shaft, Wheal Unity Wood (SVJ)

and also wound - not from Magor's Shaft, but from Trefusis Shaft, over 200 yards away, down in the valley!

The earliest production figures for Wheal Unity Wood date from 1815. It was a productive copper mine till 1843 and employed 200 people, but then seems to have fizzled out pending a reworking of the western part of the sett for tin in the 1870s. It closed in 1880, but reopened as Tolgullow United from 1882 to 1903, and one last attempt to work the northern part of it was made in 1912, in conjunction with Killifreth Mine. (The engine houses are sometimes referred to as Wheal Bush, a name that harks back to tin bounds that existed here during the 16th and 17th centuries.)

At the road, turning left will bring you to the Old Sump and stamps engine houses of Killifreth Mine, as mentioned earlier. After a little less than half a mile a short track on the left side of the road leads to Old Sump or Engine Shaft. *The engine had a 50-inch cylinder. The bob wall of the building was reduced in height for safety reasons when the consolidation work was done.* The stamps-engine house stands beside the road a little further north. *A 32-inch engine here drove a battery of 64 heads of stamps. If anything remains of the mine's dressing floors, on the slope below, it is now completely obscured, from this angle at least, by thick vegetation. On the same side of the road, near the corner with the main Chacewater-Redruth road, is the Killifreth arsenic-calciner stack, now in urgent need of stabilisation.* **Return the same way, past the Wheal Unity Wood buildings and back down to the main track in the valley.**

SOUTHERN ROUTE (for walkers only)

Turn right on the main track for the southerly option, which is the less direct of the two but includes one of the best-preserved sections of the Portreath Tramway. Most of this route is included in Round Walk 8, where it is taken in the opposite direction, and information about points of interest is given there, so if you have done or intend to do that walk you may prefer to ignore this option now.

The route, briefly, is as follows: Go almost to the end of the track running below Unity Wood, but rather than continuing to the road turn sharp-left, via a narrow gap, to walk back along the valley on the opposite side. This is where you join the course of the Tramroad. Keep beside the hedge on your right, crossing a stile; frequent granite setts mark the way. Just before you reach the road at Little Beside, a prominent siding or loop diverges to the right, but continue ahead, passing close to a short row of cottages on your left and crossing the road to walk along the narrow path opposite, between a stone hedge and a wire fence. After a few steps up, the path - still following the course of the Tramroad - passes to the left of one of the old buildings of the Unity

Fuse Works, close to which is a shaft belonging to Wheal Unity. Cross the hump and continue ahead along a wider track where you will notice several groups of setts. Go straight on at the crosstracks. The Tramroad reached its southern terminus, the Crofthandy yard, on your right at the point where the track curves left to meet another road. Turn left on the road, and take the first turning right after the right-hand bend. This brings you to the Wheal Unity Gate entrance to the Poldice Valley; from there, follow the green waymarks on the Portreath Tramroad Trail posts, passing the ruined arsenic works buildings on your right. The point at which you turn right to continue down the valley, immediately before you would reach the Todpool Gate sign, is where the southern and northern routes converge again. Pick up the directions at point 5 (ignoring, of course, the instruction there to turn left).

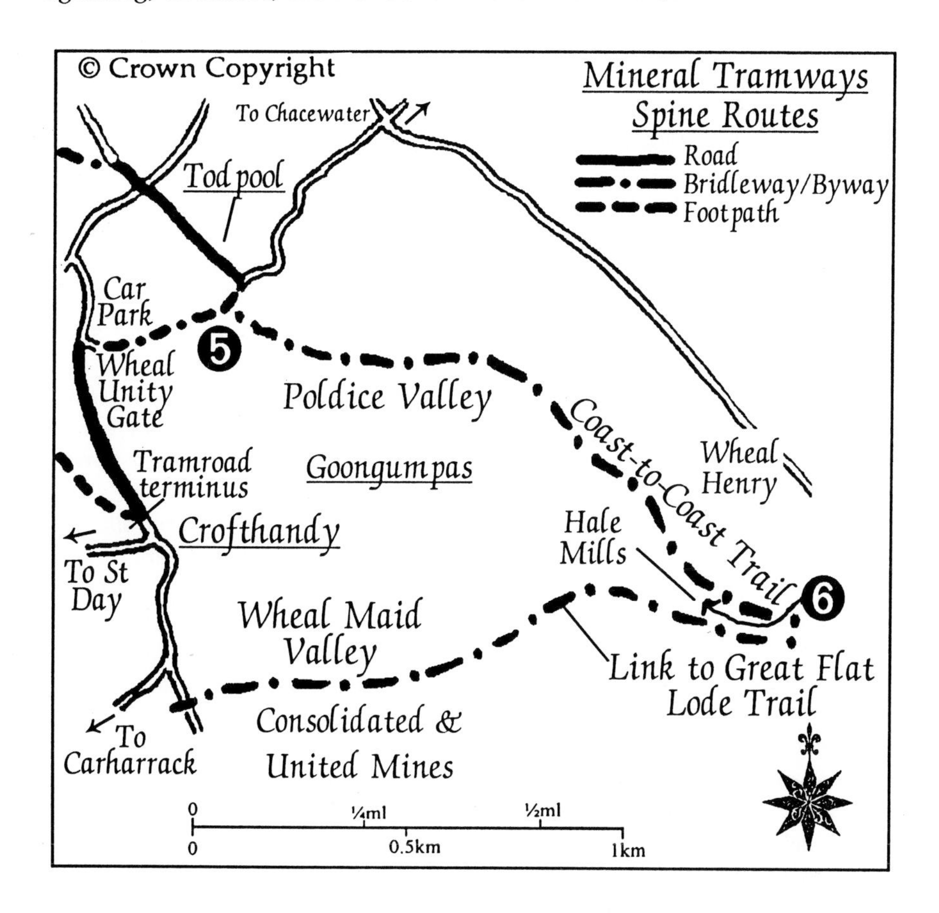

NORTHERN ROUTE (multi-use)

Turn left on the main track in the valley, which soon runs beside several buildings and brings you to a road. To the right now you can see the abandoned former parish church of St Day. For details see Round Walk 9.

Go straight on down the road, and at the crossroads continue ahead, through the hamlet of Todpool, with its attractive cottages, many if not all of which must once have been the homes of miners. The house numbered 8, just before the left corner, was formerly a pub.

The first syllable of "Todpool" derives from a personal name: "Tods House" is shown here on a 17th-century map. Presumably the hamlet was created entirely by the mines: Creegbrawse ("great barrow") was on its doorstep, as well as Poldice and Wheal Unity. Besides the pub, Todpool once had a Methodist Chapel, and more miners' cottages than we now see.

Where the road bends left, take the track on the right, passing the Todpool Gate sign. Ahead now are the ruins of the Poldice arsenic works, an interesting place to explore, like so much else in what has come to be known as the Poldice Valley. (Walk 8 takes a closer look at parts of it.)

The start of a well-known but rather enigmatic rhyme shows how the word is usually pronounced:

At Poldice the men are like mice,
The tin is very plenty.
Captain Teague is one of Breage
And he'll give ten for twenty.

(The meaning, I think, is that Poldice mine has a huge workforce because it's so rich in tin. The mine overseer is a Breage man, and he'll pay tributers the value of 10 cwt of white [i.e. smelted] tin for every 20 cwt of concentrate [tin oxide or black tin] - a good price. Since some of Cornwall's oldest deep mines were in Breage parish, near Helston, a miner from those parts would be expected to know the true value of a parcel of concentrate.)

Poldice was one of the greatest and deepest early tin mines in Cornwall. John Norden, towards the end of the 16th century, listed "Poldeese, nere Truroe" (evidently the mine's name was said differently then) among the "chiefe tynn mynes in Kirier hundred". It was described as "an ancient tin work" - and a very profitable one - in 1681, and another writer (Hals) four years later called it "that unparalleled and inexhaustible tin work ... which for about forty years space hath employed yearly from eight hundred to a thousand men and boys." Engines - presumably water-powered - were already at work draining the levels by the 1720s, and there are records of Newcomen steam engines on the site in the 1780s and four Boulton & Watt engines in the following decade. Even with all this steam power and the help of the County Adit (see pages 52-3), the problem of keeping the workings dry remained acute. It was only during the 1780s that copper began to be more important than tin at Poldice, and although it produced a very large amount of copper during the next hundred years, as a copper mine it never quite recaptured the pre-eminence it once had. In 1852 it became part of St Day United Mines; that closed in about 1867, but had another active period under the name Poldice Mines from 1870 to 1873. Hardly anything remains now of the many large engine houses; what has survived substantially intact is the arsenic works which operated intermittently between about 1870 and 1929, in association with three different mines. Inevitably, therefore, its main building has been much altered over the years; many details are now hard or impossible to interpret, and the date inscribed on it (March 25th 1897) has not, to my knowledge, been tied in with any specific event. The remains of two calciners can, however, be identified in the building, from which emerges the labyrinth flue, known in Cornwall as a "lambreth", which runs up to the stack (colour photograph 15). (A brief account of the Cornish arsenic industry and the method by which arsenic was produced is given in the Glossary of this book under the heading Burning House; for much more detail, see ECMH2; and for fuller information about this works in particular and the later history of the site see PV pages 8-10 and Round Walk 8 in this book.)

The Poldice arsenic works (SVJ)

The Wheal Unity Gate car park, the start / end point for Round Walks 8 and 9, lies to the west of the arsenic works, and is signposted from here.

❺ But to continue the Coast-to-Coast Trail, turn left immediately after passing the Todpool Gate sign, joining a fairly level track which runs along the left side of the valley.

The parallel track in the valley bottom, just down to your right, runs beside a line of tall numbered granite posts marking the boundary between the parishes of Gwennap and Chacewater, the latter having been created from parts of Kea and Kenwyn parishes in 1837.

The Poldice and neighbouring Wheal Maid valleys are often called a "moon landscape", and the phrase is perhaps nowhere more apt than in this area just east of the arsenic works, dominated by the whitish dumps known locally as "The Sands" (colour photograph 16). (The plan is to cover and vegetate these dumps to protect the environment from the dust that blows off them.) They are a legacy of the period (1928-30) when material from Park-an-Chy mine, between St Day and Redruth, was processed at the mill here. The many walled-round mouths of shafts provide the craters to complete the lunar scene. The valley is a happy hunting ground for collectors of minerals, because unwanted material brought to the surface by mining operations is scattered everywhere, much of it still in the form of spoil heaps (known in Cornwall as burrows); in particular, stone excavated during the sinking of shafts is often piled around their mouths. An old burrow which has been left undisturbed can be a valuable source of information about the mine, its methods, and the geology of the "sett" it was working; but the Poldice valley was a busy centre of industrial activity for centuries, and most of the dumps have been shifted around, or added to at various times from various sources, or reprocessed for the minerals still in them, or quarried for hardcore and other building materials. Such disturbances of the dumps tend to bring toxic minerals to the surface, inhibiting plant-growth, but when they are left untouched most of them are colonised by heather, gorse and other plants including escapes from gardens, and they become (as the Mineral Tramways Project report puts it) "rare and unusual habitats" as well as areas with a special beauty of their own.

There are a great many paths and tracks in the valley, and you are presented with an obvious choice of ways at the point where the track you have been coming along descends to the valley floor near a boundary post with obliterated number - apparently 53. Here a side path, used in Round Walk 10, goes up the hillside to the left, another crosses the valley bottom to the right, and the main one ahead splits: one branch follows the line of boundary posts and descends to what looks rather like the bed of a small lake, while the other climbs slightly. The signposted Redruth & Chasewater Trail uses this last one.

Before you proceed along it, though, notice the retaining walls, ruined buildings and massive concrete bases a little way up the slope on the south (far) side. So much use has been made of this area for industrial purposes at different periods that identifying such remains is often difficult, but stamping and ore-

dressing machinery was in use here from 1919 to 1925 as part of the operation shown in the photograph on page 106 (Round Walk 8). The Poldice branch of the Redruth & Chasewater Railway seems to have come to an end at or close to this point (part of the cutting through which it ran can be seen on Round Walk 10), and some of the masonry structures may date back to the short period when that was in use - though there is some doubt whether it ever was.

The valley bottom here (that is, to the right of the main track you have been coming along) was formerly dammed to form a reservoir known as Bissa Pool. Before the mid-18th century, when the County Adit was driven, many of the local mines drained into the Poldice and other nearby valleys, providing an energy source for numerous waterwheels. Reservoirs such as this would have served to power the wheels in dry periods, as well as probably providing a drinking-place for farm stock. "Bissa", like "Bissoe", means "birch trees"; the double-s in both is pronounced as z.

Continue now on the upper track, a short way along which is a wooden signpost with a red (byway) arrow pointing the way you are going. Coming into view now is the ivy-covered ruin of what has been claimed as possibly the oldest Cornish engine house still standing, a relic of Wheal Henry, prominent on the slope to your left.

The antiquity of this building is suggested in part by the fact that it is constructed throughout in the sedimentary rock known as killas, without granite quoins, iron tie-rods or other strengthening devices. It has been suggested (in EHA) that it dates from 1800-20 and contained a rotative steam engine, probably about 24-inch cylinder, which pumped from a shaft close to the valley floor by means of flat-rods. Wheal Henry was a tin-and-copper mine of which few reliable records seem to have survived. Despite the name of its main shaft, "Goodluck" (another name, like Wheal Bush, that derives from an old tin-bound), it seems never to have been very successful. A footpath runs up the hill below the engine house, but it is badly overgrown and hard to find. It never did join up with the track through the valley according to old maps.

Also visible from this part of the route - on the skyline straight ahead - is the Cusvey Mine pumping-engine house, about which information is given in Round Walk 10.

Keep to the main track, which gradually descends to reach the valley-bottom at Hale Mills, where the Wheal Maid and Poldice valleys converge.

Hale Mills (sometimes spelt "Hayle" or "Hail"), otherwise known as Middle Mills, appears to have been a corn or grist mill; the plural indicates that it employed more than one millstone. "Hale" probably derives from the old Cornish word for a marshy area or watermeadow, in which case the name is still very apt. The stream which powered the mills flows from the Wheal Maid valley via a narrow tunnel through the embankment built by the Redruth & Chasewater

Railway for its Poldice branch; it is now culverted under the track and eventually joins the Carnon River near Twelveheads. The bright orange deposit it leaves consists of ochre, a mixture of fine clay and iron oxide. The collection of ochre for use principally in the manufacture of paint was one of the many industries which once thrived in the Carnon Valley.

❻ A short detour here is worthwhile: turn sharp-right and go through the masonry-lined tunnel in the railway embankment to see one of the dams built across the Wheal Maid valley to create a tailings reservoir for Mount Wellington Mine. (This area is explored on Round Walks 9 and 10, and more detail is given on pages 133-5 and 153.)

The tunnels under the railway embankment at Hayle Mills

To continue towards Devoran, go on down the main track, with the ochre-stained stream and occasional walled-round shafts to your left.

Soon some of the buildings of Mount Wellington Mine come into view up on the right (unless by the time you read this they have been demolished), and on the left is the village of Twelveheads.

❼ **On reaching the road, for the official Trail route continue ahead as far as the roadside parking space on the left** which is the start / end point for Round Walks 10 and 11. **From the car park take the path on the left which runs roughly parallel with the road and brings you to the embankment which carried the Redruth & Chasewater Railway across the Carnon Valley. To take a look at the mouth of the County Adit, as described on pages 52-3, you first need to go a few yards to the right; but to continue the Trail turn left on that, crossing the stream, and continue reading from the start of the note about the railway, page 51.**

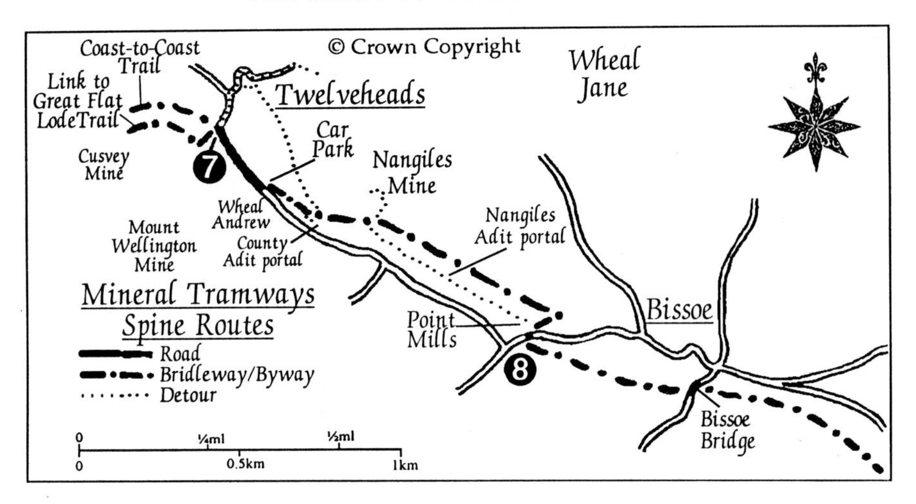

But for a worthwhile detour into Twelveheads, suitable for cyclists and riders as well as those on foot, turn left when you first reach the road.

The village is at the confluence of at least two streams. There were corn mills here, but evidently some of the available water power was used to drive Cornish stamps. The name, Twelveheads, implies that the battery of stamps here was unusually large. By the 19th century, water-powered stamps commonly had twelve heads, as illustrated for example in the Perran Foundry catalogue, but the village was called Twelveheads by the end of the 16th century, when stamps normally had three, four or six heads.

Twelveheads was the birthplace of one of the most celebrated Cornishmen, Billy Bray, and you may be interested in making the following short extension of this detour to see a couple of buildings associated with him. (If not, to return as directly as possible to the Trail route skip the next four paragraphs, picking up the directions at, "If you are on foot...".)

For the "Billy Bray extension", go on along the road past the Methodist Church at the centre of the village. Ignore the left-hand turning running up the valley to Chacewater; continue on the uphill road for about a quarter of a mile. Among some farm buildings on the left is a very tumbledown one which I shall mention again soon.

Take the first turning on the right, a track leading towards quite a large chapel. When you reach it you will see that it bears the inscription, "Bethel Methodist Chapel 1842"; adjoining it is the "Old Schoolhouse", and it is that rather than the main building which is what survives of the first chapel built by Billy Bray.

Twelveheads' most famous son, Billy Bray (1794-1868), who as a young man was a "drunken and lascivious miner" (his own words), became an inspiring evangelistic preacher of the Bible Christian Methodist Church. "Had he lived 1,000 years previously," wrote Charles Henderson in CCG, Billy Bray "would have a church and holy well called after him." One day my wife and I visited Twelveheads purposely to try to find his birthplace, half-expecting to see a commemorative plaque on a tiny cottage, but with no success. When we came to Bethel we were shown around by Alec Wiles, who uses the old chapel building as a studio for his paintings and sculptures, and he told us that Billy was born in the tumbledown shack I have referred to. (A drawing of it as it was, or may have been, is on page 66 of GIR.) Billy's own account of the building of his first chapel is given in BBKS: "The Lord put it in my mind to build a chapel. My mother had a small place; and by one of her little fields there was a small piece of common. The Lord opened my mother's heart to give a spot on that piece of common to build on. ... I began work as the dear Lord told me, and to take away the hedge of my mother's field, and to dig out the foundation of a chapel ... which was to be called Bethel." He goes on to tell of the opposition which came, not only from "the wicked" but even from some of his own sect; and of his struggles to raise enough funds to carry on. "When my little maid (daughter) was taken ill, Satan tempted me that it would take seven pounds to cover the chapel, and I had but two pounds, and our little one would die, and it would take one pound to bury her, and then I should have but one pound left." But he defied the devil, completed the work, and his daughter went on to bear ten children of her own. He tells how the original little chapel became a schoolhouse when a larger one was built beside it: "No wonder that the devil was so against me while I was building the old Bethel, and put his servants to hinder me, for I have seen at one time fifty down asking for mercy, and mercy they had." Later he built two other chapels, at Kerley Downs west of Baldhu Church, and "Great Deliverance", the largest of the three, at Carharrack. The only one still in use for worship is the so-called "Three Eyes" chapel at Kerley Downs; for some information about that and Billy's grave, see the note on Baldhu in Round Walk 12, pages 169-70.

Return the same way to resume your progress along the Trail; don't go back as far as the Methodist Church, but turn left on the signed Public Byway where the road bends right before reaching the bridge. Now pick up the directions at the top line of the next page.

If you are on foot you can take the narrow path that runs beside the Methodist Church and crosses one of the streams, soon bringing you to the tarmacked lane mentioned below; turn right on that. Cyclists and horse-riders need to continue on the road, turning right at the T-junction; ignore the left turning to Chacewater: cross the bridge, and then when the road curves left go straight on along the

signed Public Byway. Just beyond the house (Glenmoor) go right and immediately left, joining a tarmacked lane. Where this turns left, at the signs to Hillside and Wheal Widden, keep straight on along the path. This soon gives you a good view of the bridge built by the Redruth & Chasewater Railway to take its line, here running along an embankment, across the stream. The concrete structures on the left are part of a bypass section of the County Adit built in recent years; you will probably be able to hear the sound of rushing water below.

Just past these, the path meets a wider track, which is the former trackbed of the Redruth & Chasewater Railway. Turn left on that to resume the Coast-to-Coast Trail.

The Redruth & Chasewater was Cornwall's first railway to use wrought-iron rails and to employ wagons with flanged wheels. Like the Portreath Tramroad, it used granite setts rather than sleepers, but in this case the rails were attached to the setts by means of "chairs": see colour photograph 2 in "Tramway Trails" Volume 1 and the old photograph on page 7 in this book.

When mines in the southern part of Gwennap parish, such as Consols, began to be very productive, in the early 1820s, an efficient link with a south coast port became increasingly necessary, for the export of copper ore to South Wales for smelting (Cornwall having no coal deposits), and the import of coal. (During one year in the 1830s, Consols and United Mines alone consumed 15,000 tons of coal.)

As early as 1808, a plan had been put forward for a canal from Bissoe to Devoran, but the success of the Portreath Tramway during the next decade pointed the way to a better solution. In 1819, the Norwich-born businessman John Taylor (1779-1863) acquired the lease of the group of old mines known as Consols, and in 1824 his London-based company received Royal Assent to an Act of Parliament permitting the building of what was then called "The Redruth Railway". Work began at once, the engineer in charge being the Cornishman William Brunton. The new line, of four-foot gauge, was officially opened in January 1826, and by 1827 it extended from Pednandrea Mine, Redruth, to Point, a mile beyond Devoran on Restronguet Creek, with an important branch serving Wheal Buller and adjacent mines south of Carn Brea. A branch line through Twelveheads to Chacewater was planned but never built. Horses drew the wagons until steam locomotives were introduced in 1854, except on the section below Devoran. At first there were two engines, called Miner and Smelter; a third, Spitfire, was added in 1859, by which time the line was handling 90,000 tons of freight per year. The catastrophic decline in the fortunes of the Cornish copper mines that began late in the 1860s led inevitably to bankruptcy for the railway company. It went into receivership in 1877, but still soldiered on, depending in its last few years almost entirely on the income from supplying coal to the Basset mines. When in 1915 they turned instead to Portreath for coal, delivered via the Portreath Branch of the GWR, closure for the Redruth & Chasewater Railway followed almost immediately. After more than 80 years, however, most of its course can still be traced.

For a full treatment of the subject, see RCR. *Nicholas Roberts' Appendix 1 in Volume 1 of this guide puts the railway into its historical context.*

Many people are puzzled by the spelling, "Chasewater". I have heard it said that this was simply a mistake on the part of an official in London, but Barton's explanation is that it is "a legacy of the days of its (the Railway's) formation when this was the more customary spelling." Certainly Richard Thomas consistently used it in his "Report on a Survey of the Mining District from Chasewater to Camborne" (1819). (See pages 110-1 for part of the map that accompanied it.)

For a short diversion to see the mouth (more correctly, the "portal" or "tail") of the County Adit, turn right first along the railway embankment, crossing the stream, and just before reaching the bund which partially blocks the track as it approaches the road, turn down to your left. Go past the bridge, beside which is monitoring equipment set up by the NRA, **and after about another 40m the adit portal is down to your right.** (Colour photograph 19.)

By 1730, Poldice Mine was already becoming too deep for the engines available to cope with the pumping needs, and in 1748 its manager, John Williams, along with its chief "adventurer" or shareholder, William Lemon, started the construction of a deep drainage outlet in the Carnon Valley below Twelveheads. By 1768 the adit reached the western side of the Poldice sett; ten years later a branch ran through Wheal Busy to Wheal Peevor. Eventually the County or Great Adit, with its many side branches, was over forty miles in length, drained about sixteen square miles and served over sixty mines: a diagram based on research by Allen Buckley, illustrating the complexity of the system, is on page 38 in "A Second View from Carn Marth". (See also Richard Thomas's 1819 map, mentioned above.) It brought many benefits, but having many mines draining into one adit could also bring serious problems: Cyril Noall tells how in 1872 a blockage in the County Adit at the abandoned Wheal Damsel threatened to cause flooding at Poldice, and four men who were investigating the problem very narrowly escaped with their lives when the blockage gave way releasing a torrent which poured down one shaft "with a roar like that of the Falls of Niagra" CMD*). The average depth of the adit is about 160 feet, but it is at least 400 feet down in some places, such as at Wheal Hope (West Wheal Damsel). Additions and improvements to the system, such as the driving of a second adit to cope with the increased water flow as more mines were added and the original ones were extended, continued till about 1870, and even during the last few years work has been carried out to clear rock falls near the portal below Mount Wellington and construct new outlets. As Mr Buckley has pointed out, the*

County Adit was "crucial to the economic working" of Wheal Jane right up to its closure in 1991. Originally the water flowed out further down the valley, just south of Nangiles Mine, as shown on the map, dated circa 1810, reproduced on page 47 of MMC6, where the adit is called the Poldice Adit. At that time Nangiles was linked to the County Adit, but the Nangiles section of Wheal Jane now has its own independent adit a short way downstream. Directions for finding it are given later.

Return along the embankment to continue the Trail.

Soon you will see a big mine burrow up on your left, which is now the most obvious evidence of the existence of Nangiles Mine, apart of course from the water, polluted with heavy metals, that continues to spew out from its abandoned levels into the Carnon River. Part of the bob wall of the big pumping-engine house that used to stand high up on the slope has survived and can just be glimpsed from the path you are on; a short diversion to see it at close quarters is suggested below.

The Nangiles pumping-engine house as it was

Nangiles, described by J.H.Collins as "a very ancient mine", produced over 3,000 tons of copper, plus smaller amounts of tin, iron, zinc, arsenic and ochre, between 1845 and 1906. The water in this mine is said to have contained so much vitriol (sulphuric acid) that it would "rot a pair of boots off a man's feet in one day". As a result it was necessary to line the pumps with wood and brass or bronze, and the cost of this ruined the company. A unique feature at Nangiles is a railway with wooden lines seventy feet underground, and again it is thought that wood was chosen because of the acid; this seems to be confirmed by the discovery of a boot with wooden "nails" in one of the workings. (JTS No.5, 1977.) In 1905 Nangiles became part of Falmouth Consolidated Mines (see Round Walk 12), and in recent years it was worked along with Mount Wellington and Wheal Jane.

Next you come to a choice of ways, where a small group of granite setts shows that the course of the railway line ahead is now overgrown and impenetrable. (By the time you use this book, of course, the vegetation may have been cleared.)

For a diversion in order to see the mouth of the Nangiles adit, take the right fork and continue downhill, ignoring the path up on the left. The main path descends almost to the valley floor, levels off, then rises slightly. Almost 300m from the point where you forked right at the start of this detour, a few steps lead down on the right to another set of NRA equipment monitoring water quality and quantity. The ochre-stained "stream" here (colour photograph 20) is issuing from the Nangiles adit, the portal of which is just around to the right.

For an account of the events which caused the Nangiles adit suddenly, in January 1992, to assume great importance for everyone living downstream of it, see pages 168-9.

Now either retrace your steps to the point where you left the upper Trail and turn sharp-right to resume it (this is the longer route, but it enables you to see more of the remains of the railway and gives you the option of another short detour to the remains of the Nangiles pumping-engine house);
or continue ahead on the lower path. After almost 200m you will come to a group of derelict concrete-block buildings, the remains of a hardcore plant; here you can either continue at the lower level to join the road, or go up on the left just before the buildings to rejoin the course of the railway and carry on to the road as described below, immediately after the italicised note about the abortive "hot rocks" scheme.

If you take the upper path at the choice of ways, you will find that it soon brings you back down to the level track where the railway ran.

Before you reach that, however, another short detour offers itself, namely a path up the hill to visit the Nangiles engine-house remains above. It starts about 50m beyond the fork and climbs quite steeply; the path is quite narrow and tends to be slightly overgrown in summer. After about 160m, turn left, still uphill. (The path ahead runs quite close to the Nangiles stamps-engine house, in which a 36-inch engine was installed in 1871, but the path is not a right of way, and the engine house is both inaccessible and almost invisible, since it is surrounded by head-high bracken and cloaked in ivy.) **Another 150m-or-so brings you to the ruined bob wall of the pumping-engine house, perched on top of its burrow on the left, immediately beyond a capped shaft on the right.** The concrete bases, shaft cap and block structures date from the attempted reworking of 1967, when the fine engine house, a well-known landmark, was reduced to its present state. The engine was an 80-inch, which was installed in 1862 and

The bob wall of the Nangiles pumping-engine house as it is now (SVJ)

worked here for ten years. A winding-engine house a little way upslope is said to have been completely obliterated during the 1967 venture.

Return the same way to rejoin the Trail in the valley.

There are quite a few exposed setts on this section, some of which have been displaced. At the point where there is a deep excavation on the right, a row of setts have been left teetering on the edge, and in fact at least two have tumbled down.

The excavation was created by a hardcore plant, some of whose concrete structures remain in place, notably the remains of the building that housed the stone-crusher. Early in 1989, plans were announced by a company named GeoScience for drilling over 4½ miles ("the deepest hole ever bored in Britain", it was said) into the earth's crust on this site, as part of a "hot rocks project", similar to but unconnected with the one at Rosemanowes, near Stithians. Mention was made of using a "robotised drilling rig" to reach granite at a temperature of 230°C. Despite vigorous local protest, planning permission was granted. Eight years later, however, nothing has been done, and meanwhile public funding has been withdrawn from the Rosemanowes operation. The site here at Bissoe has been sold by GeoScience, and is currently subject to an application from the new owner for planning permission to be used for dumping inert materials and subsoil. A "cycle track" and cycle-hire facility feature in the application, which was given approval by the Carrick planning committee in November 1996. Whatever the outcome, the Coast-to-Coast route and links down to the valley floor will, I have been assured, be maintained.

A path descends on the right to the lower level, and for walkers this would be a convenient way to go, joining the road near the bridge; the official route, however, continues at the upper level, more-or-less keeping to the course of the railway, though the exact position of that has been obscured. Immediately before reaching the road, the track descends, and a rubble/earth bank has been placed across it; cyclists should have no difficulty with it, but for horse-riders it may be a different story.

Here you are on the edge of the village of Bissoe.

The name, as mentioned earlier, means "birch trees", and hints at a rural past which seems unlikely ever to return, despite all efforts by planters and other conservationists. Even less likely is its revival as a port. There is a strong tradition that in medieval times tin was shipped from Bissoe, but tin streaming in the Carnon Valley greatly accelerated the natural silting-up process and cut the village off from tidal waters - a fate similar to those of Tregony, Ruan Lanihorne and Treesmill, and to a lesser extent Devoran, Truro and Lostwithiel.

At the road turn right. Watch carefully for traffic here. If you have joined the road at the higher level, after about 30m you can cross it and

use the path between hedges, running parallel with the road; in that case, return to the road at the point where the path turns left beside the Carnon River. Cross the bridge.

The rambling old cluster of buildings on the right just past the bridge is Point Mills.

❽ **Turn left immediately beyond the bridge, following the gravelled bridleway** which passes close to the remains of the stack and other structures which were once part of the British Arsenic Company (later the Cornwall Arsenic Company) refinery. (Photograph: SVJ)

The square stack was tall and elegant, an important local landmark, until lightning struck it in December 1990. Bissoe played a leading part in the story of arsenic production in Cornwall: there were three important works here, two of which survived well into this century. Much of the soil downstream of this site is one-part-in-200 arsenic, reputedly the highest concentration anywhere in the world. Few if any plants can survive in that, but the Cornwall Wildlife Trust has made valiant efforts to reclaim the land; in some areas hundreds of tons of mud dredged from the Fal estuary was used to provide a cap at least six inches deep - clearly inadequate for all trees and most shrubs.

The old stack amidst the concrete-works buildings on the other side of the river seems likely to be a relic of the smelting works shown on the 1878-9 map opposite.

PLEASE NOTE At the time of writing (early 1997), the next part of the route was of FOOTPATH STATUS ONLY. Negotiations for the establishment of a bridleway were in progress, and this should be clearly signposted when available.

Until then, cyclists and horse riders will have to return to the road. The best route is probably to turn left on reaching it, continuing past Richards' filling station and taking the first turning left, signed "Hick's Mill, Coldwind Cross". Keep left at the next junction, and immediately beyond Hicks' Mill turn left along the lane that runs beside the entrance to Brayfreeze. After nearly half a mile, turn left again at the T-junction, where there is a Redruth & Chasewater Railway Trail signpost, as mentioned 8-9 lines below. Now pick up the directions from there.

The current route for walkers is as follows: Continue past the ruined chimney, along the wide, gravelled track, and over a footbridge. Ignore the stile ahead; turn right, and after about 100m cross the stile on your left. Now keep by the fence on the right at first, then beside the stream, also on your right. The path runs to the right of a small plantation of conifers and crosses the stream via a small footbridge. There are then two stiles on your right, the second of which brings you to a lane. Turn left on that. At the T-junction, where there is a Redruth & Chasewater Railway Trail signpost, turn left. This soon takes you across Bissoe Bridge (the point to which it is believed the Carnon River was once navigable); **turn right on to the wide track just beyond the bridge.** (Before doing so, however, you might care to go on up the lane for about another 80m to see where the Redruth & Chasewater line crossed - immediately beyond Hazel Villa, which has a tiny lean-to shed christened Railway Villa!) The track runs beside two batteries of reed-beds and filtration ponds which have been installed by the National Rivers Authority (now absorbed into the Environmental Agency) in pursuit of a "passive" solution to the problem of pollution following the closure of Wheal Jane. (See colour photograph 22 and the long note about Wheal Jane on pages 168-9.)

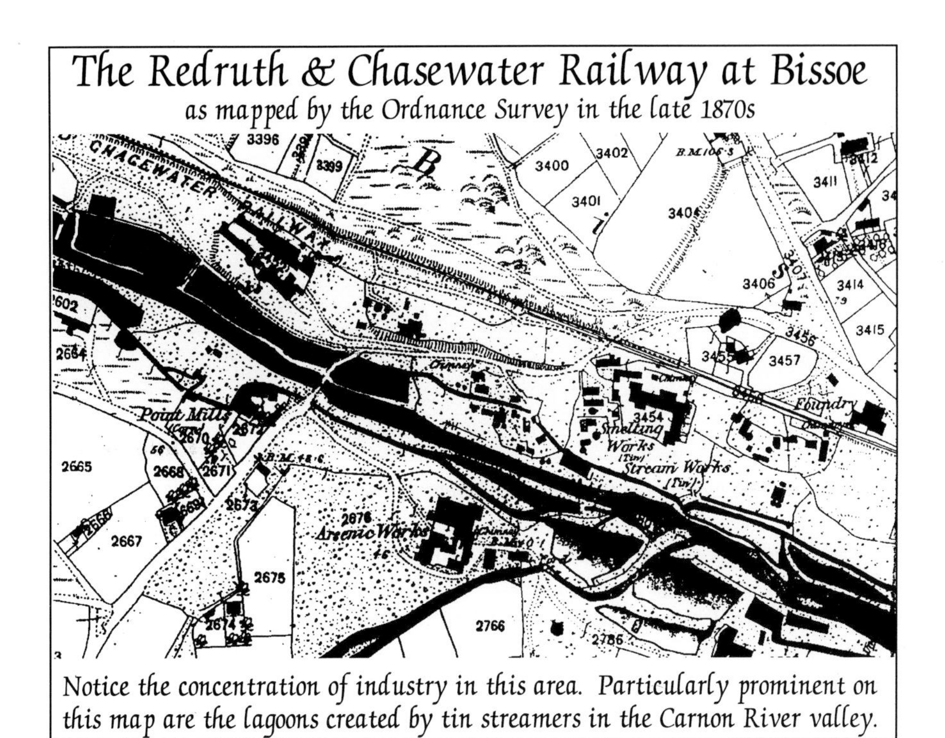

The Redruth & Chasewater Railway at Bissoe
as mapped by the Ordnance Survey in the late 1870s

Notice the concentration of industry in this area. Particularly prominent on this map are the lagoons created by tin streamers in the Carnon River valley.

During the 19th century, and possibly earlier, there was a considerable concentration of cementation pits in this part of the Carnon Valley. The 1878-9 OS map labels them as "Precipitation Works (Copper)" and in every case adds, "(Disused)". The method used involved filling pits with "any old iron". When water containing copper salts was passed through the pits, the iron was gradually dissolved and replaced by copper. The process is described more fully in "Cornish Mining" by Bryan Earl, who adds, "The water discharged from the pits at Bissoe was led into large ponds where the air oxidised the dissolved iron, which was precipitated as ochre and found a ready market."

The track crosses a minor road (Grenna Lane, the start / end point for Round Walk 12) before passing under the viaduct carrying the Falmouth branch line (colour photograph 24). *Most of the eleven buttressed masonry piers which carried the wooden superstructure of Brunel's original viaduct (1861-3) still stand beside it. The replacement viaduct was opened for traffic in 1933. As the photograph overleaf shows, the Redruth & Chasewater ran further north than the track you are on, just this side of the road. See BCV for much more detail on the viaducts.*

The Redruth & Chasewater line passing beneath Brunel's Carnon Valley viaduct

At about this point the small spire of Devoran church comes into view. The track then crosses another road - quite a narrow one, but this was the main road from Truro to Penryn and Falmouth before the construction, about 1829, of the section of the modern road that runs past the Norway Inn and crosses the Carnon Valley closer to Devoran by means of a causeway.

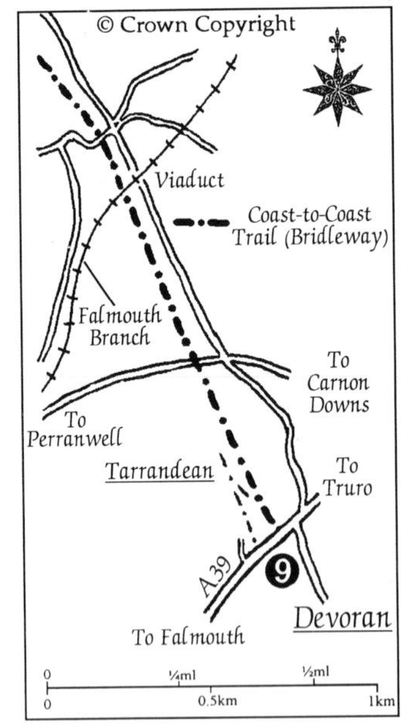

The small stack to your left is a relic of a vitriol (sulphuric acid) works, sulphur being one of the by-products of arsenic refining. It was one of the many such operations which once made the Carnon Valley one of the most heavily industrialised valleys in Cornwall. This last section of the Trail, for example, runs beside an area that has been intensively worked by tin streamers for centuries, and until quite recently tin was still being recovered here by Carnon Consolidated, the owners of Wheal Jane. Again, the long industrial building over to the right began its existence as the Basset Foundry (1858); from 1895 it was Visick's foundry and engineering works, and in 1987 it was bought by the King Harry Steam Ferry Company for the manufacture of marine parts. It has now been converted into light-industrial units. *(For more detail see Round Walk 13, pages 185-7, and HAE Part 2.)*

As you approach the main road, keep to the higher track and cross the wooden bridge, from which you have a good view of long fronds of waterweed (colour photograph 23), which remind me of the Hayle River above St Erth: perhaps it is significant that both the Hayle and Carnon Rivers have been heavily influenced by mining activity. The unusually intense green of much of the vegetation beside the Carnon may also reflect the heavy metals in the water. Several notices have been set up by the NRA warning against coming into contact with it.

❾ The main road (A39) - here running along the causeway mentioned above - is at the time of writing officially the south-eastern end of the Coast-to-Coast Trail - that is, until a safe crossing is provided, either underpass or bridge. Certainly it would be a brave, or foolhardy, person who attempted to cross it on horseback.

For walkers and (dismounted) cyclists, however, the road should present no serious problem or danger, provided that they exercise due care and patience. It would seem a great pity to have come this far along the Redruth & Chasewater Railway without seeing its terminus and the port it created and served.

If you agree, cross, turn left - luckily there is a pavement - and take the first road on the right, Greenbank Road, into Devoran.

(But if you first continue a few yards further along the main road you will reach the point where the railway crossed. On the right, half-buried now by the raised and widened road, are the remains of one of the level-crossing gates. The gatekeeper's cottage survived until the 1970s. A larger, two-storey building known locally as "The Round House" used to stand opposite; this was the turnpike road toll house, demolished in the 1950s.)

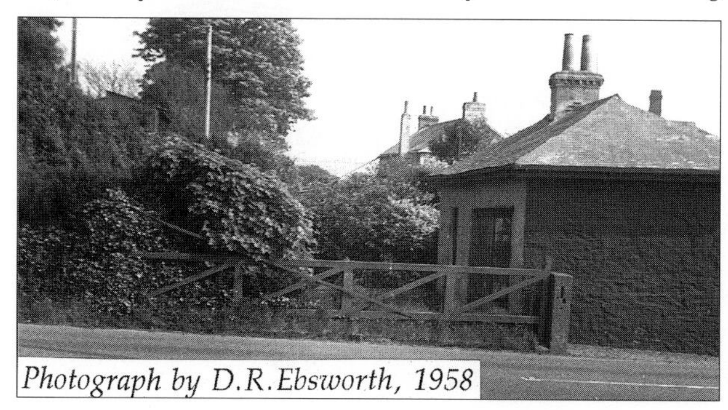

Photograph by D.R.Ebsworth, 1958

Those dependent on public transport can catch a bus to Falmouth or Truro from Greenbank Road or opposite St John's Church, at the top of Market Street.

Two Round Walks are based on Devoran: number 14 is a short tour around the village, and number 15 takes you to the terminus of the Redruth and Chasewater Railway at Point and Penpol, with an option of going on further to Feock. Both these walks start and end at the far end of Greenbank Road, where it meets Market Street and Quay Road.

ROUND WALKS 1a & 1b
TWO SHORT WALKS AT PORTREATH:
1a, THE WESTERN CLIFFS, GREEN LANE & FEADON
1b, THE EASTERN CLIFFS
1b IS WALK 1 ON THE PORTREATH TRAMROAD LEAFLET

1a: about 3 miles (5km), or can be split into walks of about 1 & 2 miles
1b: about 1½ miles (2.5km)

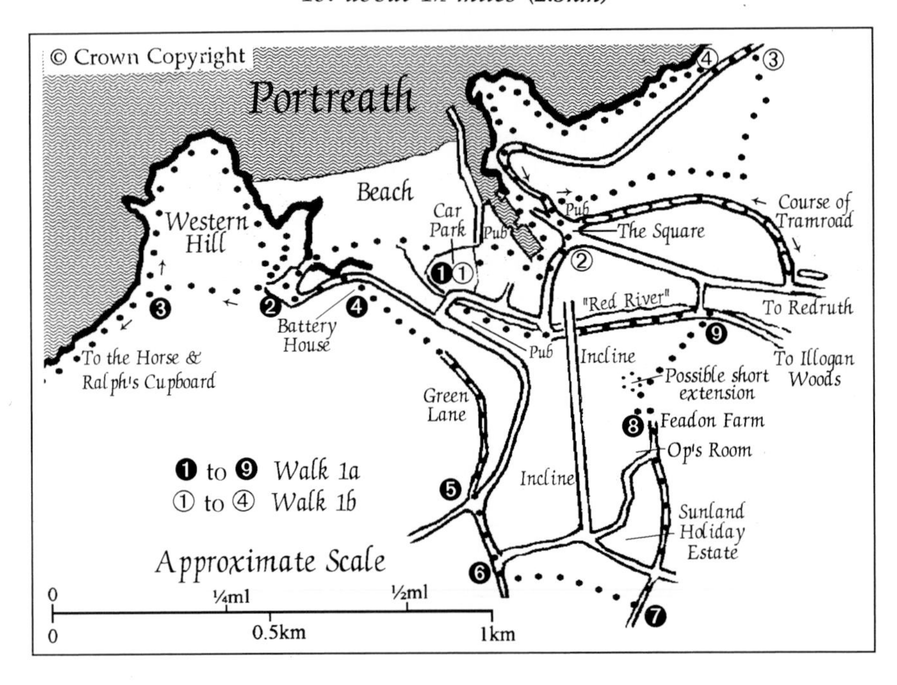

Both these little walks give excellent bird's-eye views of the village and harbour plus stunning cliff scenery. By the same token, both involve a fair bit of uphill walking. The suggested extension to the first walk gives one of the best views of Portreath, plus some very pleasant country walking. The cliff-edge path around Western Hill might be unsuitable for anyone who suffers from vertigo, but there are other paths that run a bit further inland. As you descend from the cliffs there is a very steep section where you really need shoes or boots with a good grip, or a walking stick, or both. Unless you have a severe problem with heights you are unlikely to be worried by anything on Walk b. Mud could be a bit of a problem near Feadon Farm on Walk a.

Both walks start and end at the main car park overlooking Portreath beach.

WALK 1a

❶ If the tide allows, start by crossing to the far (western) side of the beach.

Notice the old mine workings in the cliffs beneath Battery House. If you go into the small cave and look up you will see a good example of the way miners exploited mineral lodes that were exposed on a cliff face. Often referred to as "stopes", these are thought by A.K.Hamilton Jenkin to be possibly relics of a copper mine called Wheal Mary, active in the 1850s. The beach itself was a rich source of tin, deposited in the sand by the "Red River", which flowed from the heart of the mining country, and even by the little stream that reaches the beach on the far (west) side. Gold as well as tin was recovered from that stream. Michael Tangye describes how "in the 1890s horse-drawn carts with large wide wheels so that they would not sink, were filled with sand skimmed from the beach surface at low tide" and taken for processing to the tin streaming plant described and pictured on pages 66-7. As mentioned on page 82, Tehidy received dues for "Copper Ore found on the beach at Portreath."

Go up the slipway and lane to Smugglers' Cottage.

(If the tide is too high, use instead Battery Hill, the minor road that runs close to the cliff edge and passes Battery House: details in Round Walk 4. This would also be the better way to go if you want to do only the inland part of this walk; for that, take the path that cuts back sharply just before you reach Battery House, and follow the directions from section 4, line 4.)

❷ From Smugglers' Cottage take the path running up the sheltered little valley, signed North Coast Foot Path). Ignore the small path up on the right beside the National Trust Western Hill sign.

Western Hill's old name, Tregea Hill, is, suggested Charles Henderson, a corruption of "Tregear", and "gear" or "ker" in Cornish place-names indicates a fort, so the hill and headland are likely to have been the site of one of the many "cliff castles". Henderson's sketch-map of the hill indicates a "ditch" roughly where the valley path runs, or parallel with it.

Near the top, two more paths go off towards the cliff edge, and you could use either of them if you want the shortest route, but I'd recommend you to go on up to the top.

❸ On reaching the cliff edge there, if you enjoy dramatic cliff scenery I suggest that you first continue ahead for about 250m to get the best view

of the rocky promontory known as The Horse, and the gulley beyond, called Ralph's (or Wrath's) Cupboard. *A little information about this place is given on page 85, and my attempt to sketch The Horse is on page 86.* **Then retrace your steps** (notice, as you do so, the very pretty distant view of Portreath beach and harbour across the foreground of low-growing heather and gorse) **and take the narrow path which runs most of the way around the seaward side of Western Hill - or choose one of the other paths running a little further inland if you'd prefer.** (But there are only a couple of places where the left-hand path runs at all uncomfortably close to the edge.) Naturally, the path nearest the edge gives the best views, first of the small island called Gull Rock and later of Portreath and the coast north-east. **Once you start turning south-east you will see a narrow, sunken path running very close to the edge, but this soon becomes overgrown, so it's better to stick to the slightly higher path. When you come to a wide, grassy area you have what I think is the best of all views of Portreath.** The Incline for the Hayle Railway and the route of the Tramroad are both clearly seen. **From here the best way is to go down the steep slope that heads towards the bungalow in the valley; particular care not to slip is needed on the grassy first section, but later there are some helpful steps.** Notice the "summer house" half way up the slope opposite, similar to the one perched above the harbour on the far side of the cove; and further left and a little higher there seem to be the remains of another one.

Just before you reach the bottom of the slope, you might care to walk a short way along the side path going up on the left. This soon leads to a lower path which runs immediately above the site of the original small harbour (1713). *If you look right you may be able to make out what could be the remains of a wider track running up to this point from just behind Smugglers' Cottage, and this may be the route by which goods was conveyed to and from ships tied up at the quay. (See Michael Tangye's "Tehidy and the Bassets", pages 92-3, and the comments on page 86 of this book.)*

Return the same way and go on down to the valley close to Smugglers' Cottage. Continue via Battery Hill, as directed on page 86, starting at line 8.

❹ You could simply return to the car park, or make a recommended extension of the walk by taking the uphill path which starts immediately beyond Battery House, and looks at first like a private entrance to another house, West-A-Way. The path turns sharp-right, up steps, giving you a close-up view of the small battlemented walls above Battery House. Another sharp turn, this time to the left, takes you beside a small quarry, and then you are on a tarmacked surface. This is Green Lane - a good place to linger, for an obvious reason. The lane becomes a minor road passing to the right of a gaggle of bungalows.

The view of Portreath from the Green Lane area was if anything even more worth lingering over in 1895, when J.C.Burrow took this fine photograph. (Compare the slightly earlier picture on page 17.) *(Courtesy RIC)*

❺ **At the road junction go straight on. Ignore the two side roads on the left,** the second of which is a private road leading to the Sunland Holiday Estate (wooden chalets), Feadon Farm, and the Op's Room - about which more later.

❻ **Nearly 50m beyond the private road, turn left on to the signed public footpath, starting with a "Cornish stile", in other words a granite cattle-grid. The path runs beside the hedge on the right, crosses another stone grid at the corner, and continues in the same line across the next field to a third grid a little to the left of a farm gate.**

❼ **Turn left along the farm lane** (often extremely muddy in at least one patch during winter, I'm afraid), **and on reaching the buildings at Feadon Farm follow the footpath signs, turning first left, then right at the start of a concrete road.**

Feadon Farm belongs to the Duchy College and is used to give practical experience to students of agriculture. (The name, by the way, is pronounced "Faydon" according to local historian Michael Tangye.)

At the corner you can see, to the left, the long, low, flat-roofed building still known as the Op's Room, built in 1941 as a control centre for operations associated with the nearby Portreath Airfield, on the other side of the valley at

Nancekuke. In recent years it has been converted for use as a pub, but is now a private residence.

❽ **At the farmyard entrance turn left on to a narrow path, following a public footpath sign, the message reinforced by a green waymarker. After about 20m the path turns right, and then about another 20m further on another path leads off, sharp-left, down into the wooded valley. Take this path, soon passing a small pond on your left.**

When you come to a wooden stile on your left, you have the opportunity to make an attractive short extension to the walk. For this, cross the stile and go over the footbridge. The path now runs uphill and emerges briefly into the open, giving a good view over Portreath to the harbour and sea; it then re-enters the wood and zigzags quite steeply down to another footbridge. Having crossed that, turn right, walking beside the little stream, then climb some wooden steps near the first bridge to return to the stile and continue the walk as before.

Continue downhill, soon joining a surfaced lane at the mock-military "Glenfeadon Castle". Go on down to Primrose Lane.

❾ **Turn left on that.** Soon you pass the Glenfeadon House Hotel, with its rather impressive Georgian frontage.

Glenfeadon House and its neighbour, now converted into apartments and known as Bassetts Acre, were, I am told by the hotel owners, built by the Bassets of Tehidy in 1828. ("Basset" appears to be the authentic spelling of the name, and I have tried to be consistent in using it, but "Bassett" is commonly seen.) The Bain family, owners of a large merchant fleet based at Portreath, lived for many years at Glenfeadon - in fact, a member of the family informed Michael Tangye that the Bains built it. It stands on the site of the Portreath Tin Smelting House, founded in 1814. Records indicate that the smelter was busy and profitable, but it closed after only 11 years when its owners went into partnership with a larger firm of smelters. Large lumps of clinker, said to be from the smelter, have been placed on either side of the main steps leading up to the main entrance of the hotel.

Continue under the bridge through the Incline. *See the note about that on pages 78-80.* **Go straight on along Tregea Terrace,** with the small stream that was once one of Cornwall's "Red Rivers" on your right. **After passing the Basset Arms, the path climbs to the road.** *Almost opposite the point where you come to the road, once stood the Portreath Tin Streaming Plant, dating from 1887. Located just the other side of the road bridge, close to the site now occupied by the "Beach Shop 'N' Surf", it employed a waterwheel and a steam engine to drive stamps and buddles. See the photograph on the next page. When the streaming plant closed I do not know - probably not later than 1933, when, to prevent the sea from continuing to be discoloured by mine waste at Portreath, the Red River was diverted underground to reach the sea further north.*

Turn right for the car park.

The Portreath Tin Streaming Plant, where the Red River reaches the beach. It is shown on an undated postcard - probably about 1900. What is now the car park was then "The Green" or "Sunnybank". (Courtesy Paddy Bradley)

WALK 1b

❶ Follow the directions for the Coast-to-Coast Trail as far as the Portreath Arms at The Square (pages 15-18).

❷ There (before coming to the pub) turn sharp-left on to the minor road, Lighthouse Hill, which runs above the north side of the harbour and climbs towards the cliffs. (The road's name refers to the so-called "Pepperpot" daymark tower, which doubled as a look-out. A flag-signalling system was operated from it, but as far as I know it was never a lighthouse, although it may at some stage have had a lantern.) **Pass the pretty row of old cottages on your left, but just before the path that leads down to the harbour turn sharp-right up a steepish path, known as New Walk, with steps and railings.** *Michael Tangye in his book on Portreath says there is a tradition that it was originally a mule track along which ore was brought to the harbour from the small mines in the Nancekuke area. Some information about them is included on pages 73-5.*

As you climb you get an excellent overview of the landward part of Portreath to complement the one of the seaward part that Battery Hill affords on the other short walk. In particular it's very obvious from here how the modern housing in the flat valley-bottom has replaced the various railway sidings, coal yards, fish cellar, lime kiln and other paraphernalia of a working port serving an industrial hinterland. This is probably also the best vantage point for viewing the Incline on the far side of the valley, walled across near the bottom and overgrown at a higher level. (Information about the Incline is given on pages 78-80 - and see the photograph below.) As you climb ever higher, the view extends ahead to the deep valley leading towards Redruth, along which ran Portreath's earlier mineral railway, known locally as the Tram, and on the skyline can be glimpsed Carn Marth and Carn Brea, at the centre of the region which both the railways and the port served.

Eventually the path bends left and begins to level off, and now for a short while there's little to see apart from the long fence and some of the buildings of RAF Portreath, otherwise known as the Nancekuke Defence Area (details on pages 73-4). **Keep to the main path where it turns left again, ignoring a side path on the right.**

❸ **Turn left at the road,** passing a group of ugly concrete buildings, survivors of World War 2. The view ahead, in contrast, is splendid, stretching along the coast to Godrevy Lighthouse and beyond to the hills above St Ives and Carbis Bay. **After about 80m turn right to find the Coastal Footpath.**

❹ **Turn left on that. The rest of the way back to the car park, including a visit to the north side of the harbour, is described in the last few lines of Round Walk 2.**

An undated picture of the Portreath Incline in its working days (Courtesy RIC)

ROUND WALK 2
PORTREATH, THE OLD TRAMROAD, PORTHTOWAN & THE CLIFFS
WALK 2 ON PORTREATH TRAMROAD LEAFLET

About 8½ miles, or about 7 if Porthtowan is omitted

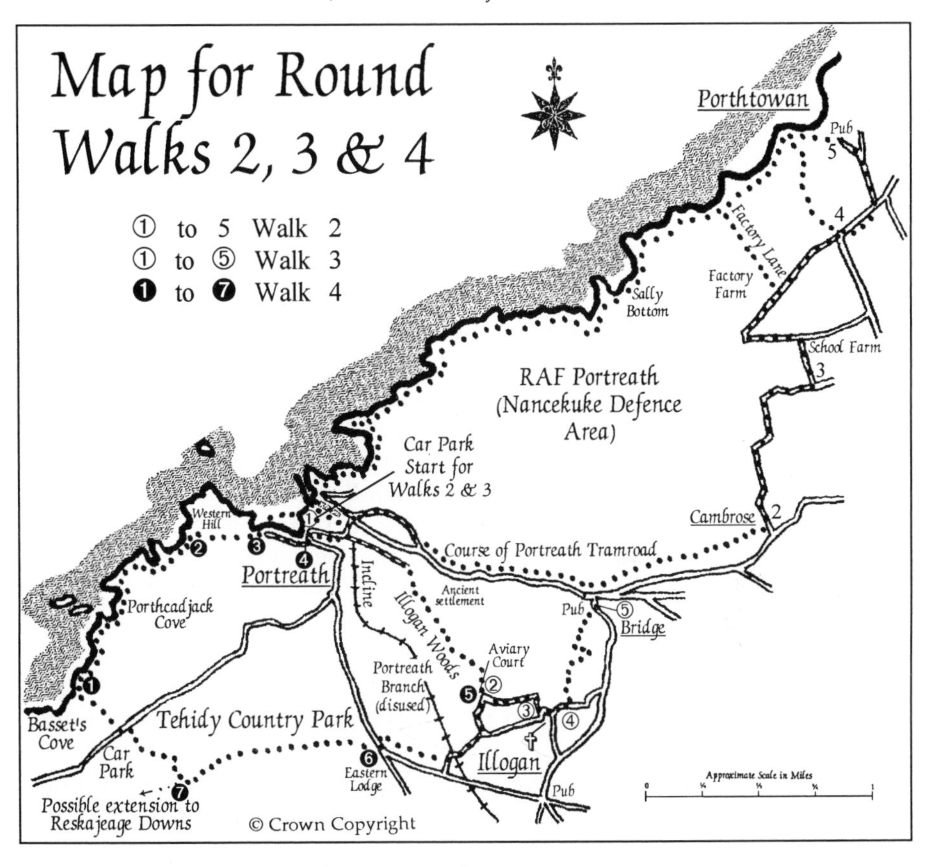

Including a lunch-stop of nearly an hour in Porthtowan, we spent about five hours on this walk, taking it at a leisurely pace, and felt at the end that we'd had a splendid day out. Over half of the inland part is along the trackbed of the Tramroad, which means level walking. At Cambrose the walk route leaves the Tramroad and follows quiet country roads with superb inland views. Porthtowan is worth visiting, whether for its fine surfing beach, its pub food, or its industrial-archaeological interest; but if you prefer you can shorten the walk by cutting across to the cliffs west of the village. The coast path between Porthtowan and Portreath offers dramatic cliff scenery plus views back to St Agnes Head and forward to Godrevy lighthouse and St Ives Bay. Most of this section is fairly level, but there are two steep descents and climbs; steps have been cut to make the going easier. Just inland is a former airfield, now a Ministry of Defence establishment; under the terms of the Official Secrets Act it has to be surrounded by a high fence, and for nearly two miles the coast path runs beside that. Luckily, it's fairly unobtrusive most of the time. You are unlikely to need waterproof footwear except perhaps early in the walk, on parts of the old railway. Shops and toilets are available in Portreath and Porthtowan, and there are several pubs along the way, at Portreath, Porthtowan and Bridge. Two little books give fascinating details about the history of this area, namely *Portreath: Some Chapters in its History* by Michael Tangye (1968) and *Memories of Nancekuke* by Ernest Landry (1978).

Directions are given from the main car park overlooking the beach at Portreath.

❶ **Begin the walk by following section 1 of the directions for the Coast-to-Coast Trail (pages 15-22).**

❷ **Turn left on the minor road. Ignore the left turning soon after; continue uphill**, with the view to the right and ahead steadily widening out till finally it includes St Agnes Beacon as well as Carn Brea. The mine stack among the houses of Redruth just left of Carn Brea is Pednandrea (when it was built in 1824, the tallest mine chimney in Cornwall at 145 feet; the brick-built top half has been demolished, but even now it dominates the town); left of that in the distance is Carn Marth, a taller hill than Carn Brea; then the triple engine houses of Wheal Peevor (Round Walk 6); next Hallenbeagle, two engine houses - one of them now little more than a stack - beside the main railway line and the A30; further left again, Doctor's Shaft, North Treskerby (Round Walk 5). **The road turns right, left and right again.**

❸ **A few hundred yards past the second right bend, take the left turning past several houses and farm buildings. Turn left at the T-junction, beside the entrance to School Farm.**

Before the hamlets of Great and Little Nancekuke were destroyed in 1939, the young children from there and other nearby settlements attended a Board Day School close to this farm. In the 1890s, when Ernest Landry attended it, it had two lady teachers and 60-70 pupils.

Now on your right you have what was once Nancekuke Common, and on your left a disused airfield, now "a prohibited place within the meaning of the Official Secrets Act", as the notice at the entrance puts it. (See the note later on Nancekuke Defence Area.) **Follow the road round,** and now you are heading towards St Agnes Beacon. On the left are the buildings of Factory Farm.

The name comes from the gunpowder factory which was once at the seaward end of Factory Lane; it closed down in 1862 after an explosion. The Tehidy Estate then dismantled the buildings and used the materials to build the farmhouse and outbuildings in a more sheltered place further inland. Until then this land had not been cultivated, except in the valley leading down to Sally Bottom.

Not far past that is Factory Lane, a wide track leading straight to the coast, and this is the way to go if you don't want to include Porthtowan on your walk - but you'll miss some impressive cliff scenery, too. **Otherwise, continue along the road as it gradually descends to the outskirts of the village.**

❹ **Here you have a choice of routes into Porthtowan.** (A) is probably a little shorter and passes a couple of shops, but (B) is more attractive and avoids any walking on a road that can be busy in summer.

(A) Go down to the main road and turn left. A short way along, to reduce the road walking you could take a path on the right - sometimes rather overgrown - which passes through the Rosehill Park caravan site and returns you to the road near the bottom of the hill. From there you could walk down the side-road on the left into Porthtowan, or continue ahead as far as the Avalon Tea Room & Restaurant and take the footpath opposite, which starts on the right side of the petrol station and ends at what was once the Porpoise Inn, then the Porthtowan Inn, and is now (1996) boarded up awaiting a buyer.

(B) Just before the main road, turn left up the steepish tarmacked lane among houses and bear left, continuing uphill on a track which passes South View Farm and West Towan House. On the right now is an area riddled with mine workings. **Soon you reach the coast path; bear right for Porthtowan.**

"Sand-dune cove" is its name: dunes overshadow it on the north side, and in winter storms often carry the beach sand well up the road. The holiday developments are quite recent and still look temporary, to my eyes at least. Perhaps some of the early settlers were fishermen, but for most of the 19th century and much of the 18th it was essentially a mining village, being surrounded by literally dozens - perhaps hundreds - of small, ancient workings extracting mainly copper. Some of these were later amalgamated or "consolidated" to form important companies such as Wheal Towan on the north side and Tywarnhayle in the valley inland. An old chimney belonging to South Wheal Towan and two spectacular engine houses of Tywarnhayle Mine are very noticeable ahead as you descend into the village from the cliffs. I have written about these fascinating mines in "Around St Agnes & Perranporth", and the remains are interpreted in detail in ECM1.

At the headland you have a good view over the splendid surfing beach and the holiday developments, many of them very tatty and flimsy, others looking like a rather half-hearted attempt to emulate the Costa del Sol. A few old cottages and Victorian or Edwardian villas remain; and notice, close at hand below you as you walk down, the New Wheal Towan engine house (though in fact no engine was ever installed in it), with its truncated castellated chimney. *It dates from 1872, when New Wheal Towan was established with the aim of retrying old workings of a mine called Wheal Lushington in the hill behind. An old adit runs from behind the engine house and emerges at the foot of the cliffs, and the plan was to run flat-rods through this adit to work pumps - but nothing came of the scheme. An engine arrived from Ireland (via Penryn!) but merely lay on the ground before it was eventually broken up. After some years in use as a café (see the photograph below), the building was splendidly restored to its original appearance and is now a private house. The bungalow next door (on the seaward side) is built around a wooden structure which was the relocated count house of Wheal Charlotte, worked early this century near Chapel Porth. Foundations for it were made using the brick upper part of the New Wheal Towan stack.*

The New Wheal Towan engine house at Porthtowan as it was in 1989 (RSA)

The Commodore Inn caters for families and serves a good range of food; during the season cafés and other pubs or bars are available closer to the beach.

❺ To return to Portreath, follow the coast path sign close to the Commodore - retracing your footsteps, if you came by route (B).

From now on, directions would be superfluous - especially along the fenced stretch! But you may be glad to have a few details pointed out.

At first there are many capped shafts of old mine workings. Several small mines exploited this area at different times, extracting mainly copper, but also some tin, lead, iron, zinc and silver; their adits (drainage shafts) opened on to the cliff face. Ernest Landry writes about an adit from West Wheal Towan which led out to a big cave where seals used to breed: "I used to take visitors to the farm (i.e. Factory Farm) down the mine shaft which was fitted with ladders ... to this tunnel to the sea ... It was a marvellous sight at the end of this tunnel watching the mother seals coming into the cave on the incoming tide to nurse their young ones." These cliffs are very unstable, as the warning notices emphasise. The large rock at the southern end of Porthtowan beach, for example, was once joined to the mainland near the top: a picture of it as it was is on the cover of Landry's book. In that form, its name, the Tobban Horse, is perhaps more understandable. The top of the huge natural arch later collapsed, obscuring many old mine workings in the cliffs below. ("Tobban" means "mound" or "bank", and probably refers to a nearby field.) The cliffs between Tobban Horse and Sally Point, about half a mile further on, were, says Landry, "the last place where the Cornish Chough was seen in this district".

Soon you approach the fence of RAF Portreath, otherwise known as the Nancekuke Defence Area.

Nancekuke was part of the Tehidy Estate. When the estate broke up, in 1916, most of the Nancekuke tenant farmers took out mortgages to buy their own farms, and then proceeded to improve them greatly. "I remember the spring of 1939," writes Landry. "It had every prospect of being a good season. All the farms on Nancekuke were a picture to look at, well-farmed by a good lot of hard-working, contented farmers."

Then the authorities announced that the area was required by the RAF as an airfield, and a Minister came down to tell the farmers that everyone had to make sacrifices during wartime. "I remember the sacrifice this Minister made sometime after was a higher position in the Government." The bitterness of Landry's account of this takeover is understandable in view of the Minister's promise that the farms would be restored to their former owners after the war, because when that time came the Ministry of Supply took the area over and added more land to it, including five acres of Factory Farm, then surrounded it with a tall fence and built, in Landry's words, "a poison factory on this lovely part of Cornwall, a disgrace and eye-sore to any country in peace-time."

Just what was produced or investigated in that building remained secret, but rumours abounded of seals dying mysteriously nearby, and several employees became ill and claimed compensation; only after many years was the justice of their claim finally recognised. John Branfield's novel for teenagers, "Nancekuke", is based on these events.

The chemical weapons research establishment closed down about ten years ago, and RAF Portreath is now part of the Early Warning System, scanning the Atlantic by radar. I'm sorry the fence is still considered necessary; at least it is less tall and ugly than before.

The name, Nancekuke, by the way, appears to mean "hollow valley" or possibly "empty, worthless valley"; food for thought there, perhaps.

Just before the fence begins there are a small concrete reservoir and a concrete chimney with a long brick-lined flue leading up to it from the foundations of a boiler house, and below, a shaft covered by an enormous newish concrete cap crowned with a "bat castle". *Around the shaft are somewhat older concrete structures, some of them the bases for horizontal pumping and winding engines, others the remains of settling tanks. The truncated rectangular wall near the shaft is what survives of the count house. The shaft is called Vivian's (or Ladder) Shaft and belonged, as stated on the metal plaque attached to the bat castle, to an old mine called Wheal Tye. It was one of many small mines which became part of West Wheal Towan, and this may well be the shaft "fitted with ladders" that Ernest Landry used to take his visitors down. The shaft was reopened in 1927; as Dines puts it, "no development ensued," but the stack and other ruins may date from then, or from the period 1920-5 when an enterprise named Sally Bottoms was reworking sections of several old mines in this area.*

"Sally Bottom" itself is the next cove, otherwise called Kerriack or Cayack Cove. Before descending to it you walk through a flat-rod trench dating from around the middle of the 19th century; the concrete shelters in it were used in World War 2 and were associated with a target for aircraft gunnery practice on the cliff nearby. As you go down to the cove, care is needed if you use the lower group of steps, because much of the soil around the vertical wooden boards has been eroded. At the bottom, notice the fenced shaft and the ancient-looking ruins of mine buildings to the left, inside the MOD perimeter fence. The site of a stamps engine can be seen (colour photograph 3). The other ruins, close to the path just after it has crossed the second little stream, are the remains of rifle butts.

Ernest Landry tells the story of Sally Peters, who was born in a thatched cottage in the valley above the cove now named after her. Both her parents were engaged in tin mining or streaming there - presumably during the late 18th or early 19th century - and she too worked as a bal maiden (breaking up ore before it was fed to the stamps machine) when young, but later married a French sailor and lived for a time at St Nazaire. She returned to her native valley, though, after many adventures and personal tragedies, and in old age became a local legend through the help she gave to the sick and aged, many of whom she saved from being consigned to the workhouse.

The valley and nearby cliffs had been mined for centuries, and tin streaming was carried out at the seaward end. Water was constantly required there to operate the waterwheels which drove the stamps and buddles, and for the other dressing processes, so the valley was dammed to create a reservoir "of quite half an acre in extent", says Landry; the small reservoir you see as you descend probably occupies part of the same site. The old mine in the valley was called Wheal Sally. In the 1920s shafts were sunk there by the Sally Bottoms company, seeking lead and zinc.

Sally Bay was once famous for its limpets and winkles; Landry tells of the old soldier with a wooden leg who used to scale the precipitous path or staircase down to the beach once a week and sell the cooked limpets, with salt, pepper and vinegar to taste, in the street near Redruth town clock. As you go up the steps on the far side, look back to see the small waterfall - except perhaps during a dry summer.

The next cove, with very sheer cliffs and a cave, is called Gollyn, Gullan or Gullyn Cove; Gullyn is also the name of the rocky island there.

"The Pepperpot" on the north side of Portreath harbour

Later there are more steps into a valley named Hayle Ulla. "Hayle" here probably refers to marshy ground, as at Hale Mills (pages 47-8). "Ulla" doesn't appear in my dictionaries of Cornish names. Look back to see the island-rock called the Diamond ... one name that doesn't require an explanation. Near the kissing-gate, the fence ends at last. Next comes Gooden Heane (or Goodern Hawne, or Goodran End) Point; whatever the name(s) mean, it's well worth going out to the farthest tip for the view of the cove and beach, with a glimpse of the white landmark at Portreath ahead and Godrevy beyond. *The landmark (or "daymark", since it contains no light), was built about 1800 and doubled as navigational aid and coastguards' and pilots' lookout; the entrance, though sealed now, is still clearly visible. Its local nicknames are "The Pepperpot" and "The Lighthouse". The latter name, like the former, perhaps simply alludes to its appearance, but it is said that a signal light used to be shone from it.*

A postcard showing Portreath harbour about a century ago. The crane was used to raise and lower the timber baulks that protected the harbour basins during stormy weather. Beyond the walled yard can be seen the Incline.

On the way down into Portreath you will pass a rather quaint little brick-built castellated "summer house" or "watchtower". *Janet Thomas in her "Illogan" states that Laurence Binyon wrote "Hymn to the Fallen" ("They shall not grow old ...") in this building; with equal confidence the "Western Morning News" (12/11/96) declares that he wrote it as he "sat on a cliff near Polzeath gazing out over the Atlantic Ocean". (Polzeath - Portreath ... was the poet's handwriting to blame for the confusion?) Later, I am told, the building belonged to a Portreath Harbourmaster, who had it rebuilt in its present position when the road on the far side of the hairpin bend started falling over the cliff.*

Next you have an excellent view in turn of the long jetty and the outer and inner basins of the harbour. *The small round hut at the end of the pier, known as "Monkey Island", was built to protect men on lookout duty when the jetty was extended in 1824. The jetty is very dangerous to walk along in rough weather, and is therefore closed to the public.*

Just after passing the house called Fairwinds, you could take the path sharp right, leading down to the harbour, and walk round to the far side and past the Waterfront pub back to the car park. *If you do go down to the north side of the harbour, notice the small round building at the top of a flight of steps at the seaward end. Officially the Lower Coastguards' (or Pilots') Lookout, this was, says Michael Tangye, "used as a mortuary for wreck victims and others" and is still called "Deadman's Hut".*

Portreath harbour today. Up on the right in the distance is "Deadman's Hut". (SVJ)

ROUND WALK 3
PORTREATH, ILLOGAN WOODS, ILLOGAN CHURCHTOWN, BRIDGE & THE TRAMWAY
WALK 3 ON PORTREATH TRAMROAD LEAFLET

Just over 3 miles (5km)
The sketch map for this route is at the start of Round Walk 2.

This is a very easy walk with many attractive and interesting features: beautiful woodland, pleasant countryside with long views, and the oldest and prettiest part of Illogan village are the main but far from the only ones. The route passes one of Portreath's pubs; in addition there is a general store at Illogan Churchtown and a pub at Bridge.

The directions are given from the main car park overlooking the beach at Portreath, but roadside parking is usually available near Illogan parish church if you prefer, or you might care to seek permission to use the car park at the Bridge Inn.

❶ **From the car park's main entrance, cross the road and turn left along the lane leading to the Basset Arms, taking the narrow path on the left at the entrance to the pub car park.** The walk route continues past the pub, along the footpath beside the stream, with a long terrace of old cottages on the right, some very tiny. The bridge ahead carries the Incline, and when you reach it it's worth looking up to the right to see the huge granite retaining wall that was built to support it.

The Incline was cut through solid rock in 1837 or 1838 as part of the Hayle Railway, which linked the Camborne and Redruth mines to the ports of Hayle and Portreath. Several rails ran from both sides of the harbour, and horses drew wagons (usually loaded with coal) to the foot of

The foot of the Incline, photographed in 1934 by B.Y.Williams (Courtesy RIC)

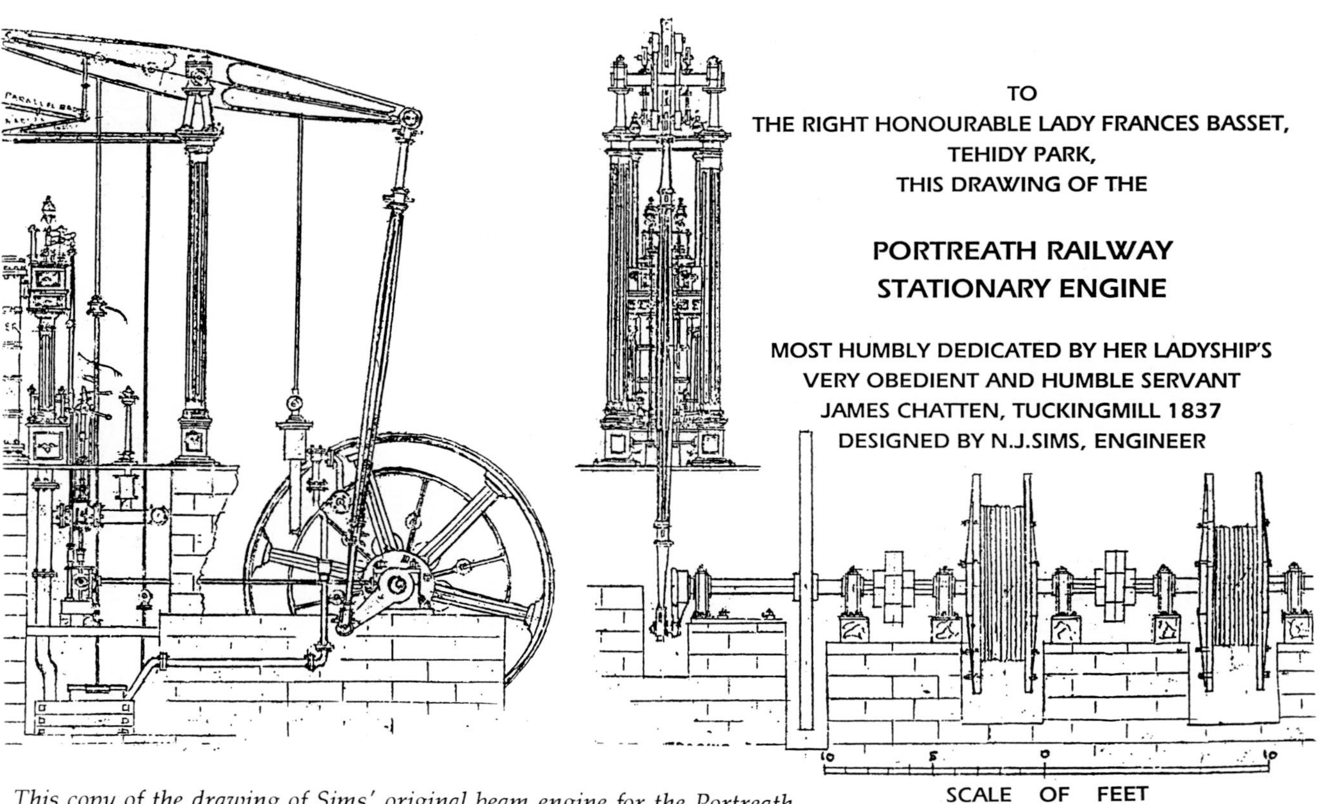

TO
THE RIGHT HONOURABLE LADY FRANCES BASSET,
TEHIDY PARK,
THIS DRAWING OF THE
PORTREATH RAILWAY
STATIONARY ENGINE
MOST HUMBLY DEDICATED BY HER LADYSHIP'S
VERY OBEDIENT AND HUMBLE SERVANT
JAMES CHATTEN, TUCKINGMILL 1837
DESIGNED BY N.J.SIMS, ENGINEER
10
5
0
10
SCALE OF FEET

This copy of the drawing of Sims' original beam engine for the Portreath Incline, though incomplete (it stops short of the cylinder on the left side), vividly illustrates the complexity and even beauty of such early machinery.

the Incline, where there were turntables. There the wagons were attached to ropes, and winding gear operated by a stationary steam engine at the top hauled them up. Locomotives took them on to the mines. The same process in reverse enabled copper ore to be taken down to the harbour and shipped to South Wales for smelting. Despite some nasty accidents, mainly in the first few days of its operation, the system worked well until the line was eventually closed in 1932. During World War 2 a wall was built across the Incline a few feet from the bottom. The reason is stated by Michael Tangye to have been to discourage German invaders from using it, though even Dad's Army wouldn't have expected Mister Hitler to be deterred by that!

Pass under the bridge and go on along Glenfeadon Terrace. *There is a brief note about the Glenfeadon House Hotel in Round Walk 1a.* **Continue ahead along Primrose Terrace, which brings you to the path through Illogan Woods. At the notice forbidding motor-cycles, continue ahead along the tarmacked path and through the narrow gap in a wall.** You will now follow a stream through a wooded valley - carpeted with bluebells in Maytime. Keep to the main track all the way, passing a few small ruined buildings on your left; there is also what seems to be an old leat. *Some or all of these are relics of a small and unsuccessful*

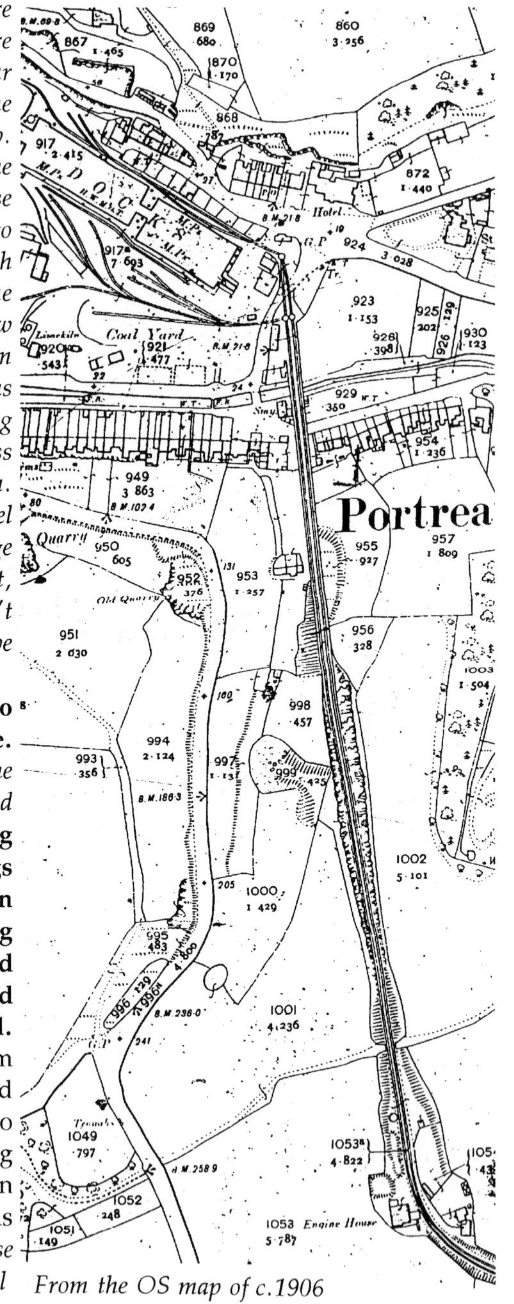

From the OS map of c.1906

mine called North Wheal Virgin which worked early last century, and the little, ochre-stained stream which flows in from the far side probably issues from the mine's adit.

This area was much used by the Bassets for pheasant shooting: there is an Iron Age hill-fort at Nance, just above the wood to the east, where shooting parties would lie in wait while the beaters went to work. In 1899 the "West Briton" reported, "Mr Basset's party had good sport last week. On Tuesday they killed 703 pheasants, on Wednesday 785 and on Thursday 1,109."

When the path emerges into the open you have a glimpse of Illogan church tower ahead. As you approach the road you have Nance Pond on your left and the well-manicured lawns of the Aviary Court Hotel on your right. *Aviary Court, otherwise called Aviary Cottage, was the home of James Tangye, one of a family of well-known engineers, towards the end of the 19th century. Janet Thomas's book on Illogan gives some entertaining details of James's inventive flair. For a little more about the Tangye family, and James's brother Richard in particular, see Volume 1 of this guide, pages 151-3. The grandchildren of the engineering brothers include Nigel Tangye, well known for his account of his life at Glendorgal, Newquay, and the prolific author Derek Tangye, whose writings mostly focus on his home between Lamorna and Porthcurno. His death at the age of 84 occurred as I was writing this book, in October 1996.*

The 81-year-old James Tangye in his workshop at Aviary Cottage, August 1906
(Courtesy Paddy Bradley)

❷ **At the road turn left.** It's a pretty little country road, which soon brings you to Illogan Churchtown. (The name refers to the church's patron saint, and is pronounced "Il -*lugg*-'n" or even just "Lugg'n".)

❸ **At the road junction just beyond the Wellbeing Centre and primary school, turn left to continue the walk ...**

... But first I suggest you enter the churchyard. (The entrance is almost opposite as you reach the road junction.) *The note about Illogan Church in Volume 1 of this guide (page 151) explains why the main body of the medieval church was demolished and replaced by a new building in the 1840s. Compare St Euny's, Redruth parish church, where all the original church apart from the tower was rebuilt to accommodate bigger congregations some 60-70 years earlier. The original intention at Illogan was to take down the tower and reconstruct it as part of the new church, but Trinity House insisted that it must stay where it had always been because it was an important landmark for seafarers. It used to be whitewashed for that reason. The clock was a gift from Frances Baroness Basset in 1836, kept time for nearly a century and a quarter, and was restored to working order in 1986.*

There are many interesting old gravestones such as the one (just left of the entrance to the churchyard as you came in) commemorating two of the six sons of Wm Willoughby, both of whom died in Ballarat, an Australian mining town, one in 1859, the other in 1861. Their father was probably the Wm Willoughby who paid 3s. 4d. to the parish in 1830 for "Portreath Stamping Mill" and dues to the Basset family of £4.6.3 in 1832 for "Copper Ore found on the beach at Portreath." (Quoted from the Illogan Rates and Tehidy Accounts by Michael Tangye in his "Portreath".) A man of note (pun not intended) in the history of Cornish music-making is buried near the north-west corner of the graveyard: Thomas Merritt (1862-1908), without whose characteristic settings of Christmas hymns no carol concert in these parts would be complete. The headstones referring to places as diverse as Tregajorran and Nancekuke are a reminder of how large the original Illogan parish was: in fact it extended as far south as Carnmenellis, east to Porthtowan and west to Hudder Down, overlooking Hell's Mouth. Notice the ancient Celtic cross, about 20m SW of the tower; it used to serve as a "station" for outdoor processions. Arthur Langdon in "Old Cornish Crosses" (1896) reports that the sexton had dug to a depth of five feet without finding the bottom of the shaft. Late in 1996 the cross was recommended to be scheduled as an Ancient Monument by English Heritage.

The new church is usually locked, though I'm told it's normally open between 2pm and 4pm on Friday afternoons. It contains several items salvaged from the old church, notably the Norman font, several carved bench-ends, and memorials to the Bassets and other important local families.

At the next road junction, where the Churchtown Mini-Market is almost opposite, turn left, following the sign to Portreath.

(If, however, you want refreshments now, other than what the Mini-Market can supply, you could turn right and continue through Illogan village for nearly half a mile. Here you will find the pub, the Robartes Arms, and almost opposite the Spar stores is the Mad Hatter's Tea Room. Its advertised opening hours are 10am - 4.30pm, Monday to Saturday - but when I called at 11am on a Thursday in August 1996 it was closed, so you might be well advised to check before making this quite lengthy diversion. Unfortunately it's not in the phone book under its trade name, so you may have to call in person.)

❹ **After about 100m turn left again, on to a signed public footpath which starts immediately past the last of the older cottages. The hedge is on your right at first, then on your left when you have crossed the first of several granite cattle grids, known in these parts as "Cornish stiles".** Now you have a wide panorama ranging from Nancekuke and St Agnes Beacon to Carn Marth (recognisable by the Pennance Mine engine house on its right-hand slope); the castle and monument on Carn Brea can just be seen above the houses behind you. **After the next cattle grid, beside a power-line pole, the path turns right to run around the edge of the field, soon bringing you back to the power-line. Here cross another grid and continue straight down the slope, following the poles at first, then going slightly left of them as the path - obvious now - runs among trees and brambles. One last grid and you are at the road in Bridge hamlet, with the Bridge Inn on your left.**

❺ **Turn left past the pub, and at the main Redruth-Portreath road left again (care needed). After less than 50m turn sharp-right on an uphill path, following the blue waymark arrow, and then after about another 80m turn sharp-left.**

You are now on the Portreath Tramroad, and should have no trouble finding your way back to the car park in Portreath. Consult the directions at the start of the Coast-to-Coast Trail if necessary, taking them in reverse of course.

ROUND WALK 4

BASSET'S COVE, THE CLIFFS, PORTREATH, ILLOGAN WOODS & TEHIDY COUNTRY PARK

WALK 4 ON PORTREATH TRAMROAD LEAFLET

About 5½ miles (9km)
The sketch map for this route is at the start of Round Walk 2.

This is a splendidly varied walk, featuring both woodland and spectacular cliffs. No road walking is involved, apart from a very little in Portreath. There are likely to be muddy patches in the woods. The cliff path between Basset's or Bassett's Cove and Portreath involves steep descents and climbs at two deep valleys. After Portreath you are well away from toilets, pubs and shops.

If you are dependent on public transport, you will need to start the walk at Portreath (point 4 in the directions). For those with cars, however, I think the best place to begin is at Basset's Cove, west of Portreath (Grid Reference: SW 638 442). By starting there you do the toughest bit of walking first, then have an opportunity to get refreshments at Portreath and maybe relax awhile on the beach. To drive to Basset's Cove from Camborne or Redruth it's best to make for Portreath first and then take the coast road south-west towards Hayle. The rough track leading to the cliffs is about 1½ miles by road from Portreath. There is parking space at the cliff end of the track, and also at the Tehidy Country Park's North Cliff Car Park, on the left a few yards further along the road.

❶ *Basset's Cove is named after the family that once owned, as far as I know, every inch of ground covered by this walk, plus a good deal of many of the other routes in this book: the Bassets of Tehidy. Portreath itself was once known as Basset's Cove, and this place was called Spratting Cove until the 1880s. Spratting Cove was a favourite recreation area for the Bassets, who built a summerhouse there.*

Turn right along the coastal footpath when you reach the cliffs, soon crossing a stile. If you have a good head for heights, it's worth taking some of the side-paths to the cliff-edge to get a better view of the splendid scenery, such as Samphire Island ahead, whose name suggests that people used to go out there gathering samphire for pickling. (Remember the imaginary clifftop scene that Edgar conjures up for his blind father in *King Lear*?

"Half way down

Hangs one that gathers samphire, dreadful trade!")

Soon come the two steep descents and climbs at Porth-Cadjack Cove. *The name is, I'm told, often said locally as "Scradjick"; what it means I don't know. In the earlier years of last century contraband, mainly brandy, was often landed at Porth-Cadjack, hidden in a cave and after dark hauled up by pulley to be stored at Trengove Farm (which you will pass later), before delivery to hotels in Camborne and Pool. An earlier name for this cove was Polscatha, meaning boat pool or - as with Portscatho on the south coast - boat cove.*

As you go up the steps on the second climb, look back to see the waterfall; in fact there were three waterfalls in January, but the two smaller ones usually dry up in summer. The valley leading down to the cove is a fine place to watch hawks. This area is called Carvannel Downs; "Carvannel", the name of the nearby farm, seems to mean "fort of the broom-plants", but I can't say I've ever noticed either fort or broom up here. Carvannel Downs is especially rich in plant life: Rose Lewis tells me that the rare, yellow-flowered dyer's greenweed (sometimes called brummel in Cornwall) and "wonderful scented burnet rose" bloom here in June, and "spring is a glory", with squill, violets, primroses, scurvy grass, thrift, blackthorn, kidney vetch, sea carrot, birdsfoot trefoil and many more, including the inevitable gorse and bluebells; later, bell heather, ling, betony and devil's bit or devil's button: a Cornish tradition was that if you picked it the Devil would come to your bedside by night. In the autumn look for field mushrooms and parasol mushrooms.

As you approach Western Cove, with its red cliffs, you may notice the group of tall masts on the clifftop in the distance; this is at RAF Portreath, otherwise known as the Nancekuke Defence Area: see pages 73-4.

Now comes the most dramatic scenery on this walk, the long, narrow promontory known as The Horse - best seen, I always feel when I'm there, by lying prone on the clifftop and peering cautiously down. Ralph's Cupboard, the gulley on the left, is thought by some to have been named after a smuggler who allegedly stored his contraband here; others say that the name refers to an ancient legendary giant called "Wrath". If you've ever seen this place on a stormy day you'll find the latter theory easy to accept.

❷ **As you approach Portreath, fork right down into the valley for the easy route, or take one of the more strenuous paths to the left round or over Western Hill.** (For details about routes and points of interest, see Round Walk 1a.)

❸ **At the bottom of the valley path is Smugglers' Cottage.**

Smugglers' Cottage once belonged to the Bassets, and descriptions are extant from about 1810 of Miss Frances Basset bathing in troughs with steps inside, still to be seen on the cliff face near the small cave. There are five of them, some with plugholes. The house, reputed to have been originally a fish cellar, is unlikely in

"The Horse" as seen from the cliff edge

fact to have been the scene of much smuggling, because for a long time the "Preventative Men" or "Preventives" were based at Portreath; indeed, the other name by which it is often known, Amy's or Amey's Cottage, apparently alludes to one Amy Jeffrey who lived there, and she was a Preventive officer's widow! Even so, there is good evidence that a tunnel led from behind a large fireplace in the cottage to a cave below ...

A possible route from here at low tide is to cross the beach and walk up from the car park to the Basset Arms. The route I would recommend, though, is to take the road above. This gives you a good view over the western side of the beach, known as Carvannel Cove.

The first harbour at Portreath was built on this side in 1713 to serve the needs of the mines. A quay jutted out 150 feet from the small headland known as "Point" or "Amy's Point", and goods presumably had to be winched to and from a clifftop track, rather like the system at Trevaunance, St Agnes. (Again, see Round Walk 1a for a little more about this.) As at St Agnes, storms soon destroyed this harbour, but its foundations are still there. Autumn gales exposed them for a while in 1983, and there is an interesting photograph of them in Michael Tangye's "Tehidy and the Bassets".

Overlooking the beach is the castellated Battery House. At this place in 1782 a battery of four 12-pound cannons was erected to protect the cove from attacks by privateers and the French. Two more cannons were positioned by the entrance to the new harbour on the east side. Only once were they fired in earnest, when a French ship in difficulties entered the harbour and was captured; otherwise they were in action only for ceremonial occasions such as the opening of the Portreath Tramroad. A cannon dated 1789 used to stand in the yard beside Battery House, but according to Clive Carter it has been "sold away". Most other remains of the battery also seem to have gone, but you can still just see where a cave was cut into the cliff, possibly as a gunpowder store. The entrance has been partially blocked now, and a concrete-block garage built in front of it. A few little castellated walls in the cliff above Battery House have also survived.

Continue down to the main road.

❹ Cross the road and continue ahead, taking the narrow path on the left at the entrance to the Basset Arms car park.

Now continue as described on pages 78-81.

❺ At the road turn right, passing a restored pump and mounting block. Soon on the left comes Glebe Farm, attractively restored and renamed "The Barnyard". **Continue along the minor road to the T-junction, and there turn right on to a somewhat busier road.**

The point immediately beyond a pair of 40mph speed-restriction signs, where the road bends slightly left, is where the Portreath Branch of the Hayle Railway crossed. You can still see where it ran: on the right a grassy lane beyond a wooden farm gate, and on the left a narrower path. **Here take another narrow path, which continues almost in the same line as you have been walking along the road. It starts with the remains of an iron kissing-gate just to the left of the entrance to a house. The path runs beside garden walls and fences for almost its entire length - nearly half a mile - and is fairly straight apart from one right-then-left manoeuvre, where there are footpath signs.**

On reaching a wide lane, turn left, and then at the road cross and turn left again. Take care - the traffic along here tends to be speedy.

❻ Turn right to enter the Tehidy Country Park at the Eastern Lodge gate.

Tehidy (said with a short i-sound, "Tehiddy") was the home of the Basset family (the Lords de Dunstanville), who were leading lights in the industrial development of Portreath, Camborne and Redruth. They acquired the Manor of Tehidy about 1150 when William Basset married into the de Dunstanville family. By 1330 they had built a large house, probably replaced in Tudor times. Mining ventures brought them great wealth by the early years of the 18th century, and work on a fine new mansion, together with a park, gardens and a lake, was started in 1734. A windbreak of trees to the north was planted, and when this was established sub-tropical shrubs were imported for the gardens. Special roads and carriageways were built, for example one to Godrevy and another to join the main Bodmin road east of Redruth. In 1779 Francis Basset earned royal favour by leading a small army of Cornish miners to Plymouth to help strengthen defences against French or Spanish invasion, and was rewarded by being made a baronet. In 1796 he became Baron de Dunstanville, and in 1797 Baron Basset of Stratton. His funeral in 1835 was probably the grandest ever seen in Cornwall, and in the following year the monument on Carn Brea was erected in his honour. Michael Tangye's "Tehidy and the Bassets" tells in some detail of the family's wealth, industrial enterprises, and "good works" such as building local schools and distributing charity. By the end of the 19th century the Basset fortunes were on the wane, largely because their income from the mines fell dramatically but their lifestyle remained extravagant: Arthur, for example, who inherited in 1888, gambled heavily at the races and spent lavishly on his own racehorses. He passed much of his time at other Basset properties "up-country", and Tehidy became increasingly neglected. In 1915 the mansion was finally vacated, and in 1916 the manors and farms were sold off. The new owners of Tehidy offered the house (plus 250 acres of the park) for sale at £10,000 for use as a chest hospital, and in January 1919 the first five TB patients were admitted. Hardly a month later, a mysterious fire devastated most of the main building. With the help of insurance money, a new, purpose-built hospital was completed by 1922. The 250-acre estate was bought in 1983 by Cornwall County Council and is being developed into an attractive woodland park with over nine miles of footpaths, some suitable for wheelchairs, and three miles of bridleways. Recent Health Service cuts have led to the closure of Tehidy Hospital; plans for future uses of the buildings were still under discussion when this book was published. A recent suggestion was for Tehidy to be the campus for a University of Cornwall, should that ever come into being, but a site near Penzance was preferred.

Continue ahead along the main track, through woods at first, then beside a fence, with the golf links on your left. *This section of the track is still called the Pine Walk, and indeed young pines have recently been planted on both sides, but the great trees that used to line it have gone now, felled by the County Council on the grounds of old age, and nothing remains of them but their sawn-off stumps, a riot of fungi.* A pictorial map of the country park, showing paths and main features of interest, is beside the seat overlooking the golf course. Almost ahead as you walk on you can see Carn Brea in the distance.

❼ Immediately after you pass through two kissing-gates into more woodland, a plentiful (and possibly confusing) choice of routes lies before you: for example, you could keep straight on, passing near the site of the Bassets' mansion, then walk along West Drive beside the Red River, and eventually reach the cliffs further west than Basset's Cove. Details are given in *A View from Carn Brea* (Walk 5) - or consult the relevant OS map.

Tehidy's Pine Walk as it was in 1989

But for the more direct route, as shown on the Portreath Tramroad leaflet, turn right. The path eventually brings you to a small clearing, at the end of which turn right, following a yellow arrow on a wooden post. This path takes you past another seat, beside which are red and yellow waymark arrows. At the "crosspaths" turn right again. Ignore the next path on the left: still follow the red arrow ahead. Where four paths meet and the red and yellow arrows point left, still go straight on for Basset's Cove. (Turning left would bring you to the North Cliff Car Park.) **Soon you leave the wood.** *From this point it's worth looking back at the profile of the woodland, shaped by the salt sea winds, with low scrub at the edge, diminutive sycamore and old coppiced beech woods next, then rather taller oak and ash, and finally big specimens of beech and other trees furthest inland.* **Cross two stone cattle-grids, and soon you will reach the main coast road. The track down to Basset's Cove is a few yards away to your left.**

ROUND WALK 5
SCORRIER, THE PORTREATH TRAMROAD, MENAGISSEY & NORTH TRESKERBY MINE

About 4½ miles
This walk, omitting the part along the Tramroad, could be treated as an extension to the longer version of Round Walk 6.

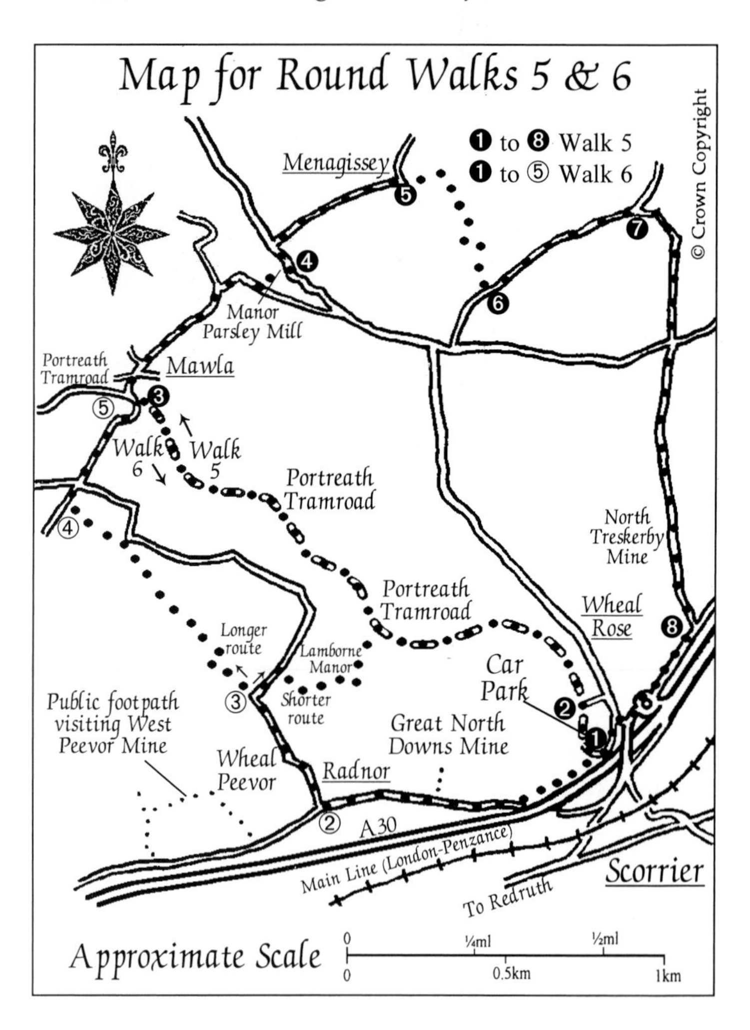

This walk begins with a substantial section of the Tramroad and then is mainly along quiet minor roads passing through attractive, quite hilly countryside. A former watermill and a well preserved engine house are on the route. One footpath is likely to be muddy. There is no shop or pub along the way.

The walk starts and ends at the small car park provided by the Mineral Tramways Project on the north side of the A30 at Scorrier. This is situated at Grid Reference SW 722 444, on the left side of the minor road which leads to Rodda's Dairies. This is the first turning on the left as you leave the A30 at the Wheal Rose / Scorrier roundabout.

❶ **The first part of the walk heads north on the old tramroad. To find it, turn left from the car park entrance, following the road as it curves right past the entrances to Rodda's and the British United Turkeys premises.**

❷ **The Portreath Tramroad is signposted ahead at the end of this road; keep to it till you come to a road: roughly 1½ miles (2½km). For information about points of interest on this part of the walk, see section 2 in the Coast-to-Coast Trail chapter.**

❸ **Turn right at the road, which takes you downhill into the hamlet of Mawla, then up past the Methodist Church. Ignore the left turn at the top of the hill, follow the road round to the right, and about 120m after the corner take the path on the left which leads quite steeply down to the Scorrier-Porthtowan road.**

❹ **Turn left** and you will see the ruined Manor Parsley mill - partially still inhabited, apparently, and by someone with a lively sense of humour. The leat is still there, on the right, and you can see where the waterwheel was: the axle-hole has been blocked with bricks. **Now take the side-turning on the right - a pretty little road leading up to Menagissey.** (The first part of this name means "hill". The rest could possibly refer to St Issey, from whom a village near Padstow takes its name; he or she is also associated with Mevagissey. T.F.G.Dexter also offers "terrible hill", but that only seems to prove he hasn't been to Menagissey! .... or was it a terrible climb?)

❺ **Where the road turns left by a post-box, carry straight on along the track ahead. After the farm, fork right, following the Public Bridleway.** Beyond Bluebell Cottage the shady path tends to be muddy except in summer, especially as you approach the stream. **Cross the wooden footbridge if necessary** (it doesn't look particularly safe!) **and turn left on to a tractor track at the T-junction.**

❻ **Turn left again at the road and go on along this for nearly half a mile.**

❼ **Take the first right turning, a very narrow, quiet road, and at the crossroads continue ahead. After about a quarter of a mile you will pass**

close to the engine house at Doctor's or Baron's Shaft, North Treskerby Mine. *It was built about 1873 for an 80-inch pumping engine; it has been stated that the engine never actually worked here, but a detailed site inspection would be required to verify this. There are also the remains of several other buildings. North Treskerby was a copper mine which also produced some tin, iron and arsenic during the period for which we have sales figures, 1859-92. Under the name of Trewan or Truan Mine it was already producing copper in the 18th century.*

Continue along the road till you reach the former A30.

❽ Turn right along the pavement. *The engine house and separate stack (in fact the remains of another engine house) on the other side of the new A30 and the railway belonged to Hallenbeagle Mine.* *For information, see page 28.* **At the roundabout turn right and then first left to return to the car park.**

The pumping-engine house at Doctor's Shaft, North Treskerby Mine (SVJ)

ROUND WALK 6
SCORRIER, WHEAL PEEVOR & THE TRAMROAD
with a possible extension across North Downs to Forge Farm
WALK 5 ON PORTREATH TRAMROAD LEAFLET

About 2½ miles (4km); with the extension, nearly 4 miles (6.5km)
The longer version can be linked to the latter part of Round Walk 5 to make one walk of about 5½ miles (9km).
For the sketch map, see the start of Round Walk 5.

The surface remains of Wheal Peevor are currently inaccessible to the general public, but this walk takes you close enough for a pretty good view of the main features. "This grouping of engine-houses for pumping, winding and stamps engines," wrote Hamilton Jenkin, "was formerly characteristic of every large Cornish mine" - but I believe it's the only remaining example where all three buildings, together with smaller structures, have survived in so complete a form. The walk there and back also skirts the vast workings of the Great North Downs copper mines. The shorter route passes the attractive and ancient Lamborne Manor, and the longer one crosses open downland with long views. Both versions of the walk as described here end with a section of the Portreath Tramroad, but the longer route could instead return to Scorrier by way of North Treskerby mine, whose pumping-engine house dominates the skyline in this part of Cornwall.

There is no shop or pub along any of these routes, but refreshments are available from several sources near the start-end point, as described in the Coast-to-Coast Trail section: see page 28.

Like Round Walk 5, this one is based on the small car park provided by the Mineral Tramways Project on the north side of the A30 at Scorrier. See page 91 for directions to it.

❶ **From the car park entrance turn left along the minor road, and where it curves right towards Rodda's take the signed public footpath ahead, a tarmacked path which runs alongside the dual carriageway.** As long as you're not too offended by the noise and fumes from the traffic below, this is quite pleasant, with views of Scorrier Woods left and the long sheds of North Downs Farm on the right, now in use for rearing battery turkeys. **At the end of the path, continue ahead along the road - now a cul-de-sac because of the bypass road.** After about a quarter of a mile you pass quite near a small stack (colour photograph 9), which seems to be the only building from Great North Downs mine (apart from the count house, at the Wheal Rose end of the sett) to have survived. *It is a quaint little structure, but not as old as it looks, dating from early this century when a horizontal engine was installed here during an operation reworking the burrows.* (There is no official right of way to the stack, but a short farm lane leads towards it from the road, and beside the gate at the end is a stile, so it appears that the landowner is happy for people to go and have a close look. If you do, take care not to get a foot stuck in the metal cattle grid just before the gate. The immediate surroundings of the stack, including two fenced open shafts, are fenced off from the Radnor Golf Centre's course.)

For information about Great North Downs Mine, see pages 24-6.

❷ Turn right opposite the disused Radnor United Methodist Church, along the road running past the trio of magnificent engine houses of Wheal Peevor.

Wheal Peevor (SVJ)

Wheal Peevor is an old mine, at work at least as far back as the 18th century as part of Great North Downs, but it lay dormant for many years before being restarted in 1872 as a separate enterprise. The new company benefited from the fact that the shallower workings were drained by the County Adit (see pages 52-3), and when a very rich body of tin was struck 40 fathoms below the adit prosperity was assured throughout the 1870s, despite the fact that low tin prices were forcing dozens of other Cornish mines to close. By the early 1880s, however, the rich ore was running out, and the directors decided to explore the neighbouring ground to the west, formerly part of Treleigh Consols copper mine. Three new engine houses were erected on what was now named West Peevor. The venture was a failure, and in about 1886 both West and Wheal Peevor were abandoned.

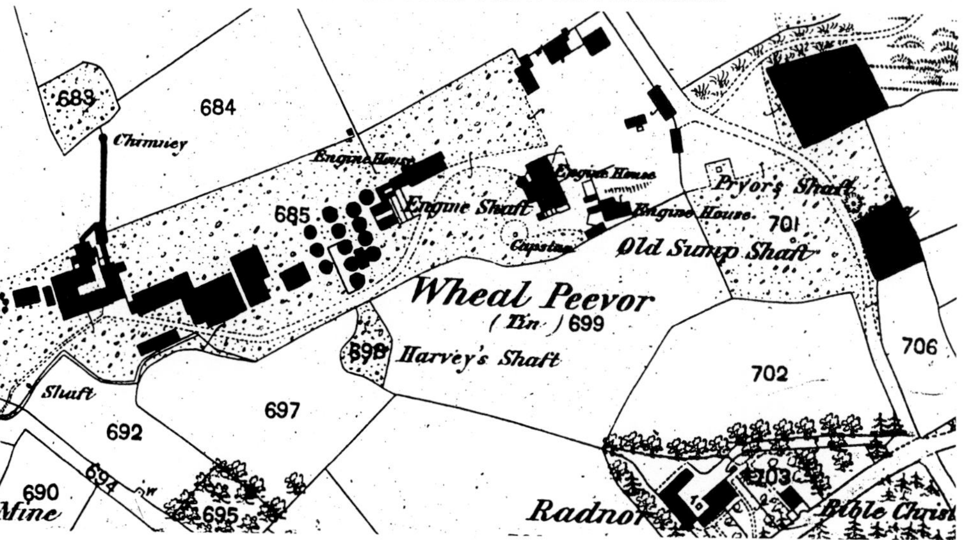

Wheal Peevor as shown on the 1st Edition OS map

Wheal Peevor was reopened in 1911 for tungsten, but World War 1 finally put paid to the mine. West Peevor was re-investigated in 1938, again about 1950 (when the top of the 50-inch pumping-engine house was removed for safety reasons), and yet again in the 1960s-70s.

The farm house by the road and the three closest engine houses belonged to Wheal Peevor. The nearest one was for the 22-inch whim (winding) engine; the middle one, built for a 60-inch pumping engine, had an old 70-inch engine squeezed into it in 1911; and the third worked the stamps with a 36-inch engine. In 1911-12 a gas engine was installed in it to drive Californian stamps, the loadings of which survive. Just beyond these engine houses are the remains of extensive dressing floors, with numerous ruined buildings including at least one calciner; a little further off are the remains of West Peevor. The West Peevor stamps-engine house is still largely intact despite the parlous-looking state of its wing walls.

West Peevor's stamps-engine house as it was in 1996 (SVJ)

PLEASE NOTE: A public footpath shown on the OS maps and on the sketch map at the start of Walk 5 runs close to the West Peevor remains, but all the engine houses are in an unsafe condition, there are still open and unprotected shafts, and no right of way exists along the track passing through the Wheal Peevor site. Negotiations regarding public access were under way at the time of writing (late 1996), but in the mean time special permission is required to enter the site, which belongs to English China Clays PLC.

Continue along the road. Once you have passed Wheal Peevor farm house (the former count house), it's worth pausing to study the view, which takes in (from left to right) Carn Brea, Woolf's engine house of Condurrow United Mine on the skyline, South Crofty Mine, Carbis Bay near St Ives, the Portreath valley, and, much further right, St Agnes Beacon. Close at hand on the right are shaft burrows of Great North Downs Mine, and on the left in the middle distance can be seen the upper part of a calciner stack belonging to Wheal Peevor and the stamps engine house belonging to West Peevor.

❸ **At the right-hand bend you have a choice of ways.**

FOR THE SHORTER WALK turn right and take the track on the right after about 150m, which has a Public Footpath sign. This takes you past the old and attractively restored manor house of Lamborne ("rushy pool"), with its fine view across the valley to the North Treskerby Mine stamps-engine and pumping-engine houses. The slightly taller section at the far end of Lamborne Manor consists of the barns. All around are the deep, uncapped shafts of Great North Downs mine. **Go on down the main track, but when it bends quite sharply left continue downhill on the slightly narrower track or path. This brings you to the old tramroad** (notice the granite sleeper-block to the left as you join it)**; to return to your car, turn right** (several more sleeper-blocks to see). **Now follow the directions for the Coast-to-Coast Trail from page 24 line 20 as far as the end of section 2 (p. 27). Turn right before the slip road for the car park.**

FOR THE LONGER WALK do not turn right, but continue ahead along a wide lane, which soon passes between two shaft burrows. *These are relics of Little North Downs, another old and productive copper mine: its recorded output (1815-71) included nearly thirty thousand tons of 8% copper ore. Its pumping and whim engines are said to have been moved to Wheal Peevor after closure.* **After right and left bends the lane narrows slightly to a tractor track. Ignore a similar track on the right. At the road continue ahead.**

❹ **At the crossroads, where Forge Cottage and Forge Villa are, turn right.** (As mentioned in the Coast-to-Coast Trail section, "forge" here apparently has nothing to do with blacksmiths but simply means "dwelling".)

❺ **Just beyond the buildings of Forge Farm the Tramroad crossed. Here again you have a choice of ways:**

TO EXTEND THE WALK VIA MENAGISSEY AND NORTH TRESKERBY MINE, continue along the road, picking up the directions for Round Walk 5 at point 3 (p91) - ignoring the first 5 words, of course.

TO RETURN VIA THE TRAMROAD TO THE CAR PARK, turn right, following a Public Bridleway sign in addition to the blue arrow on a Portreath Tramroad wooden post. Now pick up the directions for the Coast-to-Coast Trail at the words "For the Trail", line 6 on page 24, and continue to the end of section 2, except that you need to turn right just before the A30 slip road to find the car park.

ROUND WALK 7
KILLIFRETH, UNITY WOOD, CHACEWATER & WHEAL BUSY
WALK 7 ON PORTREATH TRAMROAD LEAFLET

About 3 miles (4.5km)

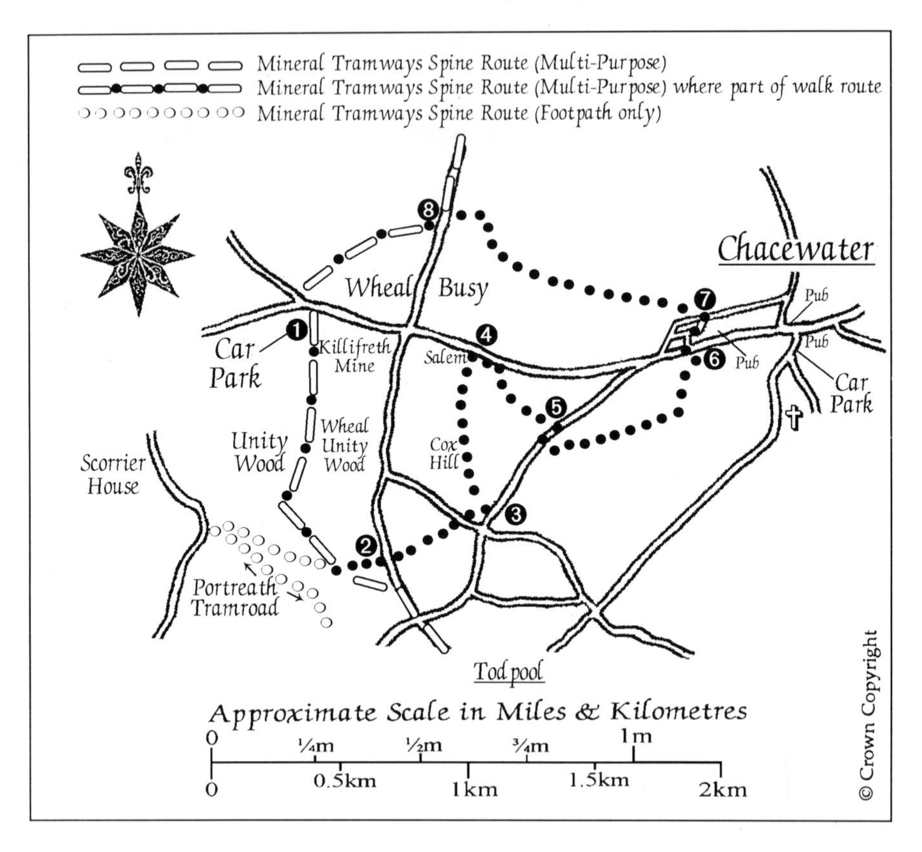

This is an easy walk linking some of the most impressive and important mine sites in the area. The route passes through attractive countryside, partly wooded and partly open with long views. At Chacewater (about two-thirds of the way along the walk) there are toilets, a general provisions shop and a choice of three pubs. Some sections of the route, especially where bridleways are used, are likely to be muddy, and a short stretch - no more than about 75m - runs along a fairly busy road where there is no verge or sidewalk.

The start-end point is the small car park close to the Hawke's Shaft engine house, Killifreth Mine, Grid Reference SW 734 445. This is on the south side of the road between Chacewater and Redruth. If you are driving from Chacewater, after about a mile continue ahead at the crossroads where Wheal Busy is signposted to the right; about a quarter of a mile further on, immediately before the road bends left, watch for the sign on the left, Killifreth Engine House. Turn into the lane beside that, and you will find the car park on the right just before the gate.

❶ **Turn right as you leave the car park and follow the directions for the Coast-to-Coast Trail, starting on page 37 at line 9 and finishing on page 42 at line 10. This includes the recommended detour up the path beside the pair of engine houses at Magor's Shaft, Wheal Unity Wood.**

❷ **On reaching the road at Wheal Bush, instead of turning left (to visit the other Killifreth mine buildings), continue ahead on the signed Public Bridleway.** Near the start of this bridleway, if you are tall enough to see over the hedge you may catch a glimpse to the left of the burrow surrounding another shaft belonging to Wheal Unity Wood, and soon the path runs beside yet another, fenced and Clwyd-capped, on the right. The farm gate on the right a little further on gives a view to the right stretching from the rather lop-sided chimney of the Cusvey (Consols) engine house on the left, to St Day church on the right, with the Consols clock tower and nearby engine houses in the centre. In the same direction as them but closer is the arsenic stack at Poldice. **At the road, cross and continue ahead beside the Truro Tractors building.**

❸ **Immediately before reaching a second road, take the signed Public Byway on the left.** Soon you pass the sad ruin of one of Cornwall's many Bible Christian chapels. *"One third of Cornish Methodism is of Bible Christian origin," according to Thomas Shaw (MGC). The founder of the sect, William O'Bryan, was born at Luxulyan in 1778, but the most famous Bible Christian in these parts was Billy Bray: see pages 49-50.* As you walk on, the Killifreth stamps-engine house comes into view ahead. **About 100m beyond the chapel you come to the cottages at Cox Hill; here the byway (indicated by red arrows) turns half-right and dwindles to quite a narrow path. Another 250m brings you to a large house on the left, and immediately past that you turn right on to a tarmacked lane which soon reaches the main Chacewater-Redruth road.**

❹ **Turn right on the road, keeping well in to the right.** As I said in the introductory note, the amount of walking you have to do on this busy road is mercifully little: **after about 75m, where the road widens immediately before the old house named Salem Farm, take the signed Public**

Bridleway on the right, which starts by passing between an old farm building and a hay barn.

The Biblical-sounding name of this district can be matched by many others in Cornwall, such as Little Canaan near Truro, several Bethels, and Jericho in Trevellas Coombe near St Agnes, not far from which is Promised Land.

The path, rather muddy at times, runs gently uphill; towards the end it tends to be rather brambly in late summer.

❺ **At the road turn right, and after about 30m take the signed bridleway on the left.** This is again uphill at first, but then levels off and becomes narrower. **Ignore the path on the right, indicated by a red (byway) arrow; the blue (bridleway) arrow seems to point left, but your way lies straight ahead.**

At the top of the slope you have a long view to the left. *The church on the skyline is Mithian Parish Church, built in Victorian times two miles from Mithian village, with little but the Chiverton Arms and the busy Three Burrows roundabout for neighbours. It has a certain interest for mining enthusiasts, since when the spire it originally had was destroyed by lightning in 1898 a new tower was built, using stone from a nearby engine house. Further left and much closer, you can see Wheal Busy's pumping-engine house and smithy.*

On reaching a gravelled lane, go left, downhill. Pass on the left side of Anzac Cottage, where the lane becomes a grassy path for a while, before running quite steeply down to the same main road you were briefly on before.

❻ Here you are on the edge of Chacewater village, and the Rambling Miner is visible, little more than 100m away; not much further along are the Britannia Inn and the King's Head. Opposite the last of these is the general store. Public toilets are in the village car park, which you will find by turning right immediately before the King's Head. A note about Chacewater is included in Round Walk 10 (pages 154-5). (If you decide to go into the village, when you are ready to resume the walk you need not return along the main road: take the side road heading north which starts between the King's Head and the Britannia, and then the first left turning, Wheal Busy Lane. After nearly a quarter of a mile, fork right on to a narrower lane, picking up the directions at point 7.)

To continue the walk without going into Chacewater, cross the road and walk up Buckingham Nip, almost opposite. At the T-junction go right, then sharp-left when you reach the sign, Wheal Busy Lane.

❼ This narrower lane runs uphill at first, soon becoming a rough track. At the top of the slope you get a distant view of St Day (note the clock tower) with Carn Marth beyond; further right are Unity Wood and the woods around Scorrier House.

When you reach the area dominated by the massive, heather-clad burrows of Wheal Busy, you are presented with a mining panorama that has few rivals. Fairly close on the right is the pumping-engine house at Wheal Busy's Engine Shaft, with the old smithy building to its left. Moving on round to the left, the twin "horns" just visible on the skyline, are the top of what remains of the bob wall at Black Dog Shaft, Wheal Busy. Much closer is the Wheal Busy arsenic stack, with the calciners on its left; and finally, the surface buildings of Killifreth mine: first the very tall chimney of the Hawke's Shaft pumping-engine house, then Sump Shaft pumping-engine, next, a little closer, an arsenic stack, and just to its left but further off, Killifreth stamps. With sharp eyes and if you choose your position carefully you may also be able to make out the two engine houses at Magor's Shaft, Wheal Unity Wood. (The skyline sketch below is from a slightly different angle - just to confuse you!)

Head for the nearest engine house at first, following yellow (footpath) arrows; before reaching the engine house turn left, passing to the left side of the smithy building.

The Wheal Busy site is of tremendous historic importance. Brief information about its history and the main mining features to be seen is given on pages 34-6. For a much more detailed account, see Walk 2 in ECM2. The flora and fauna of this site are described in Appendix 1 of this book.

Walk immediately to the right of a fenced and walled shaft and along the short track ahead.

❽ Cross the minor road and go on in the same direction along the wide, stony path, still following yellow arrows. At the end of a short stretch of "dual carriageway", your best route is to turn left: this short track soon brings you back to the main road, almost opposite the lane to the Killifreth car park. Strictly speaking, the short track just mentioned is not a right of way; I'd be amazed if anyone ever challenged your right to use it, but to avoid any risk of that, continue ahead till you reach another road. This way has the advantage of taking you quite close to ruins of the Black Dog Shaft engine house. (See page 32.) **Turn left on the road, then left again at the main road to return to the car park.**

Skyline profile looking south from Wheal Busy

ROUND WALK 8

POLDICE, THE PORTREATH TRAMROAD, UNITY WOOD & TODPOOL

WALK 8 ON PORTREATH TRAMROAD LEAFLET

About 3½ miles (5.5km)

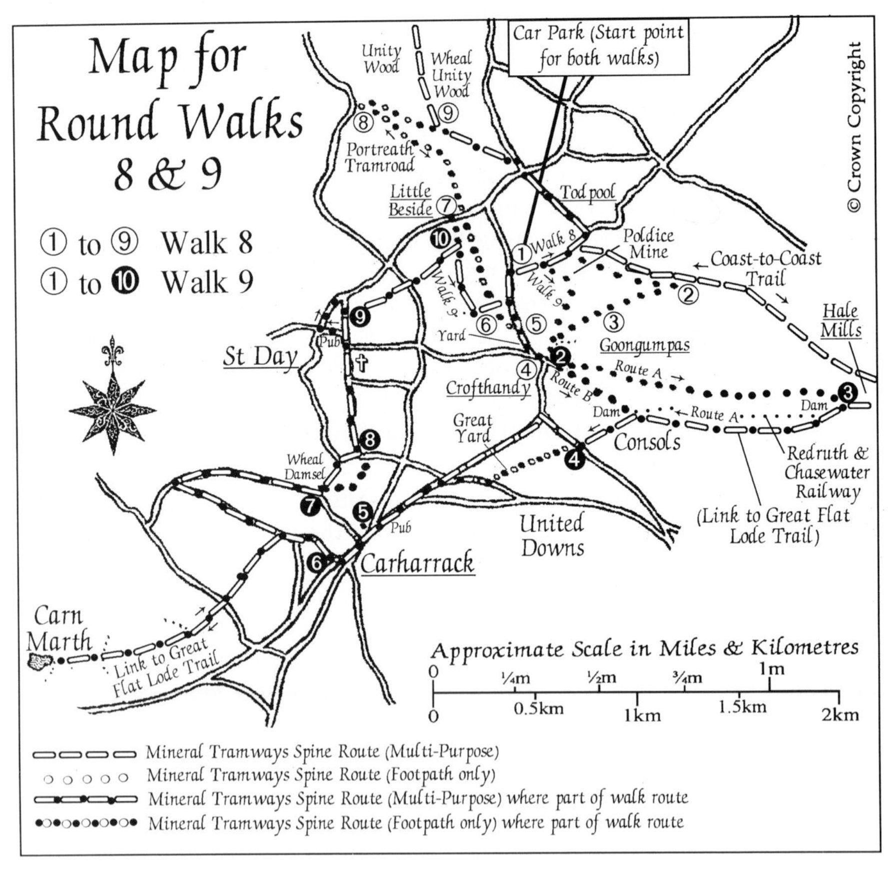

This interesting and attractive short walk includes a visit to the Poldice arsenic works buildings and associated remains, a short tour of the fascinating landscape of the Poldice Valley, and one of the best-preserved sections of the Portreath Tramroad. It is an easy walk, mostly on wide tracks and quiet roads, but in wet weather you would probably need boots in a few parts of the valley below Unity Wood. There is no pub or shop along the way.

The directions start and end at the small car park provided by Groundwork Kerrier in association with the Poldice Valley Trust (using a Derelict Land Grant negotiated via Carrick District Council) at what the Trust has christened Wheal Unity Gate. Situated at Grid Reference SW 737 429, it is on the east side of the minor road heading north from Crofthandy towards Chacewater. If you approach from Crofthandy chapel, take the first lane or track on the right, where you should see in front of you the Wheal Unity Gate sign; the car park is on the left before you reach the sign.

Before setting off on the walk, you may care to inspect the ruins of the one engine house which has survived in recognisable form in the Poldice Valley, at Sir Frederick's Shaft of Wheal Unity, later part of Poldice Mines.

To find it, go to the end of the car park furthest from the entrance, through the gap into a sheltered area with two seats, and follow the path round to the right. On your right now is the shaft, walled around and Clwyd capped, with the base of the bob wall - more than six feet thick - of the engine house almost beside it. The gap in the bob wall was the eduction (exhaust) pipe opening above the condenser. If you walk round to the back of the engine house you will see the semicircular part-base of the stack. Notice how thick the masonry was at the bottom, about five feet, necessary to support the weight; as it rose the wall became progressively thinner - hence the taper - while the vent remained roughly the same: about three feet in this case. Beyond the chimney was a boiler house, the lower part of whose end wall can still be seen. From the interior of the engine house it is clear that a second boiler lay alongside; the engine in fact had three boilers. The engine was a large one with an 85-inch-diameter cylinder; it was made at the Perran Foundry (Round Walk 13) and erected here in 1872. The engine house is thought to have been one of the many in

Cornwall that were used for target or demolition practice by the military during World War 2.

Although there is so little of Wheal Unity to see on the surface now, it was once one of the richest mines in the area. There may well have been small mines here in earlier times, but Wheal Unity itself seems, according to H.G.Dines, to have started about 1790, although Hamilton Jenkin in "The Cornish Miner" writes, "In 1773 the women breaking ores by hand at Wheal Unity ... were getting 5d a day." Already by 1798 it had made profits of over £100,000, mainly from sales of copper ore. Soon after that it was amalgamated with Poldice Mine, but its accounts continued to be recorded separately, so we know that it went on doing well: D.B.Barton claims that by 1818 it "had for some years been the principal copper mine in Cornwall, other than Dolcoath and the United Mines and, even though it declined after a peak output of almost 7,000 tons in 1816, it was still the most important mine around St Day"(ECMH2). J.H.Collins (1912) says that its total profits amounted to £400,000. By the middle of the 19th century it was dependent on selling arsenic, along with a little tin. In 1864 it became part of St Day United Mines, later reverting to Poldice Mines.

Like its neighbour Wheal Gorland (see page 146), Wheal Unity was famous for producing rare and beautiful mineral specimens such as chalcophyllite, olivenite ("wood copper") and mimetite. Examples of each, all from Wheal Unity, are shown in "Minerals of Cornwall and Devon" by P.G.Embrey and R.F.Symes (1987): see pages 94-5 and 115 of their book. Wheals Gorland, Unity and Muttrell (which became part of Gorland) were known particularly for producing "classic" specimens of the lovely blue crystals called liroconite (page 113). James King, of County Maps and Minerals in Truro, tells me that the miners, well aware of the value of such specimens, would smuggle them out of the mine by covering them with a type of soft white clay found underground. Sometimes they enlisted the help of bal maidens, who could secrete the minerals among their voluminous skirts.

❶ From the car park entrance turn left.

The information board provided by the Mineral Tramways Project beside the Wheal Unity Gate sign is well worth studying. Of particular relevance to this walk is the artist's impression of the Crofthandy coal storage yard.

The green waymark arrows on Portreath Tramroad Trail posts should be followed at first: keep left at the first fork, then left again, then right, towards the nearby old mine building, the Poldice arsenic works. Next again keep left, but when you reach the building ignore the green arrow pointing left: continue ahead, keeping to the right side of a detached wall at first. A couple of steps up on the right give you easy access to two buddles (one convex, one concave) and the main arsenic works buildings, with the remains of the labyrinth flue on the far side, leading up to the stack. On the south and east sides of the arsenic works are several more recent concrete structures. *Some of these date from 1919-26 when the Poldice* *burrows were being reworked for tin by the Berrida company. (See below.) Most, however, date from 1928-30, when this site was used to dress ore (tin and wolfram), brought by overhead cableway from Park-an-Chy mine, about 1½ miles to the north-west, where the water supply was inadequate for the purpose. The most prominent concrete remains (see Simon Vere Jones's photograph below) are the bases of Californian stamps and of the aerial ropeway terminal (the star-shaped structure), plus the floor and plinths from the power house for the ropeway, which was driven by an 18 h.p. electric motor.*

For information about the earlier industrial history of this site - Poldice Mine and the arsenic works - see the Coast-to-Coast Trail, pages 44-5.

Continue along the track at the slightly lower level, as before, and keep to the lower track running beside the large, whitish heaps, known as "The Sands" (colour photograph 16), consisting of arsenic-rich waste material from the Park-an-Chy operation. (Whenever it's windy and dry, fine dust blows off these in great clouds, so for the sake of local residents they may be covered and revegetated in due course.) **Just beyond them, take the rough path down to the valley floor.**

❷ At the end of the flat-bottomed, open area known as Bissa Pool, turn up to the right on a clear path, and at the top of that go right again on to an uphill track. *On your right soon, notice the concrete foundation, the most obvious relic of the operation shown in the accompanying photograph. Beginning in 1917, the company concerned, Berrida (Nigeria) Tin Fields Ltd., set up a tin-*

dressing mill here including a magnetic separator and Californian stamps. The latter can be seen near the top-right corner of the photograph. Once operations began, in 1919, horses drew wagons of ore along the tramway to the foot of the wooden incline, and the ore was then hauled to the top mechanically and fed to the stamps. Water for dressing purposes was pumped from Bissa Pool Shaft, below. Ore was obtained from shallow underground workings and the dumps left by earlier mining. In 1920 147 men were employed (only two of them underground) and 4,300 tons of ore were treated. The operation ceased in 1923 because of poor tin sales, but according to Eric Edmonds, to whose article in the Trevithick Society's Newsletter 75 I am indebted for most of this information, "a number of local men then acquired a sub-lease and installed 10 stamps to continue working the dumps, using the magnetic separator which had been left on site."

Bissa Pool Shaft is of great interest to mining historians, because a 90-inch engine was erected there as early as 1821, one of three Woolf engines built at Neath Abbey Ironworks. Barton tells the story of its journey here from South Wales: because of bad weather it had to be landed at Padstow rather than Hayle, resulting in the need for a difficult and costly overland trek of nearly 30 miles (CBE p.41).

Keep going uphill. From this track you get good views of the Poldice Valley, with many fenced and/or walled shafts close by, and in the distance St Day and the engine houses of Killifreth and Wheal Unity Wood.

❸ At the Goongumpas Gate sign go straight on, and still continue ahead along the rough lane which ends at Crofthandy Chapel.

❹ Turn sharp-right along the road signposted Chacewater. *The area on the left at the corner at the start of this road is the site of the Crofthandy storage yard and coal pit which marked the southern terminus of the Portreath Tramroad. The*

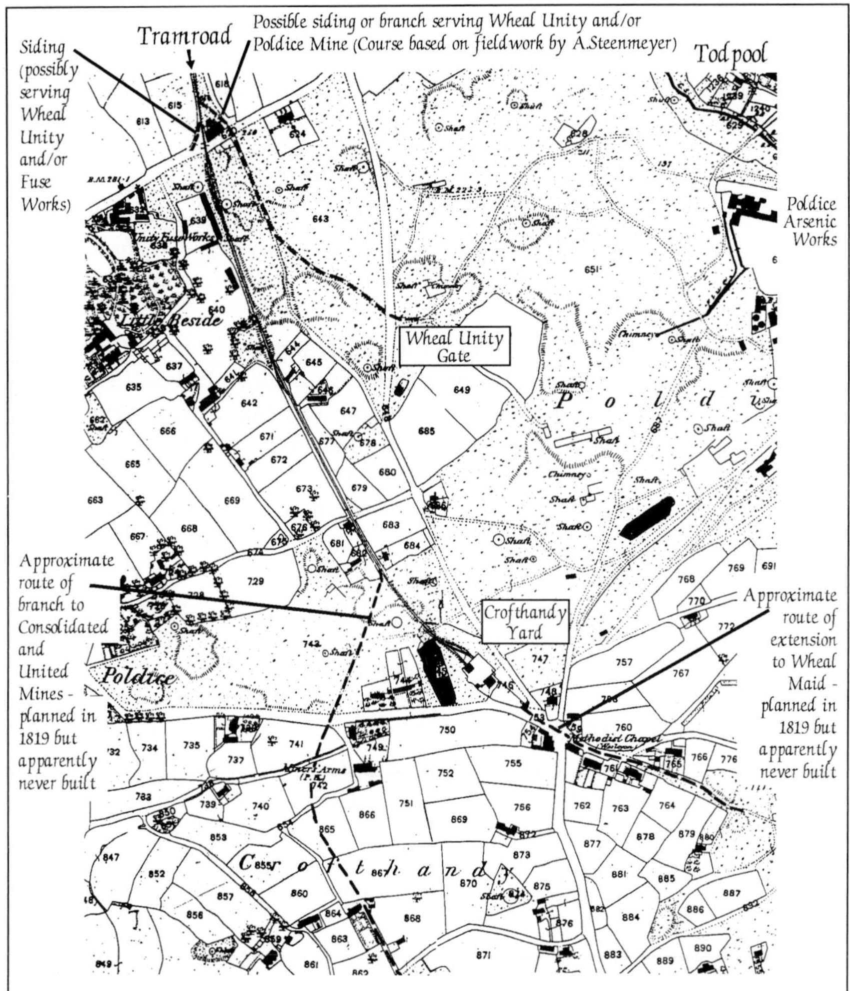

The southern end of the Portreath Tramroad as shown on the 1st Edition Ordnance Survey Map of 1878-9, with an indication of branches, sidings or extensions for which there is some evidence - documentary or on the ground.

line came in at a higher level than the floor of the yard, so that coal, timber and other bulk loads could be simply tipped from the wagons, probably via chutes, into the storage bays or waiting carts. Just to the left of the telephone box, a black, oval Mineral Tramways plaque is fixed to a low wall, part of what was once the tallyman's hut beside the Tramroad's weighbridge. Ore and other goods to be transported to Portreath would be weighed here for the carriage charge to be calculated, and then taken up a ramp to the horse-drawn wagons on the line. In April 1819 John Williams Jnr acquired the lease of land for the building of two extensions to the Tramroad. One was to have diverged westwards from the main line just north of the yard, then curved south towards United Downs. The other would have left the yard at the southern end, crossed the road near Crofthandy Methodist Church and continued along or beside Chapel Terrace, eventually reaching the Wheal Maid engine house on the south side of Goongumpas. To the best of my knowledge, neither of these extensions was actually built, in which case the coal, ore and other supplies would have had to do the first or final part of their journey by horse and cart.

❺ To shorten the walk you could continue along this road to the Wheal Unity Gate car park (the first turning right after the right-hand bend).

For the complete walk, take the first turning left, marked Little Beside, where there is a Portreath Tramroad sign. (But first you might care to take a look at the big open shaft beside the road on the right just a few yards further along the road, where there is a length of granite wall topped by metal fencing.)

The track soon joins the course of the tramroad. **Bear right**, past a house called "Silverley" where home-made honey is sometimes on sale.

❻ Where another track crosses there is a well-preserved collection of exposed granite setts. Continue straight ahead, keeping to the tramway route. You soon reach a patch of rough ground beside the Triplets Car Spares yard where the railway track has been obliterated. **The most obvious path curves to the right, around a hump, but still go straight on, over the hump, and follow the narrow path - rough, but fairly level, since it marks where the tramroad ran.** Notice the Clwyd-capped shaft on the left just before you pass a building on that side. *Old maps show at least five shafts belonging to Wheal Unity in this area. The building is probably a relic of the Unity Fuse Works, mentioned near the end of the note on St Day (page 145).* **Soon a small yellow arrow directs you to the right, but you can still continue ahead, down a few steps and then along the very narrow path between a stone hedge and a wire fence.**

❼ At the road, cross and continue ahead, following the Portreath Tramroad sign and an older sign to Zimapan. The very prominent sleeper blocks at the start of the public footpath are part of a siding heading towards the Unity Fuse Works site. *The Tramroad was near the end of its* *active life when the Fuse Works was established, about 1870, but an engine house at Wheal Unity's Old Sump Shaft previously occupied roughly the same site, and a branch line may have served that. The OS map of 1879-80 does not show any such line, but it is likely that sidings would have been constructed wherever and whenever the need existed, soon to be abandoned and either dismantled or overgrown.* After about 60m you reach the point where a complicated pattern of setts suggests that another siding or branch diverged from the main line, this time heading south-east. (See the map on page 107 and colour photograph 13.)

Take the somewhat narrower path following the line of setts as it forks left from the main track. Ahead is the tall, graceful stack of Killifreth Mine, and to the right are the twin engine houses at Magor's Shaft, Wheal Unity Wood. At the point where you are nearest to those, and also close to a large farm building in the field on the right, if you look closely at the alignment of the setts you will see that there was a passing loop on the right here. Just below the farm building is a newly-excavated area. **Cross the stile topped by a small wooden gate** just before the pond - though in summer it is often bone dry - **and continue ahead beside the wall, still following the course of the tramway.** The pond was dug only recently. On the other side of the valley is Unity Wood, part of which is explored on the main Coast-to-Coast Trail. Notice, opposite the tree that stands by itself on the right side of the track, a low arch in the wall on the left: could this have been built for the leat carrying water from Pednandrea to Wheal Unity's dressing floors? They were down on the right.

Wheal Unity's dressing floors, where the ore was crushed and prepared for smelting, were in this valley. The dressing processes required a constant and copious supply of water, and it was decided that the best source for this was the adit of Pednandrea Mine, Redruth - a surprising decision, because it entailed the construction of a leat six miles long, including over four thousand feet of tunnel. Richard Thomas's Geological Map of 1819 (part of which is reproduced in reduced size on pages 110-1) shows the leat, starting at Plain-An-Gwarry, on the north side of Redruth. It snaked its way northwards, following the contour line through Gilbert's Coombe and North Country, then still further north to Kerrow Farm, not far south of Mawla. There it turned south-east, running roughly parallel with the Portreath Tramroad and entering the tunnel just south of Wheal Rose. Next it passed under what are now the A30 and the main railway line, and surfaced close to the St Day-Scorrier road, roughly where the drive to Killifreth Farm begins. For the last mile-or-so it ran along the western side of the tramway, apparently coming to an end at the St Day-Chacewater road, at the point where the Unity Fuse Works was later built. Chris Massie of the Poldice Valley Trust says that water still flowed in the leat till the mid-1970s, when the deep cutting for the new A30 Redruth-Camborne bypass severed the tunnel.

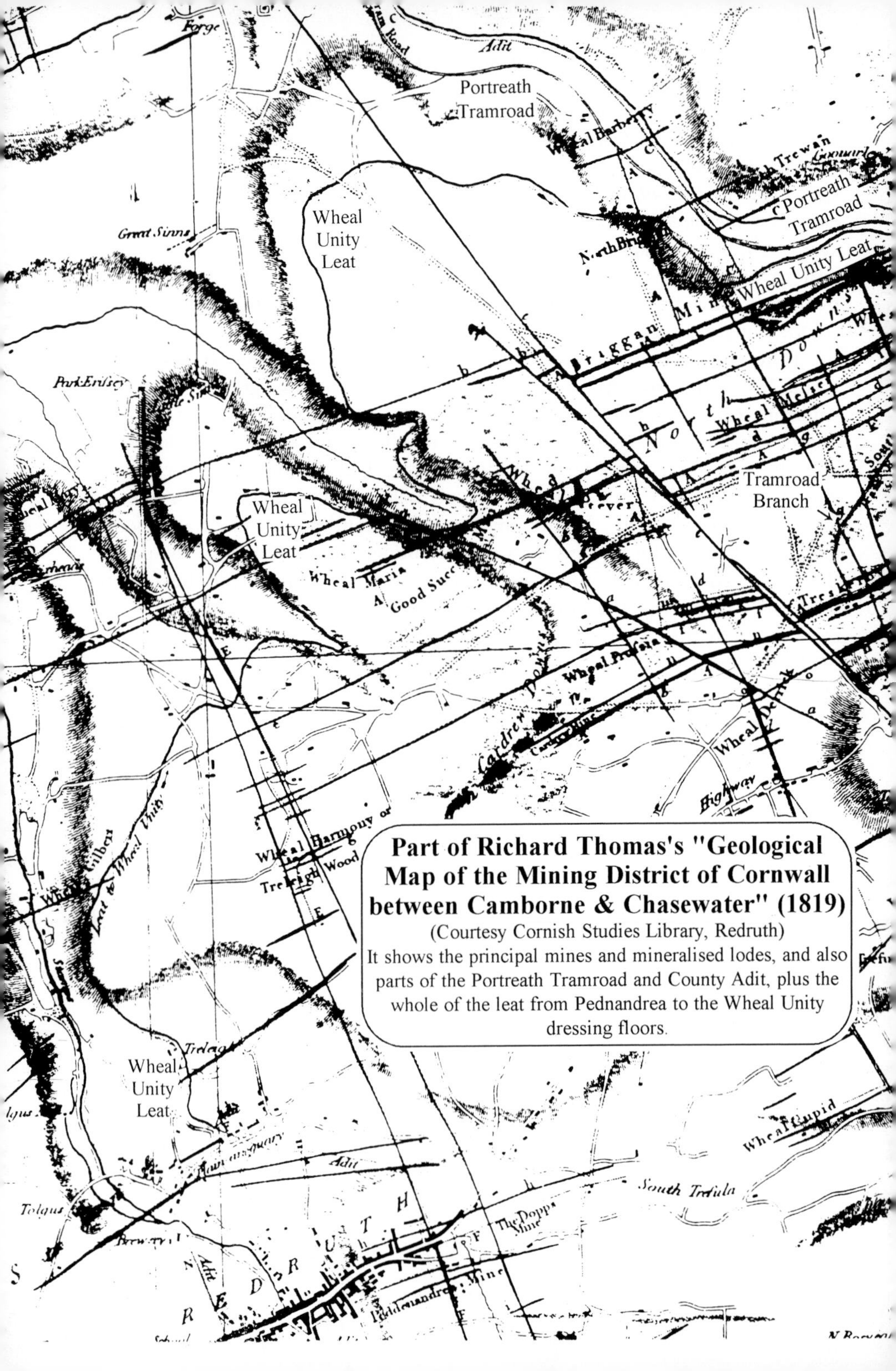

Part of Richard Thomas's "Geological Map of the Mining District of Cornwall between Camborne & Chasewater" (1819)
(Courtesy Cornish Studies Library, Redruth)
It shows the principal mines and mineralised lodes, and also parts of the Portreath Tramroad and County Adit, plus the whole of the leat from Pednandrea to the Wheal Unity dressing floors.

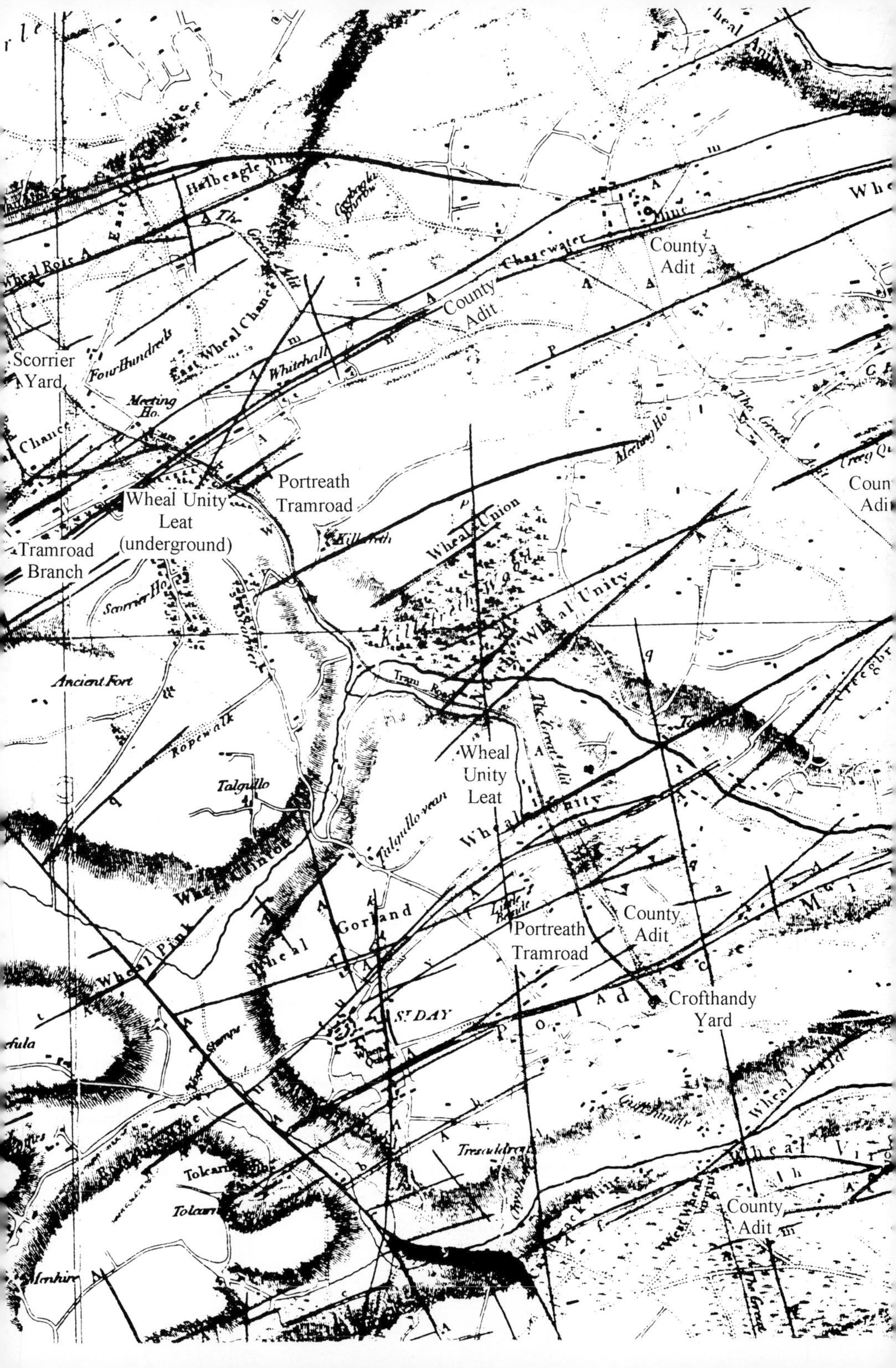
Scorrier Yard
County Adit
County Adit
County Adit
County Adit
County Adit
Portreath Tramroad
Portreath Tramroad
Wheal Unity Leat (underground)
Tramroad Branch
Wheal Unity Leat
Crofthandy Yard
Halbeagle Mine
Wheal Rose
East Wheal Chance
Four Hundreds
Meeting Ho.
Whitehall
Chacewater
The Great Adit
Wheal Union
Wheal Unity
Wheal Unity
Scorrier Ho.
Ancient Fort
Ropewalk
Talgullo
Talgullo-vean
Tram Road
Wheal Gorland
Wheal Pink
St. DAY
Tolcarn
Wheal Maid

Close to the road there's a narrow gap to squeeze through. (At present it's not possible to follow the next part of the tramway, because it passes through the private grounds of Scorrier House.)

❽ **Rather than continuing to the road, turn sharp right on the track running beside Unity Wood.**

About 150m along this track, there is a short path - really no more that a narrow opening - into the wood. If you are at all interested in the old mines I recommend a very short diversion here - no more than 50m each way, but involving a steep little climb. At the top of the slope slightly to the left of straight ahead you will be confronted with an impressive chasm, at the right-hand edge of which is Williams' Shaft of Wheal Unity Wood. The slope is well laced with old cinders from the boilers of Williams' engine.

This shaft dates from the earlier period in the mine's history, when it was a copper producer. The pumping-engine house that once stood beside it - built in 1834 for an 80-inch engine - was demolished and removed, foundations and all; the stone was probably used in the building of the two engine houses at Magor's Shaft (1872). Most interesting of all, on the level area or "plat" at the top of the slope on the far side of the hollow are some of the best-preserved remains in Cornwall of the site of a manual capstan, by which the heavy pitwork was raised and lowered in the shaft. (See ECM2 p68-70 for a detailed study and photographs of the Williams' Shaft site.) The shaft itself is marked by a square cut out at the south end of the excavation.

Return the same way to the valley path.

Continue eastwards along that, soon passing the pond again. Some parts along here are likely to be muddy.

About 350m beyond the point where you were recommended to go up into the woods to see Williams' Shaft, there's a pair of granite gate-posts on the left with a clear path up into the wood between them. Don't go that way: continue along the level track, leaving the wood behind.

❾ **A recommended short detour is to walk a few yards up the next path on the left** for a close look at the two engine houses at Magor's Shaft: see the Coast-to-Coast Trail (pages 40-2) for details. **Return the same way.**

Keep to the main track as it bears right. For the rest of the walk back to Poldice, follow the directions for the more northerly route of the Coast-to-Coast Trail, starting on page 44. After passing the Todpool Gate sign, continue uphill to the Poldice arsenic works buildings, following the Car Park sign, then turn right, as directed by the green arrow on the Poldice Tramroad wooden post. Where there is a choice of wide tracks turn left, then right at the next Portreath Tramroad sign. This will bring you back to the Wheal Unity Gate car park.

1. Portreath Harbour: looking seawards from the inner basin (SVJ)

2. The Portreath Tramroad walk near Bridge (SVJ)

3. Mine ruins on the coast, at Sally Bottoms (RSA)

4. Looking south-west over Basset's Cove to Godrevy (RSA)

5. Hallenbeagle Mine from the pedestrian crossing over the main line (RSA)

6. The smithy building at Wheal Busy, photographed in 1988 (Geof Purcell)

7. West Peevor, with the three engine houses and calciner stack of Wheal Peevor in the distance (Geof Purcell, again 1988)

8. Woodland near Scorrier in May, The path is on the Coast-to-Coast Trail. (RSA)

9. Beside the golf course at Radnor: a relic of Great North Downs Mine (RSA)

10. Killifreth Mine: inside Hawke's engine house in 1985, before restoration (Bryan Putt)

11. Hawke's engine house, Killifreth Mine, as seen from the Coast-to-Coast Trail (SVJ)

12. A Clwyd-capped shaft in Unity Wood (SVJ)

13. The Portreath Tramroad at Little Beside, showing setts diverging eastwards from the main line (Tony Steenmeyer)

14. Section of a rising main from a pumping shaft used as a culvert under a woodland path near Scorrier (Tony Steenmeyer)

15. Poldice arsenic works: the main labyrinth or "lambreth". The fumes passed through a second, smaller labyrinth, via the arch on the left, on their way to the stack. (Geof Purcell)

16. Poldice Valley's "moon landscape": "The Sands", with a parish boundary stone in the foregound and the arsenic works behind (SVJ)

17. The early Wheal Henry engine house on the slope above Hale Mills (RSA)

18. The Redruth & Chasewater Railway trackbed near Hale Mills (RSA)

19. The portal of the Great or County Adit (Derrick Phoenix)

20. Ochre deposited by mine water issuing from the Nangiles Adit (Geof Purcell)

21. The arsenic refinery site at Point Mills, Bissoe, with the headgear at Mount Wellington on the skyline (SJV)

22. Filtration ponds and reed beds in the Carnon Valley, part of the NRA's experimental scheme to deal with pollution from Wheal Jane (SVJ)

23. Waterweed (floatgrass) flourishing in the heavy-metal-laden water of the Carnon Stream (SVJ)

24. "Brunel's Stumps" beside the newer viaduct carrying the Falmouth Branch over the Carnon Valley (SVJ)

25/26. Two Views of the area long streamed for tin on the Devoran side of the A39 causeway. Above: Thrift in May - probably George Henwood's "sea daisies" (page 199) (RSA) Below: In summer (SVJ)

27. Devoran Quay: mooring posts in foreground, ore hutches hehind (SVJ)

28. A February sunset at Restronguet Creek. In the foreground and middle distance can be seen the remains of tin streamers' embankments (RSA)

29. Point Quay (SVJ)

30. The Restronguet Creek Tinworks, 1874, from an oil painting by T. May. The engine house stood in what is now "The Orchard". Point Green in the distance. (Photograph RSA, courtesy RIC)

ROUND WALK 9
WHEAL UNITY GATE, GOONGUMPAS, HALE MILLS, CONSOLS, CARHARRACK & ST DAY with an optional extension to CARN MARTH

About 4½ miles (7km), or can be cut to a little over 3 miles (5km).
The extension adds about another 2 miles (3.5km).
The sketch map for this route is at the start of Round Walk 8 (page 102).

After an exploration (which can be omitted if you prefer) of the Wheal Maid valley and the principal surface remains of the great Consols copper mine, this walk follows the course of the Redruth and Chasewater Railway across farmland and through the centre of the old mining village of Carharrack. It then turns north, along tracks and minor roads, to St Day, still interesting and attractive despite the fact that its heyday as the hub of the world's most important copper-mining district has long gone. After a brief tour of some of the most historic parts of the town, the walk returns to the starting point via tracks, one of which follows the route of the Portreath Tramroad into Crofthandy. The walk avoids roads almost completely, except in Carharrack and St Day. You will find shops and toilets in both, and each has a friendly, unpretentious pub that serves good food: both of them are "locals" in the best sense.

The directions start and end at the Wheal Unity Gate car park near Crofthandy. Directions for driving to it are given at the start of Round Walk 8 (page 103).

Note: Late in 1996 the intention was announced that "a pedestrian walkway linking Carharrack and St Day" would be created during 1997. If and when this materialises, it may prove to be an attractive alternative to the part of this walk described in sections 6-9.

❶ **From the car park entrance turn left, passing the interpretative board and the Poldice valley Trust's Wheal Unity Gate sign. Take the track ahead, signed Poldice, towards the ruined chimney at first. Keep right where the green waymark arrow points left at the fork, and just after that fork right again, passing between hefty boulders laid across the track.**

200m beyond the boulders, you could make a very short diversion on the left, where a path enters the excavated-out centre of a burrow to reveal Trussal's Engine Shaft (Poldice Mine), now capped. On the edge on the far side are a few granite blocks, the base of the bob wall of the house for the 65-inch pumping engine. Also, further right, and teetering on the side of the slope, is some old wooden planking pierced by two rusty bolts. This is part of the engine's condenser cistern, unearthed when the shaft was capped. **Return the same way to rejoin the walk route.**

This track now narrows to a rough path and brings you to a lane; turn right on that, passing the Crofthandy Gate sign. Continue ahead along Higher Goongumpas Lane, and at Crofthandy Methodist Church turn left along Chapel Lane.

Oliver Padel says the name "Crofthandy" derives from "croft", "uncultivated, enclosed land" (land, according to Charles Henderson, on which gorse was grown high for fuel), plus perhaps "hensy", "ancient house, ruins, remains"; Padel offers no suggestion as to what ruins might be meant. C.C.James suggested the name means "Hendy's croft", and thought Crofthandy "was probably a centre for smuggled goods. Old inhabitants formerly spoke of 'headless horses having been seen in the neighbourhood.' The smugglers no doubt encouraged the publication of the story as a stratagem to encourage the villagers to stay indoors when the goods were arriving." Just when this took place, he doesn't say; at first sight, Crofthandy seems an unlikely haven for contraband. Was it brought from Portreath to the depot at the end of the tramway?

❷ Where the lane divides, after about 50m,
either (A) take the left fork to include Hale Mills on the walk; in this case, pick up the directions at "Continuing Route (A)" (foot of page 131).

Or (B), for the shorter route go straight on till - some 400m past the fork - you reach the westernmost of the three dams built across the Wheal Maid Valley. *The valley's name refers to an old copper mine, sometimes called Wheal Maiden, which was at various periods linked with East Wheal Damsel and Carharrack Mine, both a little further east, and in 1864 it was combined with Poldice, Wheal Unity and Wheal Gorland to form St Day United Mines. All this makes it difficult to say how successful it was, but J.H.Collins notes that "The profits from 1800 to 1840 are said to have reached £200,000." It figures in the history books as the first Cornish mine to erect a "steam whim", a beam engine adapted for rotary use (1784).*

During 1995 CES Ltd announced plans to dump waste in the Wheal Maid Valley. The scheme met with much opposition, and the Crofthandy Area Residents' Association countered with plans to create a "major sports and leisure area" instead. Whatever the outcome, it seems certain that this much-battered landscape will be subject to further change. In the words of the Residents' Association Chairman, "Doing nothing is not an option."

Here turn right to cross the valley. Unless directed otherwise by signs, **walk on top of the dam embankment** overlooking the tailings reservoir on your left. This was, I understand, constructed not just for

Mount Wellington Mine but also as part of Billiton Minerals' ambitious but abortive scheme (early 1980s) for recovering alluvial tin by dredging Restronguet Creek. The stream flowing down this valley is led by a conduit under the dam and the floor of the reservoir; it emerges at Hale Mills. As you approach the far side, notice, down to your left, almost on the level of the valley floor, a double row of granite setts on the one short section of the Redruth & Chasewater Railway line which escaped demolition or burial when the tailings lagoons were created. The setts lie about 200m from the dam. Prior to construction of the lagoons this stretch of the railway could be walked in comfort.

The trackbed of the Redruth & Chasewater Railway in the Wheal Maid Valley, photographed by B.Y.Williams in 1934 (Courtesy RIC)

On the far side, a short detour offers itself: you could take a close look at the mine buildings at and near Taylor's Shaft (Great Consolidated Mines) by continuing ahead, uphill, from the end of the dam. Taylor's Shaft is about 250m from there, the clock tower a little further. Some information about this site is given below.

For the main walk route, after crossing the valley on the top of the dam turn right on the track. Now pick up the directions at "Continuing both routes" on page 135.

<u>Continuing Route (A)</u>: **At the next junction go straight on, following a blue waymarker near a sign, Harmony Cottage.** Soon after this you have

a good overview of the tailings reservoir and the Wheal Maid Valley, about which there is a note on page 30. The picturesque name of the island-like area you are walking through, separating the Poldice and Wheal Maid valleys, is Goongumpas, derived from the Cornish *goon*, "downland", and *compes*, "level". **You pass through a gateway on approaching a house ahead; here take the path on the left, which runs beside a wooden fence at a higher level than the house. Depending on the weather and the season, you may find this path rather muddy and brambly, I'm afraid. Where it bends 90° left, take the stony, downhill path ahead,** from which you have a view ahead of the lower part of the valley, with the engine houses at Shear's Shaft, Cusvey Mine, on the skyline half-right. **The path runs close to three Clwyd-capped shafts; immediately beyond the third one (the second on your right), fork right, heading at first towards another group of mine buildings which include the Consols clock tower. At the wide track turn left. It zigzags downhill, reaching the valley floor close to the twin tunnels (sketch, page 48) under the Redruth & Chasewater Railway embankment at Hale Mills,** built to carry a branch to Poldice Mine and possibly on to Wheal Busy. See page 152. (It's worth making the very short diversion to inspect the workmanship here: the tunnels for road and stream are lined with carefully shaped granite blocks.)

❸ **Cross the valley floor now, on the path which crosses the concrete conduit carrying the stream. A short way up the slope on the far side, you reach the trackbed of the railway's main line: here a level path goes off to the left beside a wire fence.**

From this point the walk returns up the Wheal Maid Valley, this time on the south side of the tailings lagoon.

PLEASE NOTE: The question of rights of way in this area was not finally settled at the time this book went to press. When it is, there should be signs to show it, and they may begin by taking you up the steepish path which runs straight ahead as you reach the railway trackbed. Whatever the exact course of the route, it should be of bridleway status, and will form part of the Mineral Tramways Spine Route; ideally, of course, it should keep as close as possible to the route of the railway, close to the valley floor, but at present this seems unlikely.

Meanwhile, the obvious route is as follows:

Turn right on reaching the railway trackbed and walk up the path ahead till you reach the level of the top of the dam. From here you can see the other two dam walls, with St Day old church on the skyline to the right and, further left, the ruins of the engine house and two stacks beside Taylor's Shaft, Great Consolidated Mines; the top of the "Consols" clock-tower base can also be glimpsed, just to the left of them. **Continue uphill.**

Approaching Davey's and Taylor's Shafts, Great Consolidated Mines (SVJ)

Gradually the distant view extends to include the clock tower in St Day to the right of the church and the Grambler & St Aubyn pumping-engine house to the left of it; closer at hand, the extent of the whole tailings reservoir can now be seen. **Either fork right on to the side track or continue uphill on the main one; either way, when you reach a wide, level track not far from the top of the slope turn right.** The first mining remains you pass are associated with Davey's Shaft, which like Woolf's attained a depth of 300 fathoms. On the left of the track is a fragment of the winding-engine house, and a few yards further on, on the right a little way below the level of the track, is the base of the bob wall of the pumping-engine house, in which an 80-inch engine was installed in 1832. Designed by Samuel Hocking and built at the Copperhouse Foundry, Hayle, she was, in her heyday, the "show" engine of the mine, the one visitors were always taken to see. The engine house was demolished in recent years to make way for the lorry road you have been walking along. As you continue along that, look down to your right to see a short surviving stretch of the Redruth & Chasewater Railway trackbed. Soon on your left comes the battered shell of the Taylor's Shaft pumping-engine house, one of the oldest still standing in Cornwall. It was built in 1827 for another of Arthur Woolf's engines, this time with a 70-inch cylinder; the cylinder was enlarged to 85 inches in 1833. A little further off stand the chimney, along with a few other remnants, of the whim-engine house. Both Taylor's and Davey's Shafts have twin collars to form separate pumping and hoisting compartments, a reflection of early 19th-century Cornish practice. Beyond the whim chimney stands the base of the Consols clock tower - a most unusual if not unique survival, symbolic still of the richness of this great mine. (Some OS maps mark it incorrectly as a chimney!) The clock mechanism is said to have been moved to the St Day clock tower after the closure of Clifford Amalgamated Mines in 1869, and to have worked there till well into the 20th century.

Several of the routes described in this book explore parts of the setts of the two great copper mines, Consolidated and United Mines. We do not see any part of United on this walk, but it is included in this note because its history is so intertwined with that of "Consols". (This short version of the name is almost universally used, and most people say "Cons'ls", though logically it should be "C'nsols".)

The small area stretching roughly from Carharrack to Twelveheads has been intensively mined for a very long time, and during the second half of the 18th century at least a dozen mines here proved very rich in copper. By about 1780 one group including Wheals Virgin, West Virgin, Girl and Fortune with Cusvey had amalgamated as Great Consolidated Mines, and another including Wheals Andrew, Clifford, Cupboard, Poldory, Squire, Poldory and Ale and Cakes had become United Mines.

In 1787 the novelist William Beckford visited Consols, as the former group soon came to be called, and wrote this description:

> *"At every step one stumbles upon ladders that lead into utter darkness or funnels that exhale warm copperous vapours. All around these openings the ore is piled up in heaps ready for purchasers. I saw it drawn reeking out of the mine by the help of a machine called a whim put in motion by mules, which in their turn are stimulated by impish children hanging over the poor brutes and flogging them without respite. The dismal scene of whims, suffering mules and hillocks of cinders, extends for miles. Huge iron engines creaking and groaning invented by Watt and tall chimneys smoking and flaming, that seem to belong to Old Nicholas's abode, diversify the prospect."*

Beckford contrasts the mine officials who "regale upon beef, pudding and brandy" with the miners, "woeful figures in tattered garments with pickaxes on their shoulders," who "crawled out of a dark fissure and repaired to a hovel, which I learnt was a gin-shop."

Towards the end of the century, competition mainly from Anglesey caused problems, and even though output was still quite high, both groups were closed in about 1805. In 1811, when Consols was described as "totally abandoned", United was restarted, and within a year or two Michael and John Williams of Scorrier were manager and purser. Soon after that, John Williams tried to form a company to reopen Consols; but in the event it was the Norwich-born John Taylor, armed with £65,000 supplied by his London shareholders, who succeeded in getting them working again, in 1819. The gamble paid off handsomely, and from 1823 to 1840 Consols' annual output of copper outstripped all its rivals, including Dolcoath. In 1824 Taylor took over United, and by 1830 the employees numbered over 3,000. In 1839 Taylor's application to renew the lease of Consols was refused, and his response was to "pick out the eyes" of the mine, that is, he stripped the mine of all easily accessible ore including underground stockpiles, and sold in that year the extraordinary total of 23,194 tons of ore. In the following year, the figure dropped to 13,951 tons; from then on it fell steadily, and in 1843 was overtaken by United's. In 1857 United annexed Consols, and the new group, including Wheal Clifford to the east, named itself Clifford Amalgamated. Its output during the '60s was still huge, but the great days of Cornish copper mining were over. When Clifford Amalgamated closed in 1870 it had, says Barton, "the greatest number of engines used on any Cornish mine, or indeed on any single set of mines in the world." There were over eighty miles of underground workings and eighteen engine-houses; nearly a million tons of copper, plus some tin and other metals, were brought up. Little now remains on the surface. The great waste-heaps, one of which according to Barton was "as high as Truro Cathedral", have been depleted, much of the material having been removed for road-making; some parts have been landscaped and replanted, others used as sites for modern industries.

On reaching the first of two lines of rusty iron stakes, set up to prevent the passage of four-wheeled vehicles, you can turn up to the left for a short detour to take a closer look at the mine buildings; otherwise, carry on ahead through a second line of stakes.

Continuing both routes

Fork right (on the lower track), passing through an open area scarred by recent industry, when an exploratory decline shaft, known as the Wheal Maid Decline, was sunk here by Wheal Jane to provide access to the lodes once worked by United Mines. Its progress was halted by the catastrophic fall of the tin price in 1985. The shaft mouth is now sealed with a blockwork wall, but a rough hole gouged through it allows a glimpse into the dark interior. **Take the upper track ahead,** the trackbed of the Redruth and Chasewater Railway. **This soon reaches a road, via a series of barriers designed to keep vehicles out, at the site of Crofthandy level crossing.** Old maps show a count house and stores complex on the higher ground to the left here. On the far side of the small valley to the right are two unspoilt shaft burrows of Wheal Maid. A Watt engine stood on the nearer shaft in the latter part of the 18th century.

❹ **Cross the road and continue opposite along the railway trackbed, now a narrow path between wire fences.** (Please note: this is strictly a footpath. The multi-use Mineral Tramways Spine Route uses the roads slightly to the north, as shown on the sketch map.) After about 100 yards, barbed wire crosses the path, but the passage of many walkers has ensured it's easy to circumvent. (A stile is needed here, as I pointed out in *The Landfall Book of the Poldice Valley* six years ago.) The cleared area on the right is the site of West Wheal Virgin, where more early Watt engines were employed. **Continue in the same line, beside the hedge on your right.** The ruined building ahead is the remains of the railway's Great Yard, which housed offices, stables and eight storage bays for coal and other goods. At this point there was a branch line south and east to United Mines and Consols. The exact course of the line is difficult to determine now, and indeed its route, and that of several spurs from it, probably changed from time to time according to need.

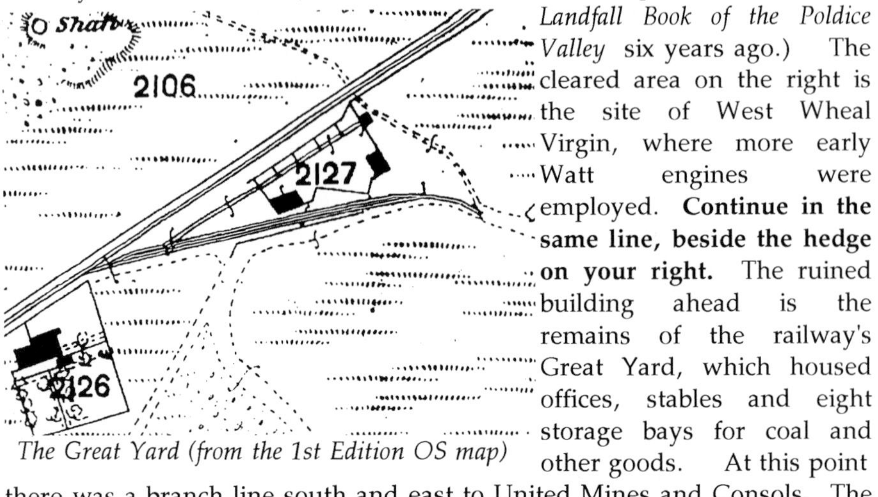

The Great Yard (from the 1st Edition OS map)

Groups of setts have survived from a few parts of this system, notably near the point where Consols Road and United Road meet (just east of Carharrack), and at two places on the Consols sett: close to the clock tower and immediately east of Pearce's Shaft. (See *Exploring Cornish Mines* Vol.1, pages 24-5 and 28.) The traffic on these lines was always horse-drawn. **The way ahead is barred by a wall, so I suggest you walk through the Great Yard.** (It is on private land, but until and unless the proper path is cleared you really have no alternative.) **When you emerge from it, continue ahead with the hedge on your left - still the course of the railway - and negotiate the farm gate where the path meets Consols Road.** (In the summer of 1996 the gate was in a state of collapse and had to be clambered over - not easy.)

Walk along the road, still in roughly the same direction. The new bungalows on the left have obliterated the railway track (a loop on this section was used as a loading point for the St Day Brick Works), but its course through the centre of Carharrack can quite easily be traced. *The name is locally pronounced "C'harrick" or "C'rarrick". Padel suggests that it means "fort of the high place". I have not come across an explanation of which fort or high place may have been referred to, but of course Carn Marth is very close, and* *it would be surprising if that has never been fortified. The setting of the village must once have looked very different: even now there is woodland close by to the south, and some historians (but by no means all) believe that oak woods once covered much if not all of Carn Marth, as with the neighbouring Carn Brea. Although Thomas Shaw in MGT states that the site of the Carharrack Methodist Church "seems to be the most likely spot where the Wesleys addressed great crowds in the 1740s and 50s", according to C.C.James there were just twelve cottages at Carharrack in 1770. The boom in copper mining caused rapid growth, however, and this was accelerated by the coming of the railway. "The railway," writes D.B.Barton, "was very much part and parcel of Carharrack's daily life. For years many of the railway horses were stabled there and almost all the working population of the village was employed in Consols, United or the other copper mines nearby." One of those, not mentioned elsewhere in this book, was Ting Tang Mine, on the railway's route between here and Lanner. In recent years, much interesting material about Carharrack has been gathered by local historians, notably Barrie May and Eric Rabjohns; their exhibition was last on display at the Methodist Church in 1996, and if it is given further airings I'd strongly recommend a visit. They have also produced interesting leaflets about the development of the village, the local remains of the mineral railway, the religious sites, and even "The Carharrack Pop Works". From the last I have learned that between about 1840 and 1970 Carharrack had at least six factories making ginger beer or "pop", the best-known of which was Jolly's, based at United Road until moving to Pool in 1971.*

At the road junction continue ahead along Fore Street (not named at this end) into Carharrack.

If you are interested in tracing the course of the railway through the village, the following may be helpful:

It crossed Fore Street before you reach the Mills' Hall (about which there is a brief note below). Notice that the wall beyond the house called Crossways, on the left, contains several granite setts, and both posts for the level-crossing gates have survived at the far end of the wall, though the one without hinges appears to have been moved. After crossing the road the line ran along what is now Croft Row, behind the site of the Hall - where one of the two railway coal yards in Carharrack once was - and the long terrace of cottages (Albion Row) on Fore Street. The gate posts on the right side of Fore Street have been moved a few yards to the entrance to the Mills Hall car park. The line crossed the main road at Railway Terrace (its course is clearly visible on the right of the 30mph sign, between two high walls, where there is another pair of gate posts),then passed close behind the shops. It crossed Chapel

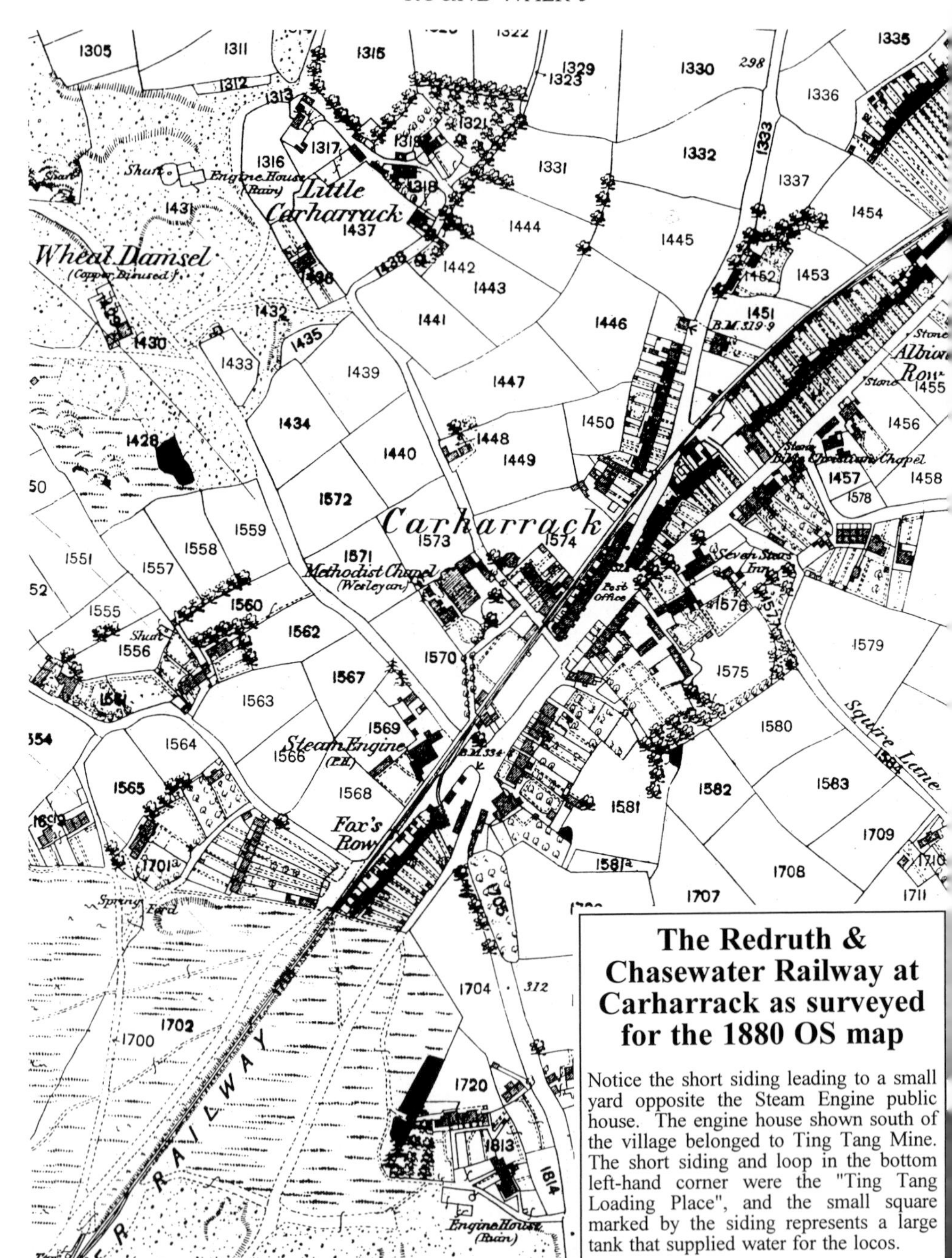

The Redruth & Chasewater Railway at Carharrack as surveyed for the 1880 OS map

Notice the short siding leading to a small yard opposite the Steam Engine public house. The engine house shown south of the village belonged to Ting Tang Mine. The short siding and loop in the bottom left-hand corner were the "Ting Tang Loading Place", and the small square marked by the siding represents a large tank that supplied water for the locos.

Terrace, and the next section of its track is now occupied by modern bungalows. Beyond them, a rusty old lamp standard marks its course. It crossed Wheal Damsel Road, ran in front of what was then the Steam Engine pub, crossed the road and went under the footbridge, then on below the slopes of Carn Marth to Redruth and Wheal Buller.

For more detailed information including a large-scale map, see Eric Rabjohns' excellent *Carharrack Railway Walkabout* leaflet, which should be available at Carharrack Post Office.

As you proceed along Fore Street you will pass the Mills' Hall, the playing field where the public toilets are, and the Seven Stars.

William John Mills, from St Day, was a successful businessman who devoted much of his wealth to local charity and other good causes, notably in 1933 by buying a complete street in St Day and converting it as free housing for elderly people. Elsewhere in the locality he provided public playing-fields and gardens, and a Village Hall for Carharrack. As you will see, this is the headquarters of the local brass band; the words "and St Day" were added to its name in return for financial help from the Mills family. The Mills Hall is built on the site of one of the railway's coal yards.

The level crossing at Wheal Damsel Road, Carharrack, in the days of the railway. On the left is the Methodist Church. (Courtesy Paddy Bradley)

❺ At the main road you need to go a few yards to the right to see remains of the railway; but for the main walk route, **turn left past the shops then first right (Chapel Terrace), then left again in front of the Methodist Church** (note its date, just when the boom in copper mining would have been causing rapid growth in village population) **and along the short path that brings you to Wheal Damsel Road.** The level crossing formerly here was the site of one of the very few fatal accidents on the railway, when an elderly lady was struck by a train. "Manor House", on the corner opposite, was once a pub, The Steam Engine. **Cross to that and continue ahead for some 200m**, past the cottages of Fox's Row, to see the original footbridge over the line, restored in 1986-7 by Carharrack Parish Council. It is of great interest in that it is composed of old rails from the line. (Why a footbridge here? The 1880 map shows two paths from Ting Tang Mine converging at this point, so it would have provided a quick way home for miners living in Fox's Row - and maybe saved a few yards when heading for the pub!) Granite setts from the old railway are plentiful around here, built into garden walls, for example, and forming some of the steps up to the bridge. Another coal yard, with a short siding leading to it, was on the south side of the road almost opposite The Steam Engine. Its site is now occupied by an animal feed store.

"Miner" taking on water at the Ting Tang loading place
(Courtesy Paddy Bradley)

❻ Return a short way along the road.

If you want to shorten the walk slightly, and are not interested in walking up Carn Marth, take the second left turning, Wheal Damsel Road. After about a quarter of a mile this will bring you to the start of the path to St Day, one of several tracks that converge at an open space on the right. This is point 7 in the directions.

But for the full recommended route, take the first left turning, a very narrow road called Hillside Terrace - uphill, and quite steep in places. Ignore the minor road on the left at a bend, opposite the entrance to Woodbine Farm.

FOR THE EXTENSION TO CARN MARTH take the stony, uphill path on the left about 100m further on, at the point where the road begins to level off. This is in fact a bridleway, despite the narrowness of the first part of it. (Quite what walkers or cyclists are supposed to do if a horse and rider come along in the opposite direction I don't know! Retreat to the road to let them by, I guess.) It is also part of the Mineral Tramways Spine Route, the vital link between the territories covered respectively by Volumes 1 and 2 of this guide.

Apart from a few slight bends, the bridleway continues straight ahead to the hilltop; and apart from one level or even slightly downhill section near the start it climbs gently the whole way. It crosses a minor road after about a quarter of a mile. Ignore all side paths.

Carn Marth is exceptionally well endowed with public rights of way, but among all the possible routes to the top this, I think, is the best. It is fascinating on a clear day to watch the panoramic view unfold more and more, almost with every step. Quite near the start, you get a glimpse of the sea horizon to the south, as well as the mining landscape of United Downs and Consols, with the modern Wheal Jane a little further off. It's not till you are about two-thirds of the way to the top that the sea to the north comes into view. (Islands have a special magic for many people, myself included, and one of the pleasures of exploring hills like Carn Marth is the illusion of being on one!) Higher still, you can see Pendennis Castle, Falmouth Harbour and Stithians Reservoir to the left, St Agnes Beacon and even Trevose Head - way along the coast near Padstow - to the right.

For information about Carn Marth, see Round Walk 7 in Volume 1 of "Exploring Cornwall's Tramway Trails", especially pages 124-5.

Once you reach the flooded quarry at the top, the whole network of round walks associated with the western part of the Mineral Tramways Project area, and the Great Flat Lode Trail itself, lie at your feet, beckoning you to come and enjoy them.

If, however, you decide to postpone those pleasures, **return the same way, turning left on the minor road at the end of the final, narrow section of the bridleway to complete Round Walk 9.**

Once you reach the top of the hill you have a fine view to the right, including St Day, Consols and United Downs, with the wind farms at Four Burrows and Carland Cross and the "China Clay Mountains" near St Austell in the distance.

The pretty road now runs downhill. **At the junction with a slightly wider road turn right and go on down this for nearly half a mile, continuing just a short way beyond the house on the right named Wheal Damsel Farm to where several tracks converge at an open space on the left.**

Wheal Damsel was a copper mine. C.C.James and J.H.Collins both call it a "very ancient mine," and James says that in 1806 it "was the richest in the parish (Gwennap), and possibly in the county." Its main shafts and surface buildings were close to the point, mentioned in the directions, where several tracks meet the road. (See the 1880 OS map, page 138.) In 1818 it was employing 240 people, and the deepest workings were about a thousand feet below surface. The last figures for production I have come across are from 1872, but it may have continued beyond that date. Incidentally, many Cornish mines bear feminine names (Jane, Frances and Kitty, for example); often these refer to the wife or daughter of the mineral landlord, the mine owner or some other official. Wheal Damsel was once linked with another mine called Wheal Spinster, both worked the same lode as Wheal Maid or Maiden and Wheal Virgin, further east, and Wheal Girl was close to those; it would be interesting to know if the same lady is alluded to in all these names, and if so, who she was.

❼ Take the rather rough and stony track passing just to the left of the cottages, which soon curves downhill towards St Day. At the broken Public Bridleway sign (almost hidden in the hedge on the right at a junction of tracks), walkers can turn right past the house called Northwethel, passing among other houses. *This is Little Carharrack. The Manor House is very old, and C.C.James suggests that it may have been a lodging-house for pilgrims travelling between the shrines of St Day and St Michael's Mount.* **Next go left and follow the Public Footpath sign. (An alternative way to go, suitable for those on bike or horseback, is to turn left at the Public Bridleway sign. The stream on the left later forms a small pond beside the road, easy enough for walkers to cross, at least in summer, by means of some makeshift stepping stones. Turn right at the road and continue for about 100m, then turn left at the wooden fencing, as mentioned in the next line.)**

❽ Cross the road, go through the gap in the wooden fencing and up the fairly steep road ahead, through the district known as Burnwithian or Burnwithen. On the left, now converted into a block of terraced houses, is the former workhouse for Gwennap parish. Further left can be seen the surface remains of West Wheal Jewel copper mine, otherwise known as

Tolcarne or North Wheal Damsel. **At the top of the hill you enter St Day, passing the school.**

Once St Day boasted thirteen pubs and its market "was a big affair with a particularly lively time on pay-days, when the miners consumed huge quantities of beef and onions accompanied by heavy draughts of ale and beer. The celebrations often continued from Saturday afternoon to Monday evening. The women also enjoyed themselves in a milder form holding on their pay day a monthly Kitty Bay Fair - with stalls around the account house." (C.C.James: "A History of the Parish of Gwennap")

An excellent symbol of the change in the town's fortunes since then is the "old" Holy Trinity Church ... not so very old, because it was built in 1828. John Betjeman described the St Day of that period as "the capital of the tin mining district" - not an exaggeration, perhaps, but as Allen Buckley has pointed out, rather than "tin" Betjeman should have said "copper". A church big enough to seat 1,500 was essential. Now it is a sad ruin: it was condemned as unsafe in 1956; the roof fell in in 1985, and the famous "Gothick" tower will inevitably follow suit unless what remains is stabilised without delay. Determined efforts have been made by members of the St Day Historical & Conservation Society to raise money for this purpose, and European grant aid, matched by funds from other bodies (principally English Partnership), has now been made available.

A little booklet available in the new church opposite gives a few details about the sixth century monk who founded the original Chapel here, and mentions how it became an important shrine on the pilgrim route to St Michael's Mount. Charles Henderson states that the shrine of the Holy Trinity survived until the reign of Queen Elizabeth I, and that the chapel at Scorrier House includes "a large crocketed pinnacle" from St Day Chapel, dating from the 15th century. Most Christmases I have a reminder of St Day's part in the history of Christianity in

The ruins of Holy Trinity Church, St Day (SVJ)

Cornwall when the choir I belong to sings the St Day Carol: "Now the holly bears a berry ..."

Paul Annear's interesting and well researched booklet, "Some Notes on the History of the Church and Chapel of the Holy Trinity, St Day", was published by the author in 1994. Profits from sales of the booklet go to support the St Day Old Church Appeal.

The St Day Feast is held on the third Monday after Whit each year: there are parades led by the local band, and a dance; traditionally, the youngest children receive a saffron bun (plus, since the early 1970s, a bottle of pop), older ones a shilling (50p nowadays), and the old-age pensioners a tea-party. A vivid account of St Day Feast and its history, again by Paul Annear, appeared in the August 1996 issue of "Cornwall Today" magazine.

The town is well worth exploring for the Georgian and Victorian houses and shop-fronts, and the granite clock tower. Annie Trevithick's tiny history of St Day (about 1890) says that it was erected in 1831, whereas C.C.James gives 1821. The wooden structure at the top was brought here from Redruth soon after the clock tower there was heightened and refurbished in 1904. In both towns, the base of the clock tower served as a "clink" in early days.

The mines helped to promote other local industries, such as an important brick works (from 1860 to 1912) and a factory manufacturing fuses for detonating gunpowder (from about 1870 to shortly before 1950). (See Round Walk 8, page 108, for more on the Unity Fuse Works.) These days, instead of benefiting the town, the old mines have brought the constant threat of subsidence. There have been several cases of holes suddenly appearing to reveal long-forgotten shafts, and one such almost led to the permanent closure of Telegraph Hill. A local committee was formed to fight this plan, a public enquiry took place, and the road was saved ... for the time being, at least ... Again, the recent grant of European money, mentioned earlier in connection with Holy Trinity Church, should be of great value in dealing with such problems.

Continue ahead at the road junction, past the ruins of the "old" church. The new one, on the opposite side of the road, has an interesting collection of photographs of St Day dating from about 1910; if the room containing them is locked, you may be able to get in by enquiring at the vicarage nearby.

The side road on the left just past the church, Carew Road, leads to Carew Close, at the end of which stands the substantial old Carew House. *This is of interest to mining historians because it was the home of Collan Harvey (d.1846) until he grew wealthy enough to move into the considerably more substantial 18th-century mansion of Pengreep, between Ponsanooth and Lanner. As the owner of the principal general store in St Day at a time when the town was prosperous he was able to invest in local mines, and when his sister married John Williams of Scorrier House he and his brother James secured what would now be called the "franchise" to supply virtually all the needs of the employees of the mines associated with the Williamses, as well as the mines themselves. As C.C.James puts it, "Men were expected to go to Harvey's for all they wanted, and if they failed to do so, were reminded. In some instances money was deducted from the men's pay (when they had taken no goods from the shop) to bring them to the latter for an explanation." (HPG) James refers to this as the "truck system", but strictly speaking that practice consisted of paying employees in goods rather than cash, and it became illegal in 1831; Collan Harvey, however, apparently continued his retailing business beyond that date, and was succeeded in it by his son Richard, who, James adds, "was reputed never to have entered a railway carriage"! (The Harveys of St Day were not related to the Harveys of Hayle, so it is an interesting coincidence that something similar applied to the employees of Harvey's Foundry, who were encouraged to buy all their goods at the Foundry's own emporium. See "A View from Trencrom" - page 70 in the 1st edition. Edmund Vale, however, states that there is no evidence that the Hayle shop "was made an instrument in the truck system." [HoH])*

Carew House, St Day

Go on along Church Street, past some shops. Turn left at Fore Street (signed Redruth), past the clock tower (toilets here) and the St Day Inn.

Turn right along Telegraph Street, with slate-hung houses on the corner, and other attractive cottages on the left later. A new road, also on the left, has been named after Wheal Gorland, whose workings extend under the north end of St Day. *This was another "very ancient and rich copper mine" (C.C.James), particularly famous for the beautiful and rare mineral specimens found in it: see the note on Wheal Unity, page 104. The Wheal Gorland dumps used to be a favourite hunting-ground for collectors of minerals, but during the 1970s the dumps were removed, thus at a stroke greatly increasing the cash value of specimens already found. A recreation ground has taken the place of the dumps. Before the mine closed in 1864, its workings had reached a depth of about 1,100 feet. As with the nearby Park-an-Chy mine, parts of Gorland were re-opened early this century for the recovery of wolfram and tin: see the note about Poldice Mine on pages 104-5.*

An old postcard of Fore Street, St Day. Notice the water-seller and his cart. (Courtesy Paddy Bradley)

Eventually you reach Scorrier Street; here go right, past a cul-de- sac, formerly Simmons' Street but now called Mills Street: see the plaque, and the earlier note about Mills' Hall (page 139).

❾ **Immediately beyond Mills Street, turn left on a track** - called Barracks Lane because the Salvation Army barracks once stood beside it. Just beyond the last house, there is a mineshaft on the left. (It was very obvious a few years ago, but not now; I presume it has been capped.) I was told it is at least 500 feet deep, and used to act as the main storm drain for St Day until recent changes resulting from subsidence on nearby Telegraph Hill. A little further on, look left beyond the hedge on the far side of the field to see a concrete structure, one of the few surviving relics of an overhead cableway by which ore from Park-an-Chy Mine was carried down to the Poldice valley for processing. **Cross the main road with care and continue down the track almost opposite**; notice the tall, graceful stack of Killifreth Hawke's Shaft engine house in the distance to your left.

❿ **Beyond the attractively restored Old Coach House, turn right among the houses at Little Beside, and keep to the main track as it bears left. At the cross-tracks, where there is a house called Kernyk, continue ahead. At the road turn left for Wheal Unity Gate.**

ROUND WALK 10
TWELVEHEADS, HALE MILLS & CHACEWATER

About 4 miles (6.5km), plus a few short optional extensions. Could be reduced to about 2-2½ miles (3-4km) by omitting Chacewater.

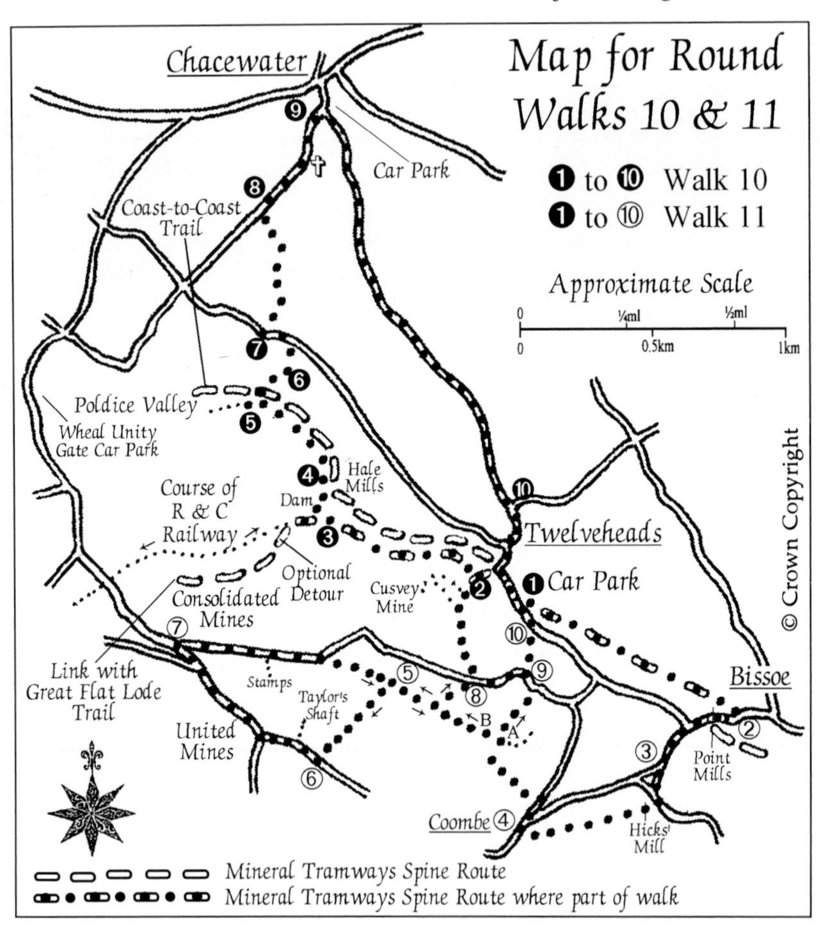

Twelveheads, despite being overshadowed by the modern mine structures of Mount Wellington (while they survive), is a charming little hamlet, full of pretty buildings and the sounds of water. The walk starts by following the course of the Redruth & Chasewater Railway into the valley leading to Hale Mills, the scene of so much industrial activity for many centuries, and yet it still has its pockets of greenery in which wild creatures flourish.

Beyond Hale Mills, after an optional detour along the side of the Wheal Maid valley to look at some remains of the great Consolidated (Consols) copper mine, the walk route re-enters the Poldice Valley, running for some distance beside the course of the Redruth & Chasewater Railway's branch line which was intended to extend as far as Wheal Busy. The walk to Chacewater, if you choose to include it, climbs quite steeply out of the Poldice Valley by means of a path used by horses and therefore likely to be muddy; it continues along paths and wider tracks, with a little road walking. Chacewater itself is much more attractive and interesting than you would suspect if you have previously seen it only from behind car windows. From there back to Twelveheads is a delightful downhill walk along a quiet road through a green and rural valley. Thus this is a very varied walk, and one which is full of interest for anyone wishing to understand the history of this important mining district.

Chacewater offers a good selection of shops and pubs, plus public toilets. The public car park in Chacewater is near the start of the valley road to Twelveheads, and would make a good alternative place to begin the walk: in that case, pick up the directions at point 9. To find the road to Twelveheads, leave the Chacewater car park by the pedestrian exit to the left of the toilets, turn left on the road and then almost immediately left again.

For those with cars, the suggested parking place is the roadside car park created by Groundwork Kerrier at Grid Reference SW 761 421. This is beside the valley road that runs north-west to Twelveheads from Bissoe. If you are approaching from that direction; the extended layby is on the right about 150m before the sharp right turn into the village. Except on Sundays, three or four buses a day link Twelveheads with Truro: Truronian service 314. Consult current timetables.

❶ If you arrived by bus, start by walking south from the Methodist Church. After crossing the bridge over the Carnon River, at the point where the road bends left continue along the stony track ahead. Continue with the directions four lines below.

From the car park, walk along the road towards Twelveheads, and at the right turn into the village take the stony track on your left, where there is a sign, "Old Cusvey House".

After almost 100m the track crosses the former route of the Redruth & Chasewater Railway. If you look left you can see that it ran along a low embankment, now marked by a line of shrubs and trees; it then crossed the road on a wooden bridge, now gone, before crossing the Carnon River on the masonry bridge which has survived intact.

For a short diversion to view at close hand the two engine houses at Shear's Shaft, Cusvey Mine, continue ahead for almost 200m. It's uphill most of the way, but just as the track begins to descend, take the narrow path which cuts back sharply on the right. It starts beside the garden wall of the first house. The path runs uphill, curving gently to the left; ignore side turnings, and after about 250m you will reach the engine houses.

Cusvey Mine was one of the old mines which amalgamated to form Great Consolidated Mines. The larger and more obvious engine house dates from as long ago as 1826, making it one of the oldest in Cornwall to have survived substantially intact. It was built for a 70-inch pumping engine, later replaced by a 65-inch. The other building, shrouded with ivy and surrounded by thick vegetation, contained a winding engine, totally enclosed in the building, which hauled from a separate shaft. The detached and distinctive stack served the boilers of both engines, and also, it would seem, a calciner some way downslope, probably for burning off arsenic as waste rather than to collect it. Vestiges of the long flue from the calciner may be seen on the right side of the path as you return.

The ruins of the pumping-engine house and stack at Shear's Shaft (SVJ)

You could go back the same way, but a more interesting and only slightly longer alternative is, having started along the path you came by, to turn left after about 150m. The path now heads downhill westwards, giving views along the valley towards Hale Mills, and beyond to the church and clock tower at St Day. After about 60m turn sharp-right on to quite a wide track. The pair of capped shafts, one for pumping and a narrower one for winding, below this track soon after you join it, belonged to Wheal Fortune, another of the old mines which became part of Consolidated Mines.

A story told about Wheal Fortune by Cyril Noall in "Cornish Mine Disasters" gives a vivid impression of miners' working conditions. In June 1853 two miners were walking along the 120 fathom level (720 feet) when falling water put out both their candles. One set off for the 90 fathom level to fetch a light, but after two hours he had still not returned. Eventually the other miner managed to improvise a light. "He went in search of Kellow, and found him lying quite dead and fearfully mutilated on the sollar (landing between ladders) at the 140. In going up the 90 Kellow had to cross a whim shaft over a roadway divided from it by a casing, but it appeared that in endeavouring to find his way in the dark, he went in front of the casing instead of behind it, and so fell down the shaft."

The track curves in a clockwise direction as it descends for some 350m, eventually returning you to the track you came up from Twelveheads; turn left on that.

❷ To continue with Round Walk 10, turn right (left, of course, if you have made the detour to Shear's Shaft) along the railway trackbed, indicated by a yellow waymarker on a wooden post. It may be somewhat overgrown during summer months for the first 150m, but then it emerges into the open. Keep an eye out for granite setts as you walk. About 350m from the start of the open stretch comes a much wider section where there was a loop line on the left, used, according to Barton, for the storage of wagons. It was probably here that the trains heading west reduced their normal load of 18 wagons to 9 before tackling the steep climb to the top of Lanner Hill. At the far end of it is a large open shaft surrounded by a fence. This is Woolf's Shaft, one of the deepest on Consolidated Mines (300 fathoms); on the valley side of it are the slight remains of the house for the 90-inch pumping engine which was moved there from Wheal Alfred, near Angarrack, in 1827. The engine was designed by Arthur Woolf, from whom the shaft took its name. (The interesting story of Woolf's work for John Taylor at Consols is told by T.R.Harris in *Arthur Woolf, The Cornish Engineer*, published by Bradford Barton in 1966.)

Continue along the attractive level path ahead, still following the course of the railway, which here ran through a short cutting. It starts just to the left of the shaft. Near the far end of the cutting it is spanned by a bridge constructed in part from old rails, possibly salvaged from the line when it was taken up during the First World War. (I understand, though, that the bridge was rebuilt in the 1930s.) As you emerge into the open again above Hale Mills you will notice a well-preserved line of granite setts.

It was here that the branch line intended to reach Wheal Busy curved off to the right to cross the valley on an embankment constructed during 1854-5. The top of the embankment can be seen, looking like a heather-clad path running between trees, but better views of the embankment are to be had from the far side, and especially from the valley floor. You may also be able to catch a glimpse from here of the cutting on the other side of the valley, but this too will be better seen later. Despite the considerable trouble and expense incurred by the railway company in carrying out these works, Barton's study of the contemporary records

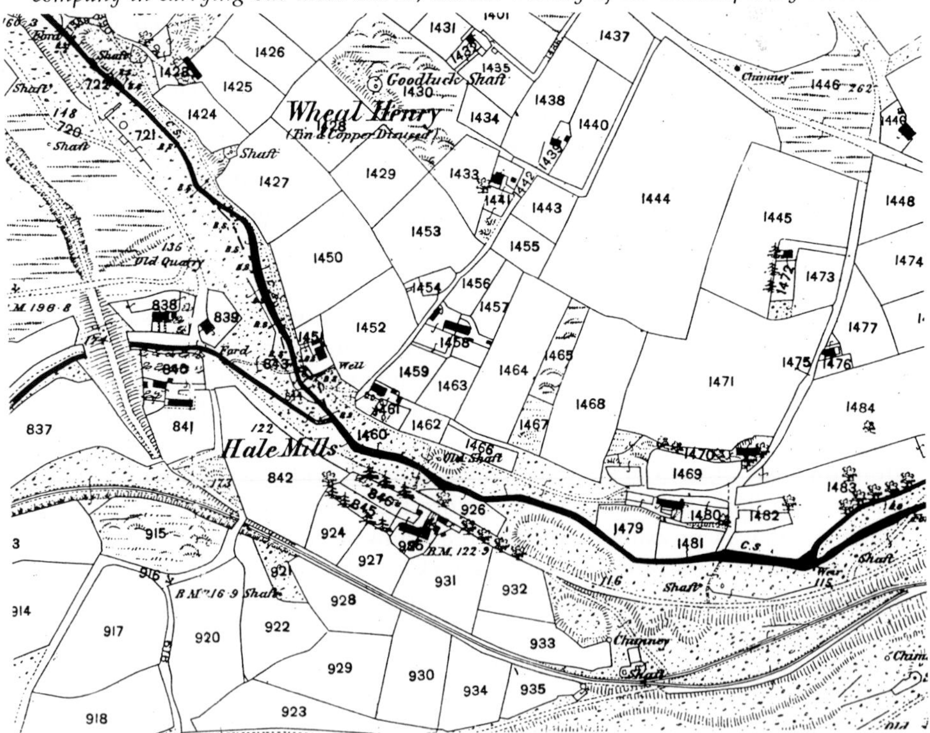

Hale Mills and the Redruth & Chasewater Railway as shown on the 1st Edition OS map. The long loop east of Woolf's Shaft is shown; so are the embankment and cutting for the Poldice branch - but no line passing over or through them.

led him to conclude that the rails were never laid. Certainly there is no sign now of any setts leading towards the embankment at Hale Mills; on the other hand, the map published by the company in 1856 (reproduced on pages 42-3 of <u>*RCR*</u>*) indicates that "Locomotives at present work" as far as Poldice Mine, with the rest of the "Wheal Bissy Branch" not completed.*

❸ The next section of the main Redruth & Chasewater line has been obliterated by the major engineering work carried out around 1977-8 to create tailings lagoons for Mount Wellington Mine in the Wheal Maid valley. Wide-bore black plastic piping was laid, mostly along the former railway track, to carry the effluent from the mill to the reservoir. The view ahead is dominated by the nearest of three dams built then, from the base of which emerges the end of the concrete conduit by which the stream in this valley was ducted underneath the tailings lagoons.

If you have not done and are not planning to do Round Walk 9, I suggest you make a detour to visit the principal surface remains of the great Consols copper mine. For this, see Round Walk 9, from the foot of page 132 to page 135; return the same way.

To continue Round Walk 10, go down the path running beside a concrete water-channel to the valley floor.

On your right the ochre-stained stream emerges from its concrete prison into the open for a few feet before passing through the smaller of the two masonry-lined tunnels in the embankment; and when you reach the path at the bottom it's worth going a few yards to the right to inspect the careful workmanship of the larger tunnel taking the trackway through to Hale Mills.

But for the walk route turn left, towards the dam wall, then after about 35m sharply right up a narrow path, quite steep at first, passing a walled, Clwyd-capped mineshaft on your left. From here you have a clear view of the railway embankment across the valley. **Now the path goes right again, downhill.** Soon you will come to the cutting on the left, which was excavated to take the Wheal Busy branch line. There is no right of way along the railway trackbed - unfortunately, from a walker's point of view, but keeping people out of it protects the birds and other wildlife living in this sheltered spot, which is a green haven amidst the industrial desolation, and seems to have its own microclimate.

Continue down the path into the Poldice Valley. On the slope opposite can be seen the stack of the little, ivy-clad Wheal Henry engine house: see page 47.

❹ **At the foot of the path, to return direct to Twelveheads, reducing the walk to less than 2 miles, turn right and follow the Coast-to-Coast Trail**

Route along or near the valley bottom. At the road go straight on for the car park rather than turning left into Twelveheads.

For the longer routes, turn left, walking either along the valley bottom or on the parallel track a little higher up the slope on the left. After about half a mile - not far beyond a wooden waymark post, where a red arrow points to the upper track - you will come to an impressive retaining wall on the left side of the valley; above this is a complex group of ruinous mine buildings, littered - at the time of writing, late 1996 - with assorted rubbish, above which are the massive foundations built for Californian tin stamps. (See pages 105-6.) At or near this point the railway trackbed seems to come to an end, well short of the heart of Poldice Mine.

❺ **Just beyond the retaining wall, if you have been walking along the upper track go down to the valley bottom. Again you could turn right to return direct to Twelveheads, cutting the walk to about 2½ miles; but for the complete walk including Chacewater take the narrow, shady path among trees more-or-less opposite, which gradually climbs the north side of the valley.** (The path begins quite close to one of the many parish boundary stones; the number on it has been obliterated, but must have been 53, since the next one downslope is 54.) Some sections of the path will probably be muddy, I'm afraid. Soon you pass a well which looks as if it might still be in use. **The path eventually joins a stony track.** Here it's worth pausing, not only to get your breath back but to admire the wide view over the Poldice Valley. In the distance, from right to left, can be seen the engine house of Grambler & St Aubyn United mine (visited on a walk in Vol. 1 of this guide: see pages 144-5), near Gwennap Pit; St Day clock tower and old church; Carn Marth; the Consols clock tower; and a restored stamps-engine house of Gwennap United Mines.

❻ **Turn left on the track, and left again at the road.** Here the view extends further east to the Cusvey (Shear' Shaft) engine houses and Mount Wellington mine.

❼ **After just over 200m, turn right on to a grassy path between hedges.** From this you can see Wheal Jane to the right. **Later the path joins a wider track, where you bear right, and then keep to the main track ahead.**

❽ **Turn right on the road, which runs down into Chacewater.** On the right before the church is the imposing Chacewater House, formerly the vicarage but now privately owned; the new vicarage is a modest bungalow a little way down the hill. Chacewater Church is worth a visit.

Oliver Padel states that "chace" means a hunting ground, and this district belonged to Goodern Manor, otherwise known as Blanchland (see Round Walk 12), which seems to have been a palace of Dark Age lords or "kings" of Cornwall. Thus Chacewater figures in the legend of Tristan and Isolda (usually called

Tristram and Iseult in Cornwall) as King Mark's hunting ground, and also in the stories of cruel King Teudar who killed many Celtic saints. (Charles Henderson, writing in 1925, makes a less colourful comment: "In the Middle Ages the whole district was barren heath land, over which various Lords of Manors had 'Free Warren.'") Although farming and trades such as thatching and brewing were important to Chacewater, the village was largely created by the mines that surround it, and its fortunes have risen and fallen with theirs. Admittedly it looks quite prosperous now, despite the parlous state of Cornish mining: its pleasant setting has attracted retirement homes, and it is conveniently placed for commuting to Truro and Redruth. From about 1760, Chacewater was the home of the celebrated Hornblower family who designed and built so many of the great steam engines. (Jonathan Hornblower, 1717-80, had 13 children: Jabez, Jethro, Joanna, Jesse, Jemima, Jonathan, Joseph, Jemima [did the first Jemima die young?], Julia, Jecholia, Jedida, Jerusha and Josiah. The search for girls' names obviously grew desperate.) An entertaining and perceptive account of Chacewater by George Henwood was published in the "Mining Journal" during the late 1850s. "When the mines were in their palmy days, Chacewater was a place of considerable importance as a mining village; a capital market-house was built for the convenience of the people, but has since been almost deserted ... Scarcely a family is to be found one member at least of whom has not been out either to Mexico, California, Brazil, New Zealand, Australia, Africa, Spain, or some mining district of less account." Great Wheal Busy had recently been re-opened, and prosperity was returning; but since the entire village belonged to Lord Falmouth and all leases were restricted to three lives, few people were prepared to build "a superior class of houses." Even so, Betjeman rightly points to its "well-built colour-washed cottages ... bow-windowed Georgian shops ... and up the valley slopes the tidy villas built in the last century by tin mine captains."

Chacewater parish was carved out of Kenwyn and Kea in 1837 - evidence of the increased population brought by the mines. St Paul's Church was built nine years earlier, in 1828, for a congregation of 1,500. A leaflet published for the church's 150th anniversary says,

> *"A local paper referred to it as one of the very ugliest churches in Cornwall and a previous Vicar said that he thought it was a factory when he first saw it. In 1866 the "West Briton" of the day reported: 'During the thunderstorm on Saturday last (Feb. 3rd) Chacewater Church which has recently been repaired, was struck by lightning which split the wall from ground to roof. Several windows were smashed into hundreds of pieces, being hurled from the west end up to the pulpit, a distance of 90 feet.' Of this original Church only the lofty tower with battlements, the second highest in Cornwall, now remains. The Church was rebuilt and completed in 1892 from the design of Edward Sedding of Plymouth. There was no gallery and the seating capacity was reduced to 500."*

That last sentence is again symptomatic of the fortunes of the mines. Incidentally, the tallest church tower in Cornwall is that of Probus, and the claim to the second tallest is also made by St Columb Minor.

Chacewater Church

Go on down past the school, founded by the National Schools movement in 1847. **To continue the main walk route, turn right on the minor road signposted to Twelveheads and follow the directions from point 9**; but if you're ready for refreshments or want to explore the village, go down to the main street first. (There are toilets in the car park on the right before you reach it.) Most of the terraced houses are at least 150 years old (dating, as you would expect, from the period when Cornish mining was at its most prosperous) but still in good order; only the rather hectic through-traffic tends to spoil the impression, and you can soon get away from that by taking one of the side-roads or paths on the far side of the main street. Chacewater Post Office was run by Mrs Annette Penhaligon until her late husband David was re-elected as MP for Truro in 1979. There are three pubs and a general store.

❾ The valley road sloping gently down to Twelveheads is pretty and usually very little used by motor vehicles. In terms of scenery it could hardly contrast more sharply with the Poldice and Wheal Maid valleys, its southern neighbours. I last walked it quite early on a Sunday morning in April, and the list in my notebook revives for me the pleasures of the experience: "Glossy leaves on trees ... Glimpse of church ... Blackthorn, chickens, pigs, ducks, cows, friendly dogs, a dung-spreader, stream, ponds (for fish-breeding?) ..." A sign announces the Chacewater Vineyard, but where are the vines? The same sign refers to a herb and garden nursery, geese and cider. Just to the right is an older notice, "Tippett's Stamps

Nurseries" - a timely reminder that when the mines were in full swing this was a very different place, because the clatter of Cornish Stamps in operation must have been almost unbearable. The stamps probably processed ore from Creegbrawse mine, just above Todpool, if I am right in guessing that Tippett was an official there: two shafts at Creegbrawse are named "Tippett's". Nearby - just a little way up the slope on the other side of the stream according to the OS maps - was a small copper mine, one of many in Cornwall given the optimistic name of Wheal Prosper. (The mine's main buildings were actually on the "Vineyard" site, and one shaft was close to the road.) Evidently it failed to live up to expectations: its recorded output is unimpressive. It closed in 1870, and it is hard now to find any surface remains. The stream presumably provided the power to drive Tippett's Stamps, and still today it is being harnessed to drive a small waterwheel. **Shortly after you have passed the track going up on the right to Rising Sun farm** (perhaps once a beer-house, judging by its name), **you could make a very short diversion by crossing the bridge on the left**; notice the small leat which has been taken off the stream beside the bridge. **Walk along the track or road on the far side of the stream for a few yards, then turn right on a footpath just beyond a corrugated building; this takes you back over the stream and past the lightweight, undershot waterwheel, apparently being used to generate electricity. Turn left at the road to continue down the valley towards Twelveheads.**

⑩ At the T-junction turn right into the village, then first left, signposted Point Mills, Bissoe. Soon you pass the Methodist Church, outside which the buses stop. Look right to see Twelveheads Mill, now almost completely rebuilt after a long period of neglect. **Continue ahead and turn left at the corner to return to the parking place.**

ROUND WALK 11
TWELVEHEADS, BISSOE, HICKS' MILL, COOMBE & UNITED DOWNS

About 5 miles (8km), or could be shortened to a little under 3 miles.
The sketch map for this route is at the start of Round Walk 10.

This walk is full of interest and variety, since it includes a valley intensively exploited by industry over many centuries, an important section of the track of the Redruth & Chasewater Railway, two former watermills with their leats, beautiful countryside which feels a world away from mines and railways, and finally a look at the surface remains of one of the world's greatest copper mines, United. The walk is mostly easy, the only exception being quite a long climb from Coombe up on to United Downs. There is no shop or pub on the route.

The walk starts and ends at the small layby car park near Twelveheads. Directions for finding it, and comments on using public transport, are given at the start of Round Walk 10 (page 149).

❶ **From the layby turn left along the road, heading away from Twelveheads village.**

About 70m from the southern end of the layby, notice the substantial granite-block wall on the right side of the road. The Redruth & Chasewater Railway crossed the road on a low wooden bridge at this point, continuing north-west along an embankment which can still be seen.

Continue along the road for about another 30m beyond the site of the bridge and turn left on a wide track with a Public Byway sign. There is a small gap at the left-hand end of the "bund" designed to bar access to motor vehicles.

After a few metres you are following the course of the mineral railway, on the embankment by which it crossed the Carnon Valley. Before walking over that you could go down the side-track on the right to see where the County Adit comes to surface. **Go past the fine bridge** under the embankment, beside which is monitoring equipment set up by the NRA, **and after about another 40m the adit portal is down to your right.** For information about the County Adit, see pages 52-3.

Then continue along the embankment, with a view up the side-valley left to Twelveheads.

The next part of this walk follows the Coast-to-Coast Trail, pages 53-7, as far as the end of section 7.

❷ **Turn right at the road, crossing the bridge over the Carnon River.** The road is quite busy, so do please use the verge wherever possible. This was once an area rich in watermills, and on the right just past the bridge is one of them, Point Mills. The truncated stack on the left is a relic of the most important of several arsenic works which operated at Bissoe until well into this century. (For more detail, see pages 57-8.) **Continue along the road, past Richards' filling station.**

❸ **Turn left at the sign, Hick's Mill, Coldwind Cross.**

Notice the well-preserved leat on the left beside the road, starting at the right-hand bend. It is carrying the water which, having powered the waterwheels at Hicks' Mill, was then needed by Point Mills. At the next left bend the leat is culverted under the road, having crossed the stream in a launder. **Walk on past the entrance to Hicks' Mill, now named The Old Mill.** One of its two waterwheels, restored and turning, is on the south side of the mill, and can be glimpsed just after you have passed the entrance. **Turn right just after that.** Beyond the line of fir trees, look down on the right to see what little remains of the other wheel, at right angles to the first one, on the west side. The leat is in good order, and the system of launders leading the water to the wheels is still more-or-less intact.

Hicks' Mill as it was a few years ago

The path passes Hicks' Mill Church, a Bible Christian chapel dating from 1821. It has strong associations with Billy Bray (see pages 49-50), and one of its early members was Samuel Thomas Tregaskis (1785-1871), who owned Hicks' Mill before taking over Sea Mills on Petherick Creek, and who in 1845 became notorious in Padstow by trying to bribe the folk there to abandon the 'Obby 'Oss custom. (See *Around Padstow*, Walk 4.) A detailed history of Hicks' Mill Church by the Rev. T.W.M.Darlington was published in 1991 with the title, *Glimpses into Renown*. (I have accepted Mr Darlington rather than the OS as the authority on the position of the apostrophe in *Hicks'*!)

The path then runs beside the leat and the stream, soon crossing the leat. Close to the weir, where the leat begins, it crosses back.

Just beyond the weir, turn right on the surfaced lane, which takes you up to the minor road from Bissoe to Cusgarne. This is one of many Cornish (and English) places called Coombe, meaning small valley - compare Welsh *cwm*.

❹ **Turn right on the road, then almost immediately left on a side-road running quite steeply uphill. After about 100m, turn sharp-left on to a narrower surfaced lane, still uphill. Beyond the house (Coombe Hill), continue ahead along a path, indicated by a blue waymark arrow.**

Eventually you stop climbing, and soon after the path levels off another one crosses it. Here you have a choice of ways:

A For the shortest walk, go straight on along a narrower path which may be somewhat overgrown for the first few metres but soon emerges into the open, running gently downhill. After passing a small car dump, turn left and continue down to the road. Turn left on that - walking with care, because traffic tends to be fast here. Where the road curves left as it approaches the headgear and mill buildings of Mount Wellington mine, take the path on the right, where there is a small gap in a line of stone blocks at the start of a wide, stony track. Now pick up the directions at point 9, line 3 (page 165).

B To extend the walk by a little over two miles in order to look at some of the more notable surface remains of the great United Mines, turn left at the crosspaths, heading slightly uphill again. Eventually, when you pass a house, the path becomes a rough lane, and not far beyond that there is a path on the right. This will be the way to go when you complete the walk, but first continue ahead.

After about 100m you will get a clear view (in a field to the left of the track) of one of the most remarkable survivals from mining days, a little round powder house (explosives store) which belonged to Wheal Clifford, one of the old mines which combined to form United Mines, and later gave its name to Clifford Amalgamated; it looks amazingly well preserved. Wheal Clifford's 76-inch pumping engine stood nearby.

❺ Take the next turning left, about 100m beyond the powder house: a wide track which runs gently downhill.

The view from this is extensive, with Carnmenellis hill on the skyline ahead (topped by a transmitter mast); further right, the closer mast on Carnkie hill and Carn Marth, with the "landscaped" United Downs public refuse tip closer in the same direction; St Day further right again; and to the left you can almost - but not quite, I think - see the sea to the south.

❻ After a little more than 500m on this track you come to a road. Turn right on that, past Highlands Farm.

About 100m beyond the farm buildings, there is a small layby on the right, bordered by an earth bund or ramp. If you are interested in seeing Taylor's Shaft on the Ale & Cakes section of United Mines, cross this ramp and follow a wide track away from the road for a few yards; turn left where another track joins, then follow it as it bears right, so that you are still walking away from the road, with a stock-car racing area to your left.

Soon you will see, in an excavated area surrounded by the remains of old burrows, the rectangular mouth of a shaft, covered with a heavy metal grid. This is the pumping shaft where a famous 85-inch engine stood. *Built at the Perran Foundry in 1840, she (Cornish engines, like ocean-going ships, are of feminine gender) soon began to outmatch all other beam engines in Cornwall for efficiency, achieving in September/October 1842 a "duty" of 107 millions - that is, an average of 107 million lbs of water lifted 1 ft high by the consumption of 1 bushel of coal. This was one of the engines chosen by the Foundry to advertise their capabilities in their Illustrated Catalogue (1870): a small version of the drawing of it is reproduced in Volume 1 of this guide (page 175). A few masonry fragments of the engine house can still be seen just north-west of the shaft. A splendid model with part of the engine house cut away to reveal the interior is on display at London's Science Museum, and an identical model survives in Ireland - for reasons which are obscure.*

This historic site along with the nearby banger-racing track was recently threatened with total obliteration by the dumping of 450,000 cubic metres of "inert waste", forming eventually a tip up to 68 feet high. The firm concerned, County Environmental Services Ltd., claimed that in the long term this would "enhance the wildlife and conservation value of the site", but opposition from local residents, Carrick District Council, local parish councils and various organisations including the Poldice Valley Trust and Groundwork Kerrier ensured that planning permission was refused.

An old mine that became part of Nangiles was called "Bread and Cheese". "Ale and Cakes" sounds like the reply: "We can do better than that!"

From the higher ground near the shaft can be seen the front of the recently stabilised Gwennap United stamps-engine house, and over to the right the slight remains of Garland's pumping-engine house; both can be seen at closer quarters later.

Gwennap United stamps-engine house (SVJ)

Return to the road and continue as before, turning right at the junction. Immediately past the entrance to the recycling centre on the left is the small engine house known as Eldon's, whose interesting history is outlined on an "interpretive board" on the far side. *The 1830s project to bring water here via surface and underground leats from a source a mile beyond Lanner is comparable with such feats as the driving of the County Adit (pages 52-3) and the construction of the Wheal Unity leat (pages 109-11). As stated on the board, the 30-inch engine in this building pumped the water 200 feet to surface, and further leats or launders then carried it another few hundred yards to a pond whose remains can be seen a little later. Eldon's engine house was reduced in height and adapted to become the office of the Gwennap United operation round the start of this century.*

Continue along the road.

❼ Take the first turning on the right.

The farm buildings on the right stand on what was the site of a pub, the Miners' Arms.

Look left at the first gateway to see the outlines of the pond that used to be filled by Eldon's engine. The water was used mainly for cooling the condensers of the United Mines' engines.

A track on the right a little further along the road leads to the conserved stamps-engine house, built in about 1900 by a company named Gwennap United whose main aim was to rework the old dumps for tin. (The venture was unsuccessful, and closed in less than a decade.) *The 34-inch engine worked a battery of stamps on the far side - the massive concrete base on which they stood can still be seen - and dressing floors were constructed on the gentle slope leading down to what is now the stock-car circuit.*

Return to the road and continue as before.

Soon you will reach the ruins - little more than the bob wall - of Garland's pumping-engine house, standing back from the road on private land. *This was built in 1851 for an 85-inch engine, and about 50 years later an 80-inch was installed as part of the Gwennap United operation.*

Where the road bends left, continue straight ahead on a track. Still continue ahead at the crosstracks near the powder house, then take the next turning on the left, as mentioned above. *The extensive burrows on the right as you descend to the road were created by Wheal Clifford.*

❽ At the road,

<u>either</u> cross and continue down the wide track or lane opposite, marked Old Cusvey House. Keep to the main downhill track, and you will emerge at the Twelveheads end of the valley road from Bissoe; turn right on that, and it will bring you back to the suggested parking place.

<u>Or</u> turn right, down the road (walking with care), past the main entrance to the Mount Wellington site.

An old mine called Wheal Friendship, part of United Mines, was previously on this site. It was last worked by two brothers called Wellington during the 1930s, and the modern mine is named after them; locally, though, it is sometimes known as Magpie Mine. Following the rise in world tin prices during the 1960s, several new mining ventures were launched in Cornwall; Wheal Jane, between Twelveheads and Baldhu, was the first into production, in 1971, and Mount Wellington began full production in 1976. By that year the main shaft was already about a thousand feet deep, and the aim was to treat 600 tonnes of ore per day, using a work force of about 300. Results were very disappointing, however, and the mine closed in 1978, but a little over a year later it was reopened by Rio Tinto Zinc as part of Wheal Jane. (The two mines are linked underground.) From then on the Mount Wellington section was used mainly for ventilation purposes. Prices collapsed in 1985, but Wheal Jane continued to function on a reduced scale, and Mount Wellington's workings also remained viable in case of a revival in the industry's fortunes. (In fact, some mining continued right up to 1991 in the Mount Wellington section, where there were some very productive stopes.) For the rest of the sorry tale up to 1996, see the note about Wheal Jane in Round Walk 12.

The Mount Wellington site as it was in 1996 (SVJ)

❾ **Where the road curves right, take the path on the left. (An old public footpath post lurks rather forlornly among tall bracken.) Start by going through the gap in a line of large granite blocks, and then after about 50m, where the stony track starts curving left, take the narrow path on the right side.** From the path you get good views, first of the huge burrow of Nangiles mine on the other side of the valley, with the bob wall of its pumping-engine house perched on top; and later of the course of the mineral railway as it crossed the Carnon Valley.

❿ **Turn left along the road to return to the parking place.**

When you come to the start of the byway on the right, where you turned on to the railway embankment at the start of the walk, notice the whitewashed cottage on the left. The sign on the gate may surprise you: "Wheal Andrew Engine House". In fact it did duty for many years as a barn, but before that contained an unusual pumping engine. Kenneth Brown thinks the engine was probably inverted - that is, the rocking beam was mounted below the cylinder - site evidence suggests this, though documentary confirmation is lacking. The house that comes next was the mine's count house. Wheal Andrew was yet another of the small mines which became part of United Mines.

The remains of a small set of water-driven stamps lying neglected somewhere in the Carnon Valley (Photograph by R.A.Curtis, 1934, courtesy RIC)

ROUND WALK 12
THE CARNON VALLEY, GOODERN & CARRINE COMMON

About 7½ miles

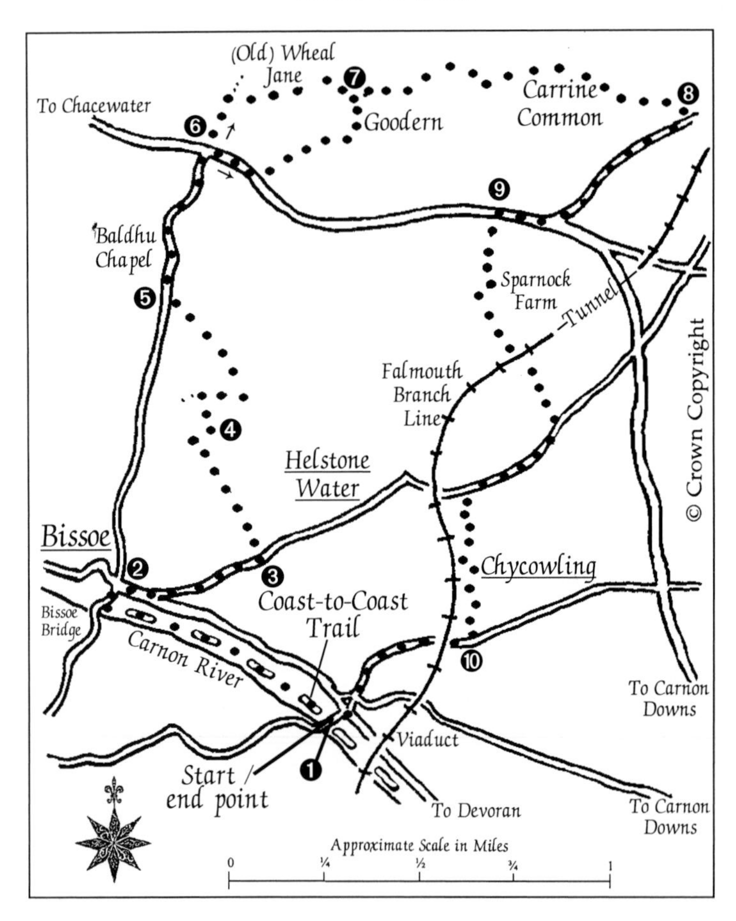

Although there are few relics of old mine buildings along the route of this walk, it neatly illustrates much of the story of Cornish mining. At the very start you have the first and one of the last two chapters of that story laid out before you, in the shape of the Carnon Valley, one of the main sources of stream tin in ancient times, and Wheal Jane, one of the last of all the great Cornish tin mines to open. An important intervening chapter concerns the earliest attempts to find "lode tin" (as opposed to alluvial tin)

and other metals, first by digging pits or "coffans" and then by sinking sloping shafts which followed the lode underground, with occasional vertical shafts for ventilation. The section of the walk around Goodern and Chygoose shows this very well. "As a classic illustration of Elizabethan mining methods," writes A.K.Hamilton Jenkin, "no other site in Cornwall can compare with this."

The walk is of considerable interest also to students of that shadowy period when Cornwall was ruled by Kings, about whom have clustered legends that may be based on historical fact.

Again, this is a walk for naturalists: for example, it crosses Carrine Common, an area of open heath which is a valuable wildlife habitat, and passes beside old shafts used by hibernating greater horseshoe bats. Above all, despite an unavoidable few hundred yards on quite a busy road, it is a delightful walk in peaceful countryside. I first walked it on a bright, snowy day in February 1991, so I associate it with sunshine lighting up the snow on every bough and across untrodden fields; but in April and May the same lanes are a mass of primroses and bluebells. In those three months and most others you will probably need waterproof footwear, and if you want food or drink along the way you'll have to take them with you.

The start/end point for this walk is on the Coast-to-Coast Trail in the Carnon Valley at Grid Reference SW 784 409, where there are a couple of lay-bys beside the minor road (Grenna Lane) which runs from Higher Carnon Farm to Grenna Farm. This lies between the viaduct carrying the Falmouth Branch railway and the southern end of the battery of filtration ponds set up by the National Rivers Authority. (Colour photograph 22.)

❶ **Start by walking up the valley (that is, away from the viaduct), taking the track which runs beside the ponds just mentioned, with the Carnon River to your left - part of the Coast-to-Coast Trail. After passing the second battery of ponds you will reach another minor road. Turn right on that, soon crossing the trackbed of the Redruth & Chasewater Railway, as mentioned on page 58.**

❷ **At the crossroads turn right again,** watching out for traffic on this much busier road. Luckily you are not on it for long: **take the first left turning, signed to Helston Water, which climbs out of the valley.**

❸ **After about a quarter of a mile a fairly wide track crosses the road. Turn left on this. Ignore the first right turning**; just past that is a marshy area with a tip, almost certainly evidence of mining *(this area was mined, mainly for lead but also tin, between about 1848 and 1870 by a mine called Great Wheal Baddern, sometimes spelt "Badden" or "Baddon"),* and then the main track curves right. At the bend you have a good view of Wheal Jane and its tailings lagoon, with Mount Wellington mine in the distance.

The new Wheal Jane was opened in 1971 after several years' research by Consolidated Gold Fields. The two shafts and the buildings housing the pumps, treatment plant and other machinery occupy the site of a very old mine called Wheal Widden. The underground workings of Wheal Jane take in the setts of several other old mines, such as West Wheal Jane and the original Wheal Jane, further north-east near Goodern, plus Nangiles in the opposite direction.

The unusually complex nature of the ores mined in this district (one mine sold as many as 17 different metals during the 19th century) caused great difficulties with ore dressing, and a crisis brought on by technical problems led to the closure of the mine in the summer of 1978. Carnon Consolidated Mines, a subsidiary of the Rio Tinto Zinc Corporation, bought both Wheal Jane and Mount Wellington (see Round Walk 11, page 164) in 1979 and decided to run them as one unit. Annual production of ore reached 300,000 tonnes in 1984, and by 1985 the main shaft had been sunk to 514m.

In October 1985 the price of tin dropped to £3,300 per tonne, having been as high as £10,500 a few months earlier. Government loans kept Wheal Jane alive then, but the Mount Wellington section closed. In 1988 the Carnon Consolidated management, controlling both Wheal Jane and South Crofty, bought the mines from Rio Tinto, and there were encouraging price rises on the metal markets in 1989, but only a year later the company announced that mining at Wheal Jane would cease in June 1991. Wheal Jane was always the more vulnerable of the two mines because of higher working costs, with as much as thirteen million gallons a day of water having to be pumped. The company proposed that "a massive £35m leisure, tourist and business complex" should be created on the site, profits from which would safeguard the future of mining at South Crofty. Meanwhile, pumping would continue at Wheal Jane, enabling underground tours to be part of the visitor attraction, and ensuring that mining could recommence if the markets warranted.

This ambitious scheme was doomed, because in February 1991 the Government suddenly cut off financial assistance to Carnon Consolidated. All mining at Wheal Jane instantly ceased, a large proportion of the workforce joined the dole queues, and the main pumps draining the deeper levels were switched off. The mill, however, equipped with all the latest plant, was retained for treating the ore from South Crofty, brought to the site by a fleet of lorries, and water for use in the mill continued to be pumped from the mine, thus postponing for a while the day when the Wheal Jane adit would start disgorging highly polluted water into the Carnon River.

Effluent from the mill ran (and still runs) into the tailings lagoon, where the solids gradually settle on the bottom and (comparatively) pure water overflows into the river. On 4th January 1992, however, gales churned up the sediment to such an extent that no overflow could be allowed. Pumping therefore was stopped, and pressure built up underground. Something had to give, and it was a concrete plug in the adit serving the Nangiles section of the workings. Tens of millions of gallons of strongly acidic effluent gushed into the river, and on contact with salt water the ferric oxide in it was precipitated, turning Restronguet Creek bright orange. (The note about Nangiles mine, page 53, refers to the notoriously acidic water in it.) The heavy metals in the mine water, such as cadmium and zinc, were invisible but potentially far more dangerous. The long-term damage resulting from the "Wheal Jane Disaster" remains to be assessed.

Emergency measures had to be taken to limit further pollution, and the "short-term solution" which, nearly five years later, is still in operation, involves the pumping of at least two million gallons of water per day (much more in rainy periods) and treating it with a daily dose of at least twenty tons of lime. It then flows into the tailings lagoon as a bright blue-green liquid, contrasting dramatically with the orange effluent from the mill, and the addition of flocculants promotes rapid settling-out of the solids. In unusually wet weather some mine water has to be allowed to flow directly into the river. Meanwhile the dam wall retaining the ever-deepening lagoon has had to be built up to an alarming level, and the time cannot be too distant when the lagoon will no longer be usable, even if the waste material from South Crofty ceases to be poured into it.

A "passive" method of treating the mine water using reed beds and various types of filtration tanks seems to be the only feasible alternative, and with the aid of government funding the NRA has set up the trial scheme in the Carnon valley which you passed at the start of this walk. At the time of writing there are confusingly contradictory reports of the outcome of these experiments, but even if they prove highly successful it is hard to see how all the effluent from the mine could ever be handled in this way.

The story is obviously far from over ...

❹ **At the T-junction turn left on the main track, at the next T-junction turn right, and then at the point where several tracks meet go left, again on the main track.** Now you should be heading roughly towards the Wheal Jane building, with a good view over the tailings lagoon on your left. **Ignore the two right turnings: continue ahead to the road.**

❺ **Turn right on that**, soon passing Baldhu Wesleyan Chapel. A little way off, to the left, is Baldhu Church; nearby, on both sides, are numerous mineshafts, some capped and others apparently still open.

Baldhu means "black mine", although Oliver Padel suggests that "bal" would more accurately be translated as "an area where surface working was carried out, perhaps a group of workings". The oldest documented use of the word was in fact in the phrase "bal dew", in 1593. Like St Day and Chacewater, it became a separate parish in the first half of the 19th century, when the populations of nearby villages such as Twelveheads and Bissoe were greatly swollen by the success of the mines; and like St Day Church, Baldhu Parish Church is now disused and falling apart. The grave of Billy Bray (see pages 49-50), surmounted by an impressive memorial, is close to the south door; it is lovingly tended, whereas the church is boarded up and deserted. Plans to demolish all except the tower and spire were put to Carrick DC in 1993, but an organisation called the Tregellas Foundation has been set up by Mrs Rita Tregellas Pope with the aim of transforming the church into a "cultural centre" which, according to press reports, will house a theatre, exhibition areas, a schools workshop for Celtic studies, facilities for a school of international puppetry and for various Cornish organisations, plus "informal eating facilities". The tower and spire will be used for "Cornwall's first observatory", and the Tregellas Tapestry depicting Cornish history will be on show in the church itself. In October 1996 the "West Briton" reported that the Queen had given her blessing to the scheme, but that less than £2,000 had so far been raised towards the £500,000 target figure.

In this part of Cornwall, nearly all the lodes of metalliferous ore run south-west - north-east, and here we have a particularly clear example, because an almost unbroken line of mine workings can be traced from Mount Wellington, through Nangiles and Wheal Jane, and continuing north-east for about another two miles. The next part of this walk will follow the northern part of that line, where the lodes of tin, copper, iron pyrites, silver-lead and zinc, along with plenty of arsenic, some of them deep but others close to the surface, have been exploited at least from Tudor times until the present day. The old shafts and "open-cast entrenchments" as Hamilton Jenkin calls them (MMC Part 6) close to the chapel are relics of West Wheal Jane.

Originally known as Baldhu, this mine was said in 1819 to have "commenced at a period so remote that no memorials of the time are preserved." In 1860 it employed 200 people, producing mainly iron pyrites; although it declined sharply after that, the shallower workings continued to be exploited for tin at least till 1919. From 1905 to about 1915 it was attached to a group called Falmouth Consolidated Mines; from 1939 till 1941 it belonged to the Mount Wellington group; and since 1971 it has been part of the modern Wheal Jane.

Continue along the road, which runs almost due north and therefore soon diverges from the lodes, although you can still clearly see the disturbed ground marking the heavily mined area on the right.

❻ At the main road, continue straight ahead along a farm track.

PLEASE NOTE: This track and the tracks and paths that lead off it are not public rights of way, and it is by kind permission of the tenant of Goodern Manor Farm that I am including them on this walk route. If at any future time such permission is withdrawn, the alternative is to turn right along the road (taking great care, since it can be quite busy), and then after about a quarter of a mile turn left on to a wide track (the second track on that side). Continue along the track, passing several capped shafts on the left and later on your right the main entrance to Goodern Manor Farm. Beyond this the track curves right. Now pick up the directions at point 7.

From the track mentioned at the start of this section, turn right after a little over 200m on to another track. (At the start of this you may have to climb over an earth bund designed to deny access to travellers.)

This track takes you into an area which has been mined over a long period. There is clear evidence, especially a little to the south of this spot, of its having been worked by "old men" (that is, before written records began to be kept, late in the 18th century). From about 1740 it was known as Wheal Jane. (It is now usually referred to as "the old Wheal Jane".) Collins records that "in 1870 it was 180 fathoms deep (on the very flat lode) and employed 300 people." It stopped work in 1884, apart from small-scale operations at the shallower levels. In 1906 it was reopened as part of Falmouth Consolidated Mines Ltd, along with Nangiles, West Wheal Jane and some other old mines nearby. ("Falmouth" acknowledges the fact that Viscount Falmouth owns the mineral rights.) The company built a mill complex in the Carnon valley including an Elmore vacuum separation plant (see the photograph on the next page), but the site you are now entering was the centre of operations, adjacent to the principal working shaft, Giles's Shaft. A substantial masonry building was erected to house gas engines to generate electricity; the other buildings appear from the photograph in MC2 (No. 64) to have been of much lighter construction, like most of those still to be seen at the roughly contemporary King Edward Mine. (See Volume 1 of this guide, p25, and ECM2 p133-8.) By far the largest of these was the mill, originally equipped with ball mills (MC2, picture 65)- a costly mistake, as these soon had to be replaced with Californian stamps, and taking legal action against the manufacturer of the ball mills drained the mine's resources. Dines records that some 860 tons of black tin and 160 tons

The remains of the power house of the old Wheal Jane

of arsenic were produced during the decade-or-so that the mine was active; closure came in 1916 following falls in the price of tin. (The above dates are those given by Mr Justin Brooke; other mining historians give 1905 or 1907 as the date for the opening of "Falmouth Consols" and 1914 or 1915 for its closure.)

Little if anything remains of the lighter buildings, apart from the mill, but the power house, though roofless now and festooned with vegetation both outside and in, is substantially intact, and Giles's Shaft is still a prominent feature at the top of the slope above. A square concrete reservoir has also survived, a little way to the south, but tall bracken and gorse hide it completely from view, at least in the summer months.

Falmouth Consolidated Mines' mill in the Carnon Valley, about 1908. On the left can be seen the track of the Redruth & Chasewater Railway, and in the distance on the right is Brunel's viaduct, with timber superstructure. (Courtesy RIC)

As soon as you have turned on to the track leading to the mine site you will see the power house ahead. **Where the track splits into three, keep straight on along the highest track, running just to the right of the power house.** About 50m past the point where the tracks divided, notice among the trees and undergrowth to your left the two lines, about 8-10 feet apart, of masonry structures mostly about six feet high - evidently parts of the mill building. **A narrow path runs down to the left immediately before the power house, and if you go down that you will get a good view of the massive base of the mill building on your left**, and also see a low, arched opening in the power house wall. **If you then turn right along the wider path at the bottom you will have a fairly good view of the north wall of the power house,** with its six arched window openings. **Return the same way to the main track and turn left, continuing in the same direction as before.**

> **As soon as you reach the far end of the power house, you could make a short detour up the wide, stony track on the right to see Giles's Shaft.** After about 75m, just after the track has curved left, there is a plat on the left, with three concrete cubes (possibly bases for the headgear shown in Trounson's photograph), and if you walk on to this you will see the fenced, open shaft on your right. **Return the same way to the track by the power house and turn right.**

To continue the walk route, go on along the narrow and probably muddy path ahead, ignoring several side-paths on the right. After a hollowed-out area on the left which looks like the result of mining activity, the path winds gently uphill. Where, after another 200m or more, there is a choice of ways, notice the Clwyd-capped shaft on the right, beside which are two huge granite blocks with drill holes, evidently once the bases of mining machinery. **At this point I suggest you keep left, following the path that runs close to the left edge of the woodland** (but if this path is too muddy you could take the other one, turning left when you reach the main track). **About 60m along the left-hand path you will pass, on your left, Wheal Tremayne Shaft.** It is partially boarded over, but temptingly easy to peer into. If you yield to the temptation, take great care! In recent years it has sometimes been used for underground visits by students at the Camborne School of Mines. On the south side of it are the remains of a stone crusher station. **Another 20m brings you to the main track, where you go straight on.**

> At the point where you join the wider track, notice the area of old - possibly very old indeed - shallow mine workings opposite (that is, on the south side of the main track). If you **make a short diversion to the right** you will see a walled shaft on the same side after about 20m, and another shaft (marked by a wooden post with the remains of a triangular warning sign attached) about 50m beyond that. A short walk further in the same direction would bring you close to the main buildings of Goodern Manor Farm.

On and around this farm on the OS maps there is a cluster of words in the Old English script indicating ancient sites: "Earthwork" or "Settlement" and "Tumulus" close to the farm buildings, and at least four other tumuli to east, south and west. As I said in my introductory note, legends tend to cluster about such places, and they find their way into print in such passages as this, from Joy Wilson's "Cornwall, Land of Legend" (Bossiney, 1989): "old *documents speak of this place (Goodern) as having been once a `castle' of irascible King Teudar who here fought a battle against Christians. During the battle he was killed by a fall from his horse, and is thought to have been buried beneath a large tree-crowned barrow that stands close by. Teudar's Christian successor King Mark is thought to have used Goodern as a hunting lodge." And from that point, those who track Tristram and Iseult (Tristan and Isolda) through the Cornish countryside conclude that Goodern was Iseult's destination when her lover, disguised as a leper, carried her across the ford at Malpas. ("Perhaps in those earlier times the Truro River was shallower," speculates Mrs Wilson, and similarly she adds to her comments about Goodern, "And in the level meadow alongside perhaps the tournament and Iseult's Ordeal witnessed by the kings was staged.") The suggestion that Goodern Manor was once an administrative centre is supported by the fact that the name of the nearby settlement of Helston Water derives from Cornish "hen-lys", "ancient court" plus Old English "tun", "manorial centre"; and by the fact that this area was once called Alba Landa or Blancheland, which is the setting of King Mark's hunting lodge in the Tristan story. Goodern is mentioned as a palace of King Teudar in the 16th-century play "The Life of Meriasek". Other stories possibly based on fact have attached themselves to Goodern and its immediate surroundings: Mrs Wilson writes of the farmer in Tudor times who "dug up at Goodern - within the enclosure - enough gold and silver to transform him from peasant to gentleman." Maybe this is in essence the same story that Sheila Bird mentions in CV: "An old legend told of a crock of gold found beneath the old cross, which was removed from the finder's possession by the landowner, who thereafter was unable to keep stock on his land, unless the animals were branded with the protective sign of the cross keys." The medieval Manor House was rebuilt about 1605, and the Tudor house was almost totally destroyed by fire late last century. Although there is so little nowadays that the casual passer-by would notice of the ancient sites at Goodern, the place still exerts a hold on people's imagination: we heard about the residents of a house nearby a few years back who went and prayed at the earthwork every morning.*

Retrace your footsteps along the track to resume the walk route.

❼ The cottage on the left soon after this is Chygoose, "the house in the woods". The track now leaves mining country, and once past the house called Fenton Goose ("fountain or spring in the woods") you are soon crossing Carrine Common, with panoramic views of the south-western edge of Truro, dominated (from left to right) by Treliske Hospital, Richard Lander comprehensive school, and New County Hall.

Carrine Common is described in NC as "a comparatively small area of dry heathland with a good growth of Dorset Heath - this species normally thrives in much wetter conditions." The name, which means "cold fort or round", may relate to the earthwork at Goodern. It is usually pronounced "Careen", but some local people say it to rhyme with "wine" or even transform it to "Cryon", and there is a legend that it got its name from the "crying" of the mothers, widows and sweethearts of those killed in the great battle between King Teudar and the Christians: see the note about Goodern. It is also firmly believed by many that the ghost of a headless woman stalks the tracks and paths on the Common; it was seen by "Mistress Sarah" of Carrine Farm, who was struck blind - though how long afterwards that happened we were not told.

Keep to the main track, curving right, which eventually brings you to a road. (There are several side-tracks and paths which are pleasant to explore and obviously much-used, but not official rights of way.)

❽ **Turn right at the road, and after nearly half a mile right again at the main road, which again "craves wary walking".**

❾ **Take the first left turning, the minor road leading to Sparnock ("thorntree") Farm. Immediately past the farmhouse, go through the six-bar metal gate on the left, and walk straight ahead along a rough, muddy track created mainly by tractor-tyres. This leads to a five-bar wooden gate, beyond which is a bridge over the Falmouth branch line, with a tunnel on the left, and then a narrow woodland path which could easily become overgrown. At the field, continue ahead (despite the waymark arrow on the wooden post) with the hedge on your right and through a metal gate to another road. Turn right on that.** It slopes gently downhill for about half a mile and passes under the railway. **Just before the railway bridge turn left at a lane signed to Kestrel Cottage and Hallego Farm, then fork right at the signs "Hannam" and "SGBawden".** This leads down to another railway bridge (notice the view of Carn Marth almost straight ahead), but **again, just before the bridge turn left**, on to a pretty but often very muddy woodland lane. Before reaching a road this becomes a path.

❿ **Turn right at the road,** which passes under yet another railway bridge and slopes down to Dunstan's Ford, with a granite footbridge. **Cross the main road to return to the suggested parking place.**

ROUND WALK 13

PERRANWELL & THE PERRAN FOUNDRY

Walks of about two, four-and-a-half and six miles

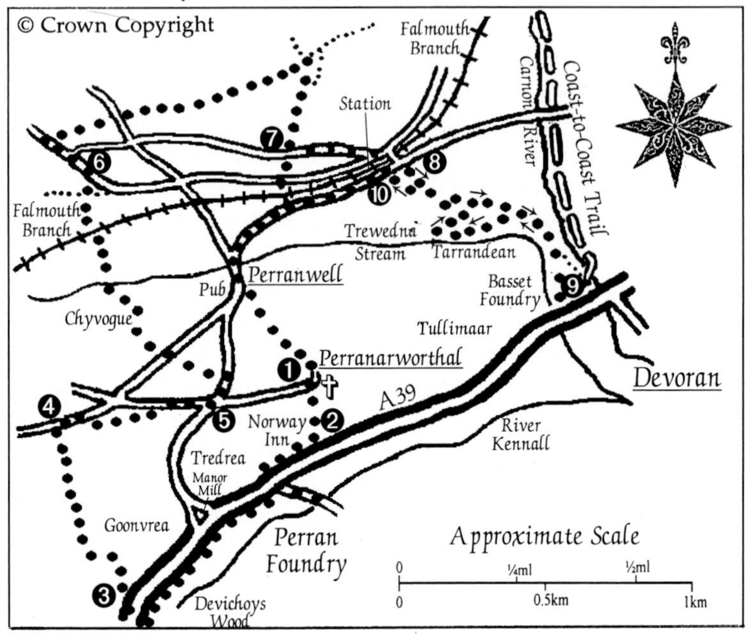

In 1870 the Rev. Francis Kilvert spent nearly three weeks on holiday in Cornwall. His base was Tullimaar, a mansion just east of Perranarworthal Church. *Although not visible from the walk route (it stands in private grounds among the trees above the main road, east of Perranarworthal Church), this house deserves mention because of its interesting history. It was built about 1828 by Benjamin Sampson, whose wealth derived both from the gunpowder works at Cosawes and from the Perran Foundry. As I have mentioned, the house features in Kilvert's diary; and in our own century another guest there was General Eisenhower. In recent years it was the home of the Cornish-born, Nobel-Prize-winning novelist, Sir William Golding, who died in 1993. He kindly supplied me with the following list of interesting people who have lived at Tullimaar. The last one, who owned the house from 1957-73, was a descendant of Napoleon.*

A *Mrs Hearle-Cock. She transferred an Italianate villa to the grounds of Tullimaar from the Isle of Wight but was in the end forbidden by the council to erect it. She died through being stung by a hornet.*

B *An illegitimate granddaughter of George III, who was, said the locals with some awe, "buried at royal expense."*

C *A daughter of David Livingstone.*

C A daughter of David Livingstone.
D Prince and Princess Ghika-Comenesti.
E Princess Bibesco, well thought-on in France as a novelist and "ornament of High Society".

In his diary Kilvert recorded what he could see from his window on the first morning: "...the brown sands, mud and shrunk stream of Restronguet, the rich sloping oak woods dark and impervious, rising from the river bed opposite. Down the river beyond the woods may be seen the back of a rounded hill, and up the river the glint of white buildings on the river side, the white walls and chimneys of an iron foundry." (The white was probably limewash, applied in order to protect the mortar from weathering. Nearly all the mine engine houses would also have been whitened in their working days, and traces of the wash can still be found on some.) This walk takes you to that foundry, one of the most important surviving groups of industrial buildings in Cornwall, already nearly a century old when Kilvert saw it, and also, if you do the full six miles, to another smaller foundry which was still working till very recently. The route includes an old church, a holy well, and attractive countryside - partly woodland and partly a ridgeway track with long views. Unlike any other walk in this book, this one includes over half a mile on a very busy main road, but there is a pavement all the way (the American term "sidewalk" seems much better, since it's not paved!), and the road runs through a valley which is full of historical interest and is beautiful despite the traffic. The rest of the walk is mostly on minor roads and well-made tracks. There is one very steep and possibly rather muddy climb, but it is mercifully short, and another section of path, beside a stream and through fields, may also be wet. There are pubs, well known locally for good food, at Perranwell (the Royal Oak) and Perran Wharf (the Norway Inn), and Perranwell has a shop.

The walk starts at Perranarworthal Church. To drive there from Truro, take the A39 Falmouth road. After about six miles, shortly after the Norway Inn, take the right turning signposted to Perranwell. At the crossroads, turn right again, following the sign to the church. The church is at the end of this road, and there is a car park at the corner on the left just before you reach it. The Vicar is happy that walkers should use it, providing they avoid times of Sunday services. Bear in mind, too, that if there's a wedding or christening in the church while you're parking, you could get boxed in. There is also some room to park by the road just past the church, but please be careful not to impede farm vehicles.

❶ Before setting off, you may care to look round the church. It is usually kept locked, but a small notice by the main door explains how you can get a key.

Piran, an Irish saint who is supposed to have floated to Cornwall on a millstone, gave his name to Perranporth, Perranzabuloe and Perranuthnoe, and here his name is linked to that of the ancient manor of Arworthal (probably meaning "beside the marsh, creek or estuary"). The spelling often seen, "Perran-ar-Worthal", is therefore historically incorrect. The church dates from Norman times: above the south door, behind glass on the inside of the church, is a Norman tympanum (defined in my dictionary as "a space between a lintel and an arch over it") depicting the Lamb and Cross. The tower was built about 1450. Most of what we see now, however, is the work of Victorian "restorers". The pinnacle on the corner of the tower nearest the car park is a modern replacement for the original, destroyed by lightning. As has been pointed out to me, the new workmanship is far cruder than the old.

To start the walk, return along the road you came by for a few yards, past the entrance to a nursery, and go down the footpath signposted to Perran Wharf, which starts on the left via a turnstile. After a short distance, where the path widens, there is a side-path on the left, signposted to St Piran's Well. The well is only a few yards away, down a flight of steps, and worth a look. *Any actual connection with St Piran is highly dubious, but "the water is said to contain considerable amounts of iron salts and to have `general medicinal qualities'"(HW). Francis Kilvert visited it on 6 August 1870, and in his diary wrote a beautiful description, adding, "It is called St Katharine's Well, or the Holy Well"(KCD, p.102). I'm told it is still the source for baptismal water at Perranarworthal Church.* Return to the main path, now a metalled drive, and **descend to the main road.** As you reach it, notice the large limekilns on the right, now serving as stores for the Norway Inn. Elisabeth Rowlands mentions that there was "a little arm of the river which gave access to the lime-kilns"; hence the little hump-back bridge on the main road (FRV).

The remains of limekilns are common in Cornwall - a reflection of the high acidity-level of the soil. There were far more on the south coast than the north, mainly because sand containing lime-rich shell fragments was more readily available on the north coast than limestone, most of which came to Cornwall by boat from Plymouth. Kilvert, returning at 3am from one of the many exhausting expeditions the Hockin family took him on, was still sufficiently awake to notice when they reached Perran Wharf that "A sailing lighter had come up the creek at high tide with a load of limestone, and was lying at the quay waiting to unload and go down again with the next high tide." (KCD) The memories of an elderly resident at Calenick, near Truro, are relevant here: "The lime used to come up the river in boats - brown rocks, it was ... They set fire to them somehow in the kiln, and poured water, and then - oh my dear life! - the smoke used to come up and the lime would be white as snow, like dust, and the farmers would come and collect it for their fields." (Quoted in "Calenick Village, A Case Study", a Project Pack published by the Truro Research Project in 1988.) The way "they set fire to them" was in fact by feeding into the kiln from above alternate layers of coal and limestone and then lighting a coal or wood fire underneath; finally the burnt lime was hydrated or slaked, thus making it suitable for agricultural or building use. The kilns were usually built into the sides of hills or low cliffs so that access from above was easy: see Walk 15 (Point Quay area) for a good example of this. After the middle of the 19th century, limekilns gradually fell out of use, largely because burnt lime was superseded as a fertiliser by crushed limestone brought in by the railways.

The Norway Inn ("Norway Hotel" in early days) is said to have got its name from the Norwegian vessels which once brought loads of timber to Perranwharf, largely for use in the mines. A great deal was used underground - for ladders and lining shafts, for example, though not normally for pit-props since these were not usually necessary in hard-rock mining; the pump-rods and in the early days even the beams for the huge steam-engines were wooden. The inn dates from about 1830, the time when the main Falmouth to Truro road was rerouted to cross the Carnon River on an embankment just above Devoran; the bridge about half a mile further upstream carried the previous turnpike, which passed through Perranwell and Calenick. (A later section of this walk passes along the old turnpike.) In the days of the Falmouth Packets, the Norway was the first point at which horses were changed by the Falmouth mail coach on its way to London.

❷ **Turn right.** You are now close to Perranwharf.

In 1769, George Croker Fox, a member of the Quaker family which was already deeply involved in Cornish industry (and which has also bequeathed to Cornwall a legacy of beautiful gardens), bought the lease of what was then a large area of waste land in Perran Creek, the lower Kennall valley. He then proceeded to develop it into a port to serve the Gwennap mines, creating jetties, quays, timber ponds and warehouses. The problem of shallow water at most states of the tide in Perran Creek was overcome by the provision of several quays downstream where seagoing vessels could transfer their cargoes to flat-bottomed barges. For many years the project was highly successful, but the eventual demise of Perranwharf was ensured by the development of Devoran when the railway came, and by the silting-up of Restronguet Creek.

You are also approaching the even more important later development, Perran Foundry. **Cross to the far side of the road; the safest place to do so is where keep-left bollards form an island in the middle, just before the left turning signed to Carclew.**

A recommended short diversion is to walk a little way along the Carclew road. *In the Foundry's working days , a canal ran beside the main* *road to your left, flanked by quays; it has been filled in now. A little further south on the same side, what looks like a flat watermeadow was a timber pond. The Kennall River curves south beside the road on your right, then runs beneath it. Before you reach the bridge you have quite a good view on that side of the eastern end of the Foundry complex, notably the three-storey building, originally the Foundry's New Pattern Shop, adapted as a grain mill by the Edwards brothers when they took over the site about a century ago.*

Return to the main road and turn left.

The buildings on your right include the former Wharf Offices and the Foundry's Counting House, "where the men queued for their pay," says Elisabeth Rowlands, who also suggests that behind the building were stables "where some at least of the twenty four horses needed for hauling heavy castings up the hill in the early days may have been stabled." Even if you have to view the Foundry itself from the road, from its two entrances you can get a fair impression of the extent of the buildings. The famous cast-iron lintel bearing the name of the foundry and dated 1791 is over the entrance to the forge building. (There are in fact three such lintels; one of the others, above a bricked-up entrance a little further left, is visible from the road but very battered and scarcely recognisable from a distance.)

Perran Foundry was built on part of the site of Perranwharf by Fox's two sons, George Croker Junior and Robert Weir. It was not Cornwall's first large engine-factory (that was built by John Harvey at Hayle in 1779), but it followed close behind, in 1791, and remains one of the most interesting and impressive monuments to the heyday of Cornish industry, despite recent neglect.

The most interesting accounts of the history of Perran Foundry that I have come across are those by W.Tregoning Hooper in Journals of the Royal Cornwall Polytechnic Society dated 1929 and 1938 (particularly the later one) and the chapter by Elisabeth Rowlands in ERV. For another good source of information, seek out HAF, Vol.1. T.H.Bradley's article concentrates on the water-power at the foundry, but the plan on pages 40-1 gives a clearer picture of the extent and layout of the works than any words could. A second leat was taken from the Kennall River close to the Manor Mill leat but on the south side, and on its way down to the foundry this was joined by the stream from the old gunpowder works at Cosawes and another stream at Treluswell. It was then sufficient to run at least five waterwheels at the foundry.

Business flourished. As early as 1815 the great beams for the steam engines were being cast at Perran. In 1840 the foundry supplied an 85-inch pumping engine for Taylor's Shaft, United Mines, one of the finest ever made by Cornish engineers (see Round Walk 11, page 161), and three years later the "West Briton" reported that "the largest piece of wrought iron work ever forged in Cornwall" had been made here in 1842 for another 85-inch engine, this time for Tresavean Mine, Lanner. Between 1843 and 1846 the Hayle and Perran foundries in partnership

The Perran Foundry, from an engraving made probably in the 1830s, soon after the Norway Inn was built. (Courtesy RIC)

built the enormous compound engines required by the Dutch government to drain the Haarlem Meer.

By 1860 the works covered 6 acres and had 400 employees. Tregoning Hooper remarks on the excellent relationship between management and "work-people", and on the inventiveness and enthusiasm of the mechanics. The engines for export were loaded on to flat-bottomed barges and transferred to sea-going vessels at a quay near the Pandora Inn which the Foxes had acquired, or further down-river. For more information about the engines and other equipment made at the foundry, see Hooper's articles, BE, CBE and the recent reprint of the foundry's catalogue of about 1870. The name of the company at that time, Williams' Perran Foundry Co., reflects the fact that the Williams family of Scorrier, who had been involved in a small way with the project from the beginning, had gradually increased their share holding over the years, finally taking over as sole owners in 1858.

The slump in the mining industry during the 1870s hit Perran Foundry badly, and it closed in 1879. As described by Ivy Edwards in FRV, the buildings were later adapted for the milling and storage of grains and animal foods, and also cloth-dyeing; another waterwheel was added. More recently the old foundry has belonged to the Bibby group, who used it mainly as a store.

In 1988 Devington Ltd put forward plans to convert the buildings without destroying their original character, into a 4-star hotel-cum-restaurant at the western end of the site, residential apartments and cottages at the eastern end, and a "Heritage Centre" in the middle, including a museum and facilities for exhibitions, concerts, presentation of plays and public meetings. In August 1990 the Carrick Planning Subcommittee approved this scheme in principle, but with several conditions, one of which required that before building work started time should be allowed for the Cornwall Archaeological Unit to carry out a survey of the

Part of the Foundry's forge building as it was in 1996 (SVJ)

site. Ten trial trenches were accordingly dug during October and November 1991, and several interesting discoveries were made, including the remains of a mid-19th-century reverberatory furnace.

Almost five years later, little if anything has happened at the Foundry site apart from the gradual deterioration of the buildings. The owners, now known as Perran Foundry Ltd, have abandoned the plan for a hotel, and instead propose to fund the heritage centre by setting up "retail facilities", a restaurant, craft shop, blacksmith and a "food village" featuring various demonstrations of food processing. The estimated cost is over £8m. Grants and private investment are being sought - and meanwhile the likelihood grows ever greater that the Perran Foundry complex will go the same way as those of its one-time illustrious rivals at Hayle and Copperhouse. The latest bad news (February 1997) is that the National Lottery Heritage Fund has refused to make a grant, a decision which is likely to mean that other funds being held in reserve cannot be made available.

Continue along the left side of the road. *Notice the old building at the bottom of the road on the right, Cove Hill: this was Manor Mill, a corn and grist mill which had two waterwheels served by a leat taken from the Kennall River close to where the Ponsanooth railway viaduct now is. The date of the mill is uncertain, but there are records of its existence in 1692. Ivy Edwards refers to it as "Little*

Mill" in <u>*FRV*</u>*. ("Big Mill" was the converted New Pattern Shop on the former Foundry site.) On the opposite side of Cove Hill from the mill is Tredrea, the house built about 1740 as their own home by the Fox family, founders of Perran Wharf and Foundry. The Manor Mill leat also once powered a waterwheel for water pumping at Tredrea. (In our century Tredrea became a hotel, and is now divided into flats.) The next turning on the right, which joins Cove Hill higher up, is the old turnpike road to Truro, as mentioned in the note on the Norway Inn. Soon after this, also on the right, is Goonvrea, another house built by the Foxes; this too became a hotel. Recently it suffered a bad fire. The Kennall River is on your left; the water-meadows beside it and Devichoys Wood above are now under the protection of the Cornwall Wildlife Trust. (Devichoys Wood is a delightful place to explore on foot, but unfortunately I cannot recommend that you walk to it now because the sidewalk beside the A39 gives out well before you would reach the entrance. If, however, you wish to drive to it, you will find the entrance at Grid Reference SW 773 376, a few yards along a minor road towards Mylor Bridge. The wood's name derives from the Cornish "dywys cos", "burnt wood", almost certainly a reference to charcoal burning. The Wildlife Trust has found evidence of early charcoal burning in the wood, and is experimenting with a scheme to produce charcoal there again in order to raise funds to continue its programme of active management of the woodland.)* **Continue on the left side of the main road, past the large layby opposite, where farm produce is usually on sale. Soon you will come to a bus stop on your side; a few yards beyond that, cross with the aid of another central island.**

❸ Turn right on reaching the far side, and after a few yards turn left up the public footpath to Perrandowns (though the name is hardly legible now on the wooden post at the start). Follow the path as it bends right and left. After the entrance to Polpentre it becomes a very steep, narrow path up among trees. The OS 1:10,000 map indicates a shaft to the left of this path, near the bottom, apparently a relic of Perran Vale Mine, a very small operation which closed in 1832. **At the top, turn right on a wider track -** but before turning right, notice the view to the left. The small cluster of "mobile homes" in a wooded valley is at Cosawes, the site of Cornwall's first gunpowder works. **Keep to this track as it curves left and right.** At the right-hand bend, beside farm buildings, you can catch a glimpse in the distance to the left of Ponsanooth village. **Go straight on where a metalled drive on the right leads to a bungalow.** The view here includes Perranwell to the left; Perranarworthal Church further right with Carnon Downs on the hill above; and Devoran further right again. Also visible, if you're tall enough to see over the hedge to your left, outlined on the skyline is the Gwennap United stamps-engine house on United Downs. (See page 163.) Notice the pump on the left beside the track later.

❹ At the road turn right, passing the lodge at the entrance to Goonvrea; after about fifty yards take the path on the right, and at the road turn right again.

❺ At the crossroads, to return straight away to Perranarworthal Church take the minor road ahead, Church Road; but for the full 5- or 6-mile walk, turn left on to St Piran's Hill. Soon on the left there is a side-road (Treworthal Road). The walk continues along the footpath on the left immediately after that.

At the next road is Perranarworthal County Primary School. *The area opposite the school appears to have been the site of an old mine, referred to in early documents variously as a lead mine, "a rich tynn mine", "Perran Downs Old Tin Mine", and in the 1850s as "South United Copper Tin and Lead Mine" (MMC6).* **Cross and continue along the path opposite, signposted Rissick. At the junction, bear slightly right (not sharp right), then keep to the lane as it curves left beside the entrance to Chyvogue House.** *There is some evidence that tin stamps were once sited at Chyvogue, which means "the place of the furnace" (compare Vogue, on the edge of St Day). The 1908 OS map shows a "Woollen Factory" here - it manufactured mainly blankets - and by 1900 there was also a sawmill.*

Turn right beside the Old Mill, over a footbridge and along to the left beside the Trewedna Stream, which served this mill. (It continues through Perranwell to Mellingey Creek, where it provided power for a smelting works and Basset Foundry: some details are given later.) **Cross the stile and then go more-or-less straight on, diverging from the stream and crossing the field to a high stone stile topped by a metal rail. (The decaying remains of one or more felled trees lay on either side of the stile when I was last there.) Next, bear left, keeping wall and hedge on your left, to another stone stile, and pass under the bridge** carrying the Falmouth-Truro branch line (1863). **Soon another track cuts across; here, cross the stile straight ahead, walk by the hedge on the right** (where the path was a little overgrown in June 1996, but perfectly passable) **and go through the gate to the road.**

❻ Turn left. Walk with care on this road, which can be quite busy at times. Ignore the signed Public Byway on the right after about 150m; some 130m further along, just past Hawthorne Farm, turn right past a bungalow's entrance, taking the shady, slightly sunken track which leads off uphill on the right. At the road, carry straight on along this ridgeway which later gives you good views south. Where the unsurfaced lane narrows to a (probably muddy) track, the house on the right is called River View, and at the farm gate just beyond you can see why: an attractive glimpse of Devoran and Restronguet Creek. **As you approach a farm on the right, watch for a high stile on that side. Cross this and walk to the**

right side of the farmhouse, where there is another stile; pass along the house-side, then by the hedge till you come to a stile to the narrow road on your left. Cross on to this and turn right. Now again you have views over Devoran and Restronguet Creek. (See Round Walks 14 and 15.)

❼ **At the T-junction, you could take the direct route back to the church, as follows: Cross the road and continue down the footpath, signposted to Perranwell. At the next road turn left and then immediately right, through a kissing-gate to cross the railway line (with due care!). Turn right at the road - watch for fast traffic here. Now pick up the directions at line 3 of point 10.**

But for the full walk, turn left, and at the next T-junction turn left again. *As hinted by local place-names (Silver Hill, Silverdene Farm), this part of Perranwell once witnessed silver-lead mining. Silver Hill Mine is recorded as having been active during the 1830s.* **Follow the main road as it bends right across the railway bridge,** giving you a glimpse of Perranwell station.

❽ At **the following T-junction take the rough lane opposite. Fork left where the lane splits into two, beside the house called Newlands.**

The Basset Works, early this century (Courtesy RIC)

This takes you alongside the part of the Bissoe Valley where tin-streaming was still being carried out by Carnon Consolidated in 1989: the lane itself runs along one of the embankments created by tin streamers perhaps as much as two centuries earlier. A new bridleway on the left crosses one of the former tin-streaming lagoons and provides a handy link with the Coast-to-Coast Trail; and finally - just before the lane meets the A39 trunk road - you pass fairly close to the engineering works generally known as Visick's (say "vie-zix"), which began life in 1858 as Basset or Bassett Foundry. After a period of prosperity it succumbed, like its larger neighbour at Perranarworthal, to the problems created by the mining depression, and in 1876 was converted into the Cornwall & Devon Chemical Manure and Bone Works. The largest building was the bone mill, and its walls are still visible. This new enterprise survived only six years, and the buildings lay derelict till 1895 when Walter Visick, a former Perran Foundry employee, took out a 60-year lease and risked making large investments in a new engineering works at a time of general decline in Cornish industry. He rebuilt the two existing waterwheels on the west side, and made a dam on the east side to control the flow of the Trewedna Stream, converting Mellingey Creek (see below) into a large

A photograph taken at the Basset Foundry site, probably during World War 1. The women appear to be cleaning trench mortar bomb warheads. (Courtesy RIC)

millpond, thus providing a reliable source of power for another waterwheel, built in 1905. The remains of this can still be seen from the footpath, on the opposite side of the Trewedna Stream. By manufacturing a wide range of smaller items like lamp-posts, manhole covers and Cornish ranges, the new factory prospered. (For most of the information in the last two notes, I am indebted to T.H.Bradley's article in HAF, Part 2.) In 1987 it was bought by the King Harry Steam Ferry Company, and over the next couple of years reportedly had a healthy order book for the marine parts it manufactured, but the buildings have now been converted into small industrial units.

❾ Return the same way at first. The marshy area to your left close to the point where the link with the Coast-to-Coast Trail comes in from the right is what was once Mellingey Creek, now usually known as Tarrandean.

It is hard now to believe that until at least the end of the 18th century Mellingey ("mill house") Creek was navigable, and that timber and mining supplies could be landed. By about 1650, a blowing house for smelting tin was built beside the creek; about 1690 it was enlarged, and from 1733 onwards it was known as "Perran Smelting House". In 1774 it was described as having five furnaces, two stamping mills "with buddles and every convenience for dressing tin" and a house with stabling for eight horses. Before long, though, the Bissoe Valley tin-streaming had completely cut off Mellingey Creek to boats, and the smelting house closed, to be converted in 1812 into an arsenic works - in fact, according to D.B.Barton, this marked "the first beginnings of industrial arsenic production in Britain". In 1840 it began dealing with heavily contaminated ores, and at once local people started complaining of bad smells and the poisoning of bees and even livestock; the owner was brought to court in 1851, lost the case, and by 1856 had closed down the works. (See PV, page 41.) Despite one attempt to revive it (1866-70), it became derelict, and now it is difficult to find any trace of its existence.

Turn left at The Stables, a house on the left a little over 200m beyond the Coast-to-Coast Trail link. The surfaced lane becomes a grassy path - attractive but possibly a little overgrown at some times of year - after passing the last house, and about 125m beyond that point it comes very close to the Trewedna Stream. It seems to have been at or close to this spot that the early blowing house, referred to in the above italicised note about Mellingey Creek, was sited. Take a sharp right turn here. This path goes gently uphill, bends left on reaching a house, and eventually becomes a surfaced lane. At the junction (Newlands again) continue on the wider lane, slightly left of straight ahead. It soon brings you to the road, opposite the entrance to Perranwell railway station.

❿ Now turn left and walk with care along this fairly busy road, which is the original turnpike linking Truro with Penryn, Falmouth and Helston, as mentioned earlier in connection with the Norway Inn. Some 175m along the road, a gate on the left affords a good view of Mellingey Creek below. **After about 600m you reach Perranwell Methodist Church** Just beyond it, notice the attractive old house on the same side, bearing the slightly surprising name of Prince Regent House. It dates from the mid- to late 18th century, and was originally a pub, called at one time The Prince Regent's Arms; at other periods it was The Prince of Wales and The Plume of Feathers. Mr D.Endean Ivall, the historian of Cornish heraldry, who lives close by, tells me it was the place where local miners met to discuss business. A plume of feathers was the house mark stamped on ingots of tin at the Treyew smelting works in Truro; one of the partners who owned Treyew took a lease on the Perran smelting house at Mellingey Creek in 1733, and from then on it too used the plume of feathers insignia. "This," writes H.L.Douch, "was no coincidence for smelting-house and inn were frequently owned and managed by the same man" (OCI). As you cross the bridge over the Trewedna Stream, notice on your left the sluice gate marking the start of a leat. This dates back to at least the 17th century, when it served the Mellingey blowing house, and long before that it probably supplied at least one corn mill; in 1858 it was extended to power the waterwheels at the Basset Foundry. On the right side of the road just beyond the bridge was the village smithy, demolished to make room for a pair of cottages. **Now take the public footpath to the church on the left just before the Post Office and general store.** (The Royal Oak, a deservedly popular pub, is a little way beyond the Post Office, on the right.) **The path to the church, which crosses two stone cattle-grids, is about 600m long.**

ROUND WALK 14
A DEVORAN VILLAGE WALKABOUT

About ¾ mile (1km)

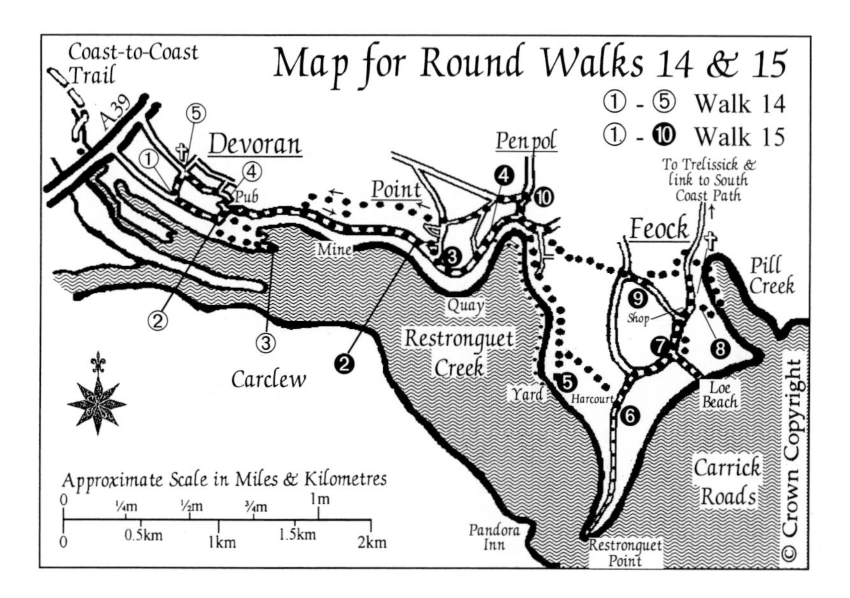

A short tour of this attractive and historically very interesting village. Pub fare can be had at the Old Quay Inn, roughly half-way around. There are no public toilets in the village.

Devoran does not have a car park, but careful roadside parking should not cause any problems, and there is usually space for a few cars in the area between the bottom of Market Street and the village hall - but please do not obstruct the access to the rear of the doctors' surgery - and be careful not to collide with any of the granite posts! There is quite a good bus service to Devoran from both Truro and Falmouth.

The start/end point for the walk is the foot of Market Street, where it meets Greenbank Road and Quay Road.

The name, Devoran, means "waters": very apt, since here three streams (the Carnon River, the Kennall and the Trewedna stream) meet the tidal waters of Restronguet (or Devoran) Creek - though in fact the Carnon River was tidal and even, it is said, navigable once as far as Bissoe Bridge.

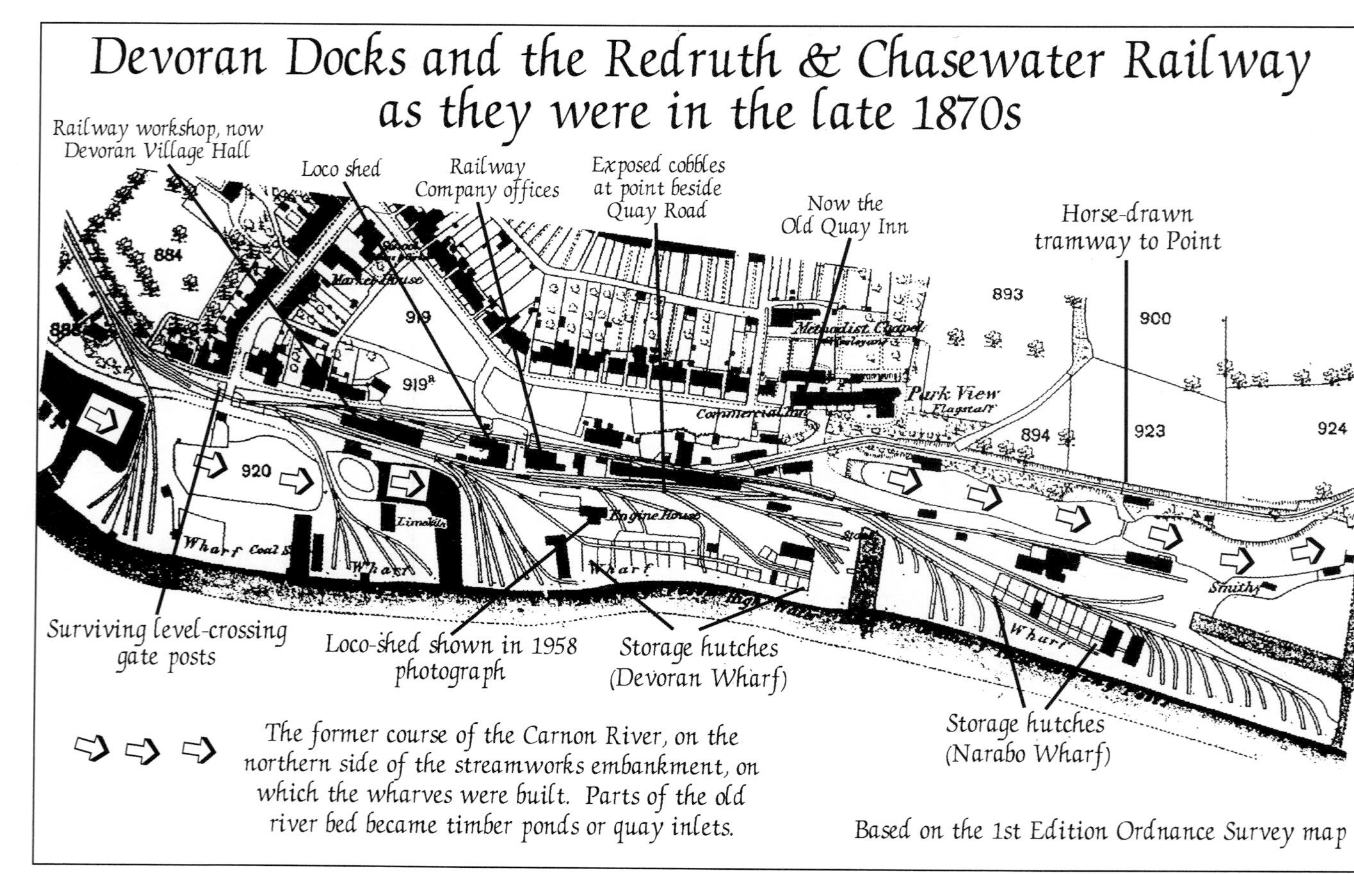

Devoran Docks and the Redruth & Chasewater Railway as they were in the late 1870s
Railway workshop, now Devoran Village Hall
Loco shed
Railway Company offices
Exposed cobbles at point beside Quay Road
Now the Old Quay Inn
Horse-drawn tramway to Point
Surviving level-crossing gate posts
Loco-shed shown in 1958 photograph
Storage hutches (Devoran Wharf)
Storage hutches (Narabo Wharf)
The former course of the Carnon River, on the northern side of the streamworks embankment, on which the wharves were built. Parts of the old river bed became timber ponds or quay inlets.
Based on the 1st Edition Ordnance Survey map
884
893
900
919
919ª
920
894
923
924
Market House
Methodist Chapel
Park View
Flagstaff
Engine House
Smithy
Wharf

It is scarcely an exaggeration to state that Devoran owes its very existence to the Redruth & Chasewater Railway and the docks built by the railway company. The first edition Ordnance Survey map (1813) indicates nothing besides Lower Devoran Farm on the site. The 1841 census (17 years after the coming of the railway) gives the population of the village as 250, and by 1871 it had risen to 1500.

❶ The walk begins by going along Quay Road, but first I suggest you walk a few yards along Greenbank Road, as far as the entrance to the Devoran Boatyard, the first turning on the left.

Greenbank Road runs between the old Redruth & Chasewater Railway track - which ran just this side of the older houses on the right - and the foreshore of Devoran Creek, to your left. Much of this part of the foreshore is now occupied by industrial buildings. One of the many railway sidings which ran to the quays lining the foreshore went along the left side of what is now the boatyard entrance: 14 granite setts can still be seen.

Return to the junction with Market Street.

Notice, in the garden on the left at the corner, the posts of a level-crossing gate, not quite in their original position now. *(See the photograph on page 196.)* *The line itself ran parallel with Carclew Terrace, a few feet away from the houses.*

Continue ahead along Quay Road.

Just past the foot of Market Street the line divided into three. The branch to the left ran beside the wall along the left side of what is now a parking space, passed to the left of the workshops (now the Devoran Village Hall) and continued beside the creek as a horse-drawn tramway for about a mile and a half to Point and Penpol. The one on the right ran along what is now Quay Road, with many sidings to quays on the right, and ended at what is now known as Devoran Quay. The short spur between them served the workshop and the engine shed beyond it. All three lines, plus the siding near the modern boatyard, are seen in the drawing, based on an old photograph.

Some of the older buildings on the left on Quay Road are relics of the railway: as already mentioned, the Village Hall originated as the workshops (it was a good deal longer then than now, extending as far as the further

Railway workmen outside the workshop, now Devoran Village Hall (Courtesy Paddy Bradley)

end of the doctors' surgery), and the attractive Old Quay House, with the picture of Spitfire at its gate, was once the Company's offices. (The big arch in the end-wall of the block at right-angles to the house, now used mainly as garages, appears to confirm that this building was the loco shed in the photograph of "Smelter" on page 34 of Barton's book about the railway.) The incorporation of some granite setts in the lower parts of both the Village Hall and Old Quay House suggests that they were erected after the railway's conversion to locomotive traction, when heavier blocks would have replaced the smaller ones that were adequate for horse-drawn wagons; possibly, though, the setts were used to repair or decorate the buildings after the railway closed. The large house now called Hazeldene was formerly the Crown & Anchor Hotel. The start of one of the sidings appears to be revealed in the parking space in front of the bungalow on the right called Smelter's Rest, named after the loco in that picture.

❷ Where the road makes a double hairpin-bend up to the Old Quay Inn, take the narrow path bearing right on to Devoran Quay.

A fine job has been done during the past few years by the Devoran Quay Preservation Society in restoring much of the quay to something close to its original form. On your right when you first walk out on to the quay are the upper parts of what was once a complex system of wharves and docks, now gardens and bungalows. Downriver, only one modern building has encroached on the quay area, a bungalow which stands on the site of a loco shed. On the waterfront side of it are the ruins of eight of the original twelve "hutches" in which copper ore was stored ready for shipment to South Wales. The railway line ran on a wooden structure behind them, level with the tops of the walls (then about 10-12ft high), so that the ore could be tipped in. It was transferred to the ships by barrow, although horses were used to haul wagons along the numerous sidings to the quayside.

Ruined hutches on Devoran Quay (SVJ)

The quay itself was wooden, because stone walls were hard to build on the shifting mud; wood faggots were used to bind the mud, and then 16-ft-long piles were driven in. Several granite mooring bollards have survived. In the early days vessels of about 100 tons could dock here, with an average water depth of 10ft alongside the main wharf at neap tides, but as time went on the ever-encroaching silt was an increasing problem.

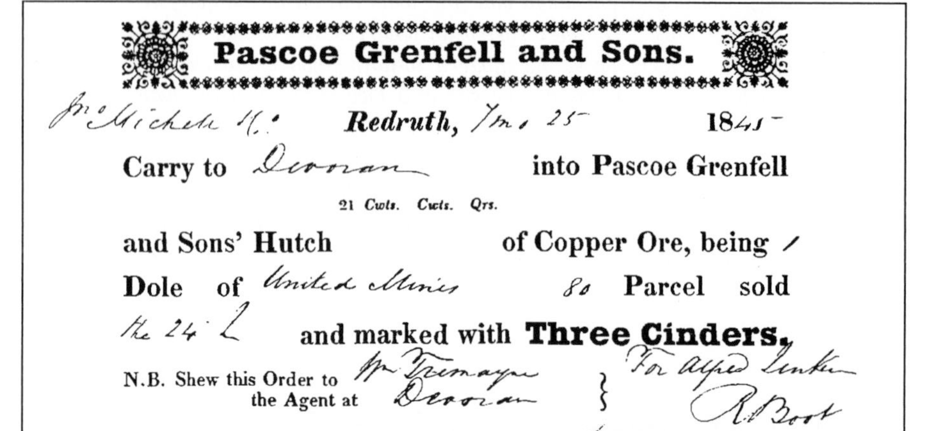
Pascoe Grenfell and Sons.

Mr Michell & Co. **Redruth,** 7mo 25 **1845**

Carry to Devoran **into Pascoe Grenfell**

21 Cwts. Cwts. Qrs.

and Sons' Hutch **of Copper Ore, being** 1

Dole of United Mines 80 **Parcel sold**

the 24 L **and marked with Three Cinders,**

N.B. Shew this Order to Wm Tremayne
the Agent at Devoran

For Alfred Jenkin
R. Boot

Wm. Tremayne Carr

A ticket dated 25 July 1845 detailing delivery of copper ore from United Mines to one of the hutches at Devoran. 21 cwts (2352 lb) was a ton in Cornish mining circles. The weight of this particular "dole" is not given. Does anyone know what the mark of the "Three Cinders" was?

After about 1870 the decline of the Gwennap copper industry spelt trouble for Devoran Quay. In 1876 the County Adit became blocked near its mouth at Twelveheads; the following winter was very wet, and when the pent-up waters in the mines finally broke free so much silt was deposited down-river that from then on ships had to discharge much of their cargo at Point before proceeding to Devoran. The last ship delivered coal at Devoran in 1916.

A model of part of Devoran Quay, including the hutches and tramway, is currently (December 1996) on display at the County Museum in Truro.

An engine shed on the former Devoran Wharf, its site now occupied by bungalows. (Photograph by D.R.Ebsworth, 1958)

From the far end of Devoran Quay you have a fine view of Restronguet Creek, with the woods of the Carclew estate on the right, the engine house of the Carnon Stream Mine on the left, and close at hand in the bed of the creek the remains of embankments. Some of these were created as part of the huge tin-streaming operation which occupied much of the creek bed from the late 18th century till 1812, when the dam at the seaward end was swept away during a storm; probably others are evidence of attempts by the docks and railway company to divert the Carnon River and its silt away from the wharves. (For more information about these features see Round Walk 15.)

❸ **From the end of the quay follow the foreshore to the left, round a small inlet** (notice the sleeper blocks scattered about, mainly in the low walls)**, and then beside the larger one, Narabo Creek.** This appears to have been the original course of the Carnon River before the quays were built. **Now the path runs beside several ruined buildings -** probably warehouses and stables for the railway. **Turn right on the gravelled drive, and soon you are back at the road below the Old Quay Inn -** originally called The Commercial, and then until recently the Devoran Inn. **Go round the hairpin bends to that.**

❹ **From the pub** - unless you feel the time is right to make your way along the Old Tram Road to the terminus of the Redruth & Chasewater Railway

St John's Terrace, Devoran

(Round Walk 15) - **I suggest you head back towards the centre of the village, along St John's Terrace.**

Like Belmont Terrace, up to the right, this was built about 1850; both are attractive, but the upper one, slightly less imposing, was presumably built for the company's humbler employees. St John's Terrace takes its name from the church, built in 1855-6 and designed by J.L.Pearson, the architect of Truro Cathedral later in his career.

❺ **Unless you want to take the bus to Truro or Falmouth, which stops opposite the church, turn left down Market Street**, originally named Lemon Street, after the owners (at the time it was built) of Carclew, the great house on the far shore. At the corner as you turn into it is Devoran School, founded in 1846; it recently took over the old Market House, a little way down the street.

This completes the short tour of Devoran.

A faded but fascinating reminder of Devoran a century-or-so ago: looking up Market Street from the level crossing (Courtesy Paddy Bradley)

ROUND WALK 15
DEVORAN, POINT & PENPOL
with a possible extension to FEOCK

About 3 miles (5km), or about 6 miles (10km) including Feock
See the start of Round Walk 14 (page 189) for the sketch map.

This is a very fine walk in terms of both scenery and historical interest. Those who have enjoyed discovering the remains of the Redruth & Chasewater Railway will want to follow it to its southern terminus at Point Quay, and the visit to Feock includes a look at Pill Creek, one of the places from which copper ore was shipped to South Wales before the railway was built. Other "industrial archaeology" *en route* includes visible relics of tin streaming, three underwater mines, a smelting works and a tide-operated bone mill. Among many other points of interest are a pretty village green and a medieval church.

Much of the route is on minor roads, but some of the paths and tracks are liable to be muddy. Feock has a shop, but there is no other source of provisions along the way except the pub in Devoran.

To drive to Devoran from Truro, take the A39 south towards Falmouth. At the end of the Carnon Downs bypass you reach the main turning to Devoran on the left, but continue a little further, past the Bissoe turning (right). Take the next turning left, and where this road turns left into the village, go straight on for a few yards, into Quay Road. You should find parking space here, either beside the road on the right, or in a space on the left. If not, roadside parking elsewhere in the village should be possible.

❶ **The walk starts as directed for Round Walk 14.** For comments on points of interest along Quay Road, see pages 191-2. **On reaching the end of Quay Road you will see the Old Quay Inn up on your left.** Here you could go down on to Devoran Quay, on the right, and follow the little circular tour described on pages 192-5; but **to walk to Point, Penpol and Feock, go left and then right on to the Old Tram Road**, which follows the course of the horse-drawn tramway to Point. Although the rails were taken up in 1919, the tarmac surface was not laid over the granite setts till 1951, and in the intervening decades the track became so rough and muddy as to be almost unwalkable in places. The unspoilt woods and farmland on the opposite side of the creek are parts of the Carclew estate.

The great house at Carclew was built in 1728 for Samuel Kempe, a gentleman from Penryn. In 1749 it was bought, together with its deer park, gardens and plantations covering more than a square mile, by William Lemon, who had made a vast fortune, mainly from the copper mines. Carclew House was burnt down in 1934, and little remains except part of the Ionic façade. The splendid gardens, noted for their rhododendrons, lily pond and lake, are occasionally opened to the public.

After a quarter of a mile or less, the road curves round Tallack's Creek. At the end of this part, just beyond the letter box fixed to a telegraph pole, go down on the right to look at the remains of the engine house of the Carnon Stream Mine. (Hamilton Jenkin calls it the Upper Carnon Mine, but this would have been a very odd name to give it at a time when there was no other mine in the Creek! A document of 1827 refers to "the Carnon Stream adventurers" and another of 1828 names "the Carnon Stream Tin Mining Company". To add to the confusion, in the *Engine House Assessment* publication it is called "Lower Carnon Mine"!)

The ruined engine house of the Carnon Stream Mine (SVJ)

From the late 18th century until 1812, a big area of the Carnon Valley, from Carnon Gate (where the old main road from Perranwell ran to Truro) to Tallack's Creek, was sealed off by embankments, with a dam at the seaward end: the remains of the dam can still be seen at low water, just to the seaward side of the engine-house wall. Inside this enclosure tin streaming was carried out; ancient tools made of wood and antler were found, plus some gold: a nugget 5.5cms long is displayed in the County Museum, Truro. George Henwood, lecturing in 1853, recalled the scene here: "a machine in a desert of red sand heaped into vast piles and hollows, the only herbage being a few tufts of sea daisy, while here and there in the trenches might be seen tinners working knee deep in water and a few squalid, half-clad boys wheeling the tin ore to the stream head in barrows." (See colour photograph 25 for the "sea daisies" still there.) In 1812, the dam was swept away during a storm, and now almost the only visible remains of that huge enterprise, which yielded profits of about £5,000, are the low-tide footpaths near the Carclew side and across Tallack's Creek, which follow the lines of embankments. Plenty of tin remained, and by 1818 plans were afoot to sink a shaft in the middle of the creek just below where the tin streaming had ceased, and to erect a powerful steam engine and water pump on the shore. These were complete by 1824. In 1828 the railway company officially complained that the new mine-workings were impeding shipping, and the mine seems to have closed soon after that, but during its short lifetime it made a profit of £28,000. The remaining wall is among the oldest substantial relics of an engine house surviving in Cornwall.

Return to the road and continue. The old pump on the right a little later is a reminder that mains water came to the houses near here for the first time only recently; they all have their own wells.

❷ Nearly half a mile beyond the engine house, immediately past the cottage on the right called The Salt Box, go up the narrow tarmacked lane on the left. At low tide this is the best vantage point for seeing the "Iron Shaft" in the middle of the creek - explained a little later. **The lane soon becomes a path.** Point Green, at the top, is one of the few genuine "village greens" in Cornwall, and a very pretty one. The right-hand pair of cottages facing you across the green was formerly a pub, the Bell Inn: part of an arch in the middle, now filled in, probably marks the original entrance to the pub. Its name is said to allude to the ringing of a bell to summon the ferryman for a link with Carnon Yard, on the other side of Penpol Creek - an attractive suggestion, but there seems to be no solid evidence for it.

Go down the short flight of steps near the post box, a little way to your right from the place where you came up from the Tram Road. The steps lead down to a small orchard with a well preserved limekiln on the right. The orchard and nearby bungalow, "Gulls Haven", mark the site of a later underwater mining enterprise, the Restronguet Creek Tin Works.

In 1871 a shaft (Taylor's Shaft) was sunk here to a depth of 108 feet and a cast-iron ventilation shaft (Charles Shaft) was driven down 78 feet to the tin-bearing level in the middle of the creek. Flanged cylinders 6 feet in diameter, 6 feet long and each weighing 2½ tons, cast at the Perran Foundry, were forced into the mud by fastening barges loaded with 250 tons of stone to the top at high tide; when one cylinder was in place, another was fitted to the top and driven down in turn, and so on till the shaft was complete. The top of the "Iron Shaft" can still be seen at low tide. During the next eight years a complex pattern of "levels" was mined between here and the old Carnon Stream Mine, and the workings remained dry even though there was 14 feet of water above them at high tide. For the full story, see Volume 2 of ECMH. A fascinating painting showing the multi-purpose engine house which was built where the orchard now is in the possession of the Royal Cornwall Museum, Truro. (It is reproduced in the colour section - No. 30 - and on a larger scale in my wife's book, "Life by the Fal", now out of print but available through libraries.) The rotary beam engine pumped from Taylor's Shaft by means of flat-rods, wound to the surface the wagons which also ran along rails in the levels out under the creek, and probably also worked the stamps, of which there were only two heads, since alluvial tin needs little stamping.

This was the last mining venture on (or under) Restronguet Creek, but as recently as the early 1980s an international company, Billiton Minerals, caused much local controversy by putting forward a scheme to dredge the creek bed for the wealth of minerals that still remains. Falling tin prices put paid to that, as to so many earlier and later enterprises.

❸ **Continuing to the left along the creekside road, you immediately reach what was once known as Daniell's Point**, with its long old building, the near end of which is shown as a coal store on the 1908 map. More recently it housed a small shop. During 1990 was converted into two houses.

Point was where the railway line ended (although by 1906 there was an extension towards Penpol to serve the smelting works there); the Daniell family had built a quay here before 1800, capable then of taking ships over 160 tons. The quay, now known as Point Quay, was purchased as a public amenity in 1989 by Feock Parish Council with the aid of £33,000 raised locally through the Point Quay Association. At the same time the orchard opposite "Regatta Cottage" and "Point Quay House" was also bought, and the limekiln there has been brought out of hiding by the voluntary effort of members of the Association and other local people. The name, "Regatta Cottage", alludes to the fact that Point Quay is the setting for the Point and Penpol Regatta, one of the leading annual events in the local yachting calendar and justly famous for the excellent teas provided by the local WI.

Opposite the quay is a brick-built pair of houses - a quite unusual sight in these parts. As our copy of the 1857 painting shows, there was a tall stack here, part of the Penpoll smelting works, and when this was demolished the bricks were used to build the houses.

Continue round into Penpol (or Penpoll) Creek. Soon after Black Lane, on the left (perhaps so named because of the smoke from all the industrial chimneys once here: the old painting shows seventeen!), you reach the site of the main smelting works buildings, now occupied by the

Where the Tramway ended

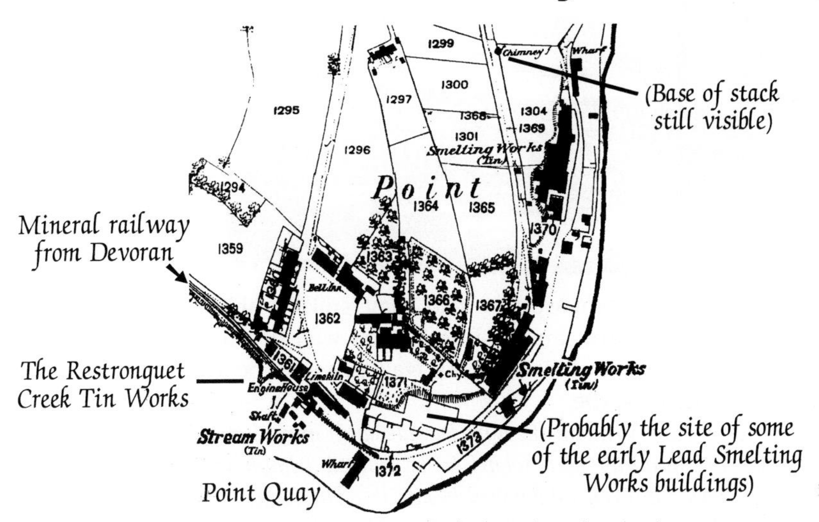

Above: The southern terminus of the Redruth & Chasewater Railway as shown on the OS map of 1878

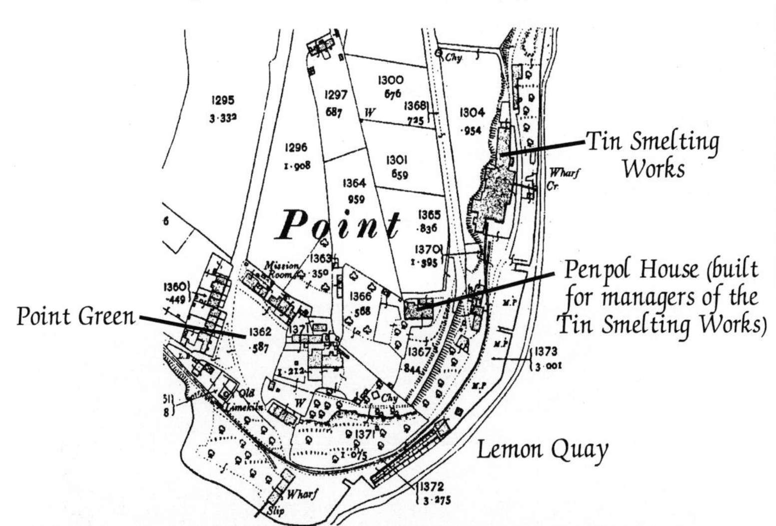

28 years later: the mine and the southern section of the smelting works have gone, and the railway has been extended to serve the smelter, and apparently also storage hutches on Lemon Quay.

The smelting works at Penpol - sketch based on a watercolour dated 1857. (The original is reproduced in colour in Viv Acton's "Life by the Fal" and in black-and-white in ECMH2.)

bungalow called "Polmarion". You may still be able to see relics of the concrete floors or yard, and of flues in the wall behind. On the right here was another wharf, and close to the wall you may be able to make out what could be a small buddle.

In 1817, Sir William Lemon leased land immediately north-east of Point Quay, for the building of a wharf to be named Lemon Quay. By 1827 a lead smelting works had been established beside it. The painting shows that during the next three decades this expanded northwards along the western shore of Penpol Creek. Long flues were built up to tall stacks on the higher land. By 1880 the works was owned by a London-based company which had converted the buildings for tin smelting. The 1906 OS map indicates that by then work was concentrated on the northern part of the site, that the Redruth & Chasewater line had been extended to serve the smelter, and that storage "hutches" had been built on Lemon Quay. As at Devoran, these were probably at a lower level than the line, so that the contents of the horse-drawn wagons could be simply tipped in. Closure of the smelting works came in 1921.

The working tin smelter after 1910, by which time the lead smelter stack had been demolished. (Courtesy Mr & Mrs R.Michell)

Go on for another couple of hundred yards, until you come to stepping stones on the right - perhaps submerged. In their place was once a tide mill used to power bone-crushing machinery; beyond it was Bone Mill Pool. ("Stock of bone ashes" was listed in 1828 among the assets of Penpoll smelting works.)

The stepping stones at Penpol,
beside the site of the waterwheel of the former tidemill

❹ Now the time for a choice has come: either return directly to Devoran now, or continue to Feock.

For the shorter walk, go to the bridge at the head of Penpol Creek and on past the chapel to a left turning; then follow the directions from point 10.

To walk to Feock (and it's very worthwhile), cross the stepping stones if the water is low enough; if not, walk to the head of the creek and take the track on the right beside the foreshore. Follow track or foreshore round to Penpol Boatyard. (At exceptionally high tides you may have to walk round to the boatyard via the road above, through the Trevallion Park estate.) *This part of the foreshore has a heavy scattering of clinker, the most obvious surviving physical evidence of the former smelting works. The boatyard carries out repair work, builds boats from scratch, and places a special emphasis on restoring old timber vessels. During the winter as many as about 60 boats are usually laid up on the hard and foreshore.*

Immediately after passing the boatyard take the lane straight ahead (blessed with a wealth of signs: "Private Road", "Public Bridleway" and "Unsuitable for heavy goods vehicles"), or at low tide continue along the

foreshore. (This is probably the more attractive way, but rough underfoot, and you may have to bestride or duck under a good many mooring ropes.)

❺ The foreshore route will bring you to the small headland called Carnon Yard or simply Yard; if you are using the lane, bear right where it forks, after nearly half a mile, to reach the headland.

This point takes its name from a boat-building yard which appears to have been situated on or very close to the beach. Many locally famous vessels were built here and at Pill Creek (visited later on this walk) by the Ferris family in the earlier part of the 19th century, and even after their yard here was bought by John Stephens in 1858 William "Foreman" Ferris was in charge of the actual boat-building. When Stephens sold the yard in 1880 it was probably taken over by Frank Hitchens, who had already established his own boat-building business in the walled yard, part of which can still be seen, beside the lane leading down to Carnon Yard.

Carnon Yard once had an engine house on it, together with an "Account House" and, no doubt, assorted other mine buildings. They belonged to the Carnon Mine (1835-42). An island was created out in the creek and a shaft twelve feet in diameter was sunk into this "by the laborious expedient of covering the cylinder top and shovelling sufficient silt on to it that the weight - as much as a hundred tons - forced it down in successive stages" (TMSC). A small pumping-engine was then erected by the shaft. By 1838 212 people were employed, but this was a costly operation, and tin prices fell, so the mine lost about £16,000. The island, known locally as "The Mine Bank", is still visible at low tide and a hazard for yachtspersons when it is submerged, as at least one discovers to his or her cost during most Point & Penpol Regattas.

From Yard take the lane leading inland. The original Hitchens' boatyard was on the right opposite the old cottage named Carnon Yard. At the junction, turn right, following the sign to Harcourt (spelt "Harket" on some old maps, and probably meaning "beside or facing the rock"). **At the bungalow called Tweseldown, go straight on ahead to a narrow path and over the stile.** You will have occasional glimpses of the Pandora Inn across Restronguet Creek to the right: see Walk 3 in *Around the Fal*. **After the farm buildings, follow the lane past the houses at Harcourt till you reach the road by a telephone box.**

❻ If you want to visit Restronguet Point - about a mile there-and-back - turn right. Otherwise, turn left and take the road to the right just past Porthgwidden gatehouse, into Feock. *Porthgwidden is an old house (c. 1830) built by Edmund Turner, one of Truro's MPs. Its estates used to extend as far as Restronguet Point; it is now converted into flats and maisonettes.*

❼ Soon you come to a right turning signposted Loe Beach, a pleasant spot with a lovely view of Carrick Roads. Even if you don't want to go right down to the beach (and you may be deterred from doing so by the steep climb back), **I suggest you go a short way down this road to join the path to the church**, to take advantage of the view over the beach and out to sea. **The path, which is marked "Feock" by a rather elderly and not very legible sign, is on the left just beyond a wooden garage. At first keep close to the hedge on the left**, then continue ahead, eventually passing between a house and the churchyard. **Turn right at the road** (look left to see the former school, closed in 1983, when the roll of pupils had fallen to thirteen) **and continue past the post-office-cum-shop and the lych gate.**

St Feoca's church is said to have been where the last sermon in the Cornish language was preached. The church itself was so heavily "restored" in 1874 that hardly anything old remains, but the detached tower dates from the 13th century. There is also a Norman font and in the south porch a set of stocks. In the churchyard is an old Celtic cross.

Whether there ever was a saint called Feoca is doubtful. The name suggests a female, but if a man perhaps he was the Irish or Scottish Fiacc or Fiacra, said to taken up residence in France as a scholar at the court of Charles the Bald. His garden on the outskirts of Paris became famous, and he became known as the patron of gardens, or of garden birds. There is a tale that a Parisian cab proprietor had a sign bearing the saint's name above his door; "hence the 'fiacre', or covered horse-drawn cab which was understandably preferred by courting couples for a romantic ride in the Bois de Boulogne and gave rise to the popular song of the 'Naughty Nineties'." (Quoted from an entertaining article by Barry Simpson in the 1997 Newsletter of the Restronguet Creek Society.)

A less colourful suggestion is that the name may derive from the Cornish "feage" or "vegue", "a lofty place". This gains some support from the fact that the upper part of the village is called La Feock, pronounced "La Vaig". The "La" is not French but probably derives from "Lan", "church-site or hermitage". For more on this, see the later comment on the well near The Old Grange.

❽ **After the right and left bends, take the tarmacked footpath on the right, beside the entrance to the Church Hall car park, which brings you down to Pill Creek**. The square concrete-and-glass house overlooking the head of the creek from the far side is regarded as an architectural gem and has been recommended for Grade 2 listing.

Pill Creek (oddly named, since "pill" means creek) was for a time important to the copper mines as a port for shipping ore and importing coal. Look across the creek from the point where the path brings you down. The right-hand house of the attractive pair was a pub, and the ships docked at the quay below it. The problem with ports like this one and Roundwood Quay, a little further up-river (see Walk 4 in "Around the Fal") was the land communications. (A letter of January 1817 reads, "... such frequent rains for the last month - the roads from the mines to the wharf are so badly cut up, particularly those to Pill, that all the wheel carriages are stopped and the mules are the only conveyance at present.") Canals were considered, but engineers declared them impracticable, and the hills precluded a railway. The arrival of the Redruth & Chasewater Railway at Devoran ensured that Pill Creek would return to peace and quiet.

If the tide is low enough, go down the steps to the foreshore and walk along to the left - but if not, see the note in brackets a few lines below. Near the head of the creek there is a wooden boathouse on the left; go up the tarmacked path just beyond this to return to the road. There turn right, and after a short distance turn sharp left on to a concreted lane, signposted to La Feock. Just past the house called Gelvinack, take the footpath on the right, again signposted to La Feock. (If the tide is too high for walking on the foreshore, return up the same path, turn right at the road, and after about 70m, at the top of the slope, take the footpath on the left, turning left again where signposted to La

Feock, just past houses called Seascape and Landfall. *Snap!*) **Keep by the hedge on the right - a good view down Carrick Roads from here - and go through the small gate; now the path curves left and becomes a tarmacked lane before turning right. After the second house, The Old Grange, notice the pump on the left, and the well at the bottom of a short flight of steps.** *Mrs S.M.Satchwell, who has written a brief history of the village, "Introducing Feock", suggests that an unnamed monk may have set up his hermitage beside this well and become known as "the holy man on the hill" or "Saint Feock". (See the last part of the note about Feock above.)*

❾ **Turn right at the road, and at the T-junction cross the stile (concrete steps beside a gate) immediately opposite. Walk straight ahead, keeping the hedge to your left.** At and just after the next stile you have a good panoramic view of Penpol Creek and beyond to Restronguet Creek and Devoran, with Carn Marth on the skyline. The Carn Brea monument is also visible, just left of the Pennance engine house. **Continue straight on down the field, emerging via a farm gate on to a lane. Cross the stile almost opposite,** by Trolver farm, where two formerly dilapidated old barns have been transformed into impressive-looking houses, **and go on in the same direction. After the next stile you walk among modern bungalows and come to a road. At the road, continue downhill into Penpol, passing the chapel on your right.**

❿ **Turn left over the bridge.** Notice the attractive Bridge Cottage on the left, famous locally for its well-tended traditional cottage garden. The house was built in about 1635 "towards the Relife of the poore people". **Walk quite steeply uphill past more old cottages at first, then new houses. Take the first left turning, signed Public Bridleway, and where it joins a tarmacked lane turn right.** This is called The Rope Walk, but no-one seems to know just where the rope walk itself was; perhaps along the side-lane on the left leading to Rope House.

At the road, turn right, then immediately left on to a track, usually muddy. (If it is too muddy, you could instead walk back down the road towards the creek, to rejoin the Tram Road via Point Green.) If you decide to brave the mire, walk along the track behind houses. It dips into a valley at Chycoose Farm and then continues ahead. Still a little more mud to come, but the view of Restronguet Creek a bit further on will compensate. **At the end of the field with a hedge to your left, you could cross the high stile just before a gate and go down to the Tram Road; or go through the gate, keep by the hedge, and turn left down the drive at the next house. Turn right on the creekside road to return to your starting-point.**

A VISIT TO KENNALL VALE

A stroll of about ¾ mile (1km)

This is a place you mustn't miss, whether your taste is for natural beauty or industrial archaeology or both. As the site of the most important gunpowder works serving the local mines and quarries, it is an essential part of the story unfolded by the other walks featured in this book.

After heavy rains the Kennall or Kennal Vale is even more dramatic than usual, with the water in full spate, not only in the river itself but in the leats above, from which it sometimes spills over at several points in waterfalls and cataracts. Come at such a time if you can; but in any case do come!

The devastating gales of February 1990 did great damage to the trees, and in the next few years uprooted stumps were still everywhere to be seen; here and there the trees in their fall dislodged granite blocks in buildings or the side walls of leats; but the Cornwall Wildlife Trust has made repairs and planted saplings, and new plant-growth is starting to flourish where more light has been admitted. One small consolation for the loss of trees is that some of the impressive remains of the gunpowder works are now more visible than before. The second half of Appendix 1 consists of a study of the flora and fauna of Kennall Vale.

Following the tour described here involves a certain amount of scrambling in damp, possibly slippery places, so waterproof footwear with a good grip, and maybe also a stick, are recommended.

An exploration of this site is also included in *A Second View from Carn Marth*, where I have been able to give fuller detail, especially about the quarry that was established here after the gunpowder works closed. Walk 9 in that book also features a visit to the site of the slightly earlier and much smaller gunpowder works at Cosawes; it includes, too, an impressive railway viaduct in another beautiful part of the Kennall valley, close to which was the old Magdalen tin mine; and the village of Ponsanooth, which has many attractive and interesting features, probably unsuspected by at least 95% of the motorists who hasten through.

To reach Kennall Vale by car, take the main Redruth-Penryn road (A393) and drive to Ponsanooth. Turn on to the side road which starts between the bridge and the post office / store, which stands a little way back from the road, on the right if you are coming from the Redruth direction. The entrance to Kennall Vale is on the right about half a mile up this road, almost opposite Cotwood Cottage (Grid Reference SW 754 376). Although people do park beside the road just beyond the entrance, it is

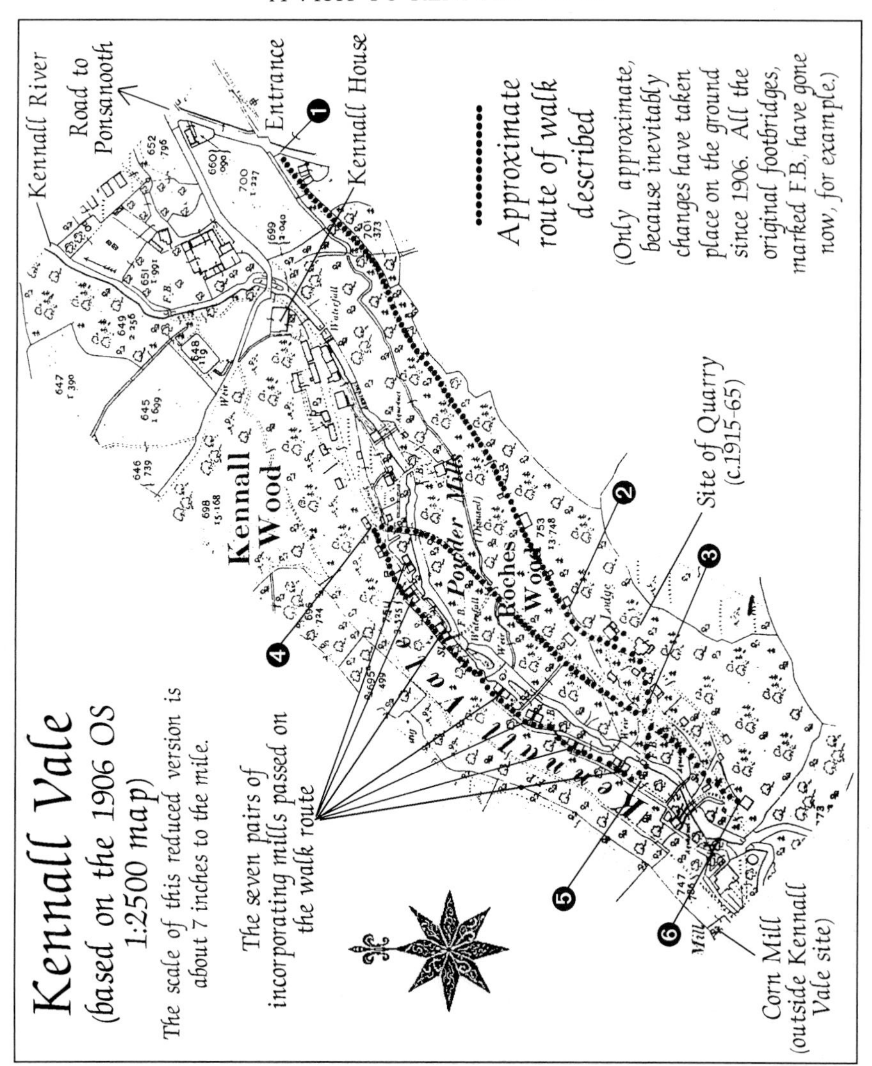

very narrow there, and parking is much more practicable a few hundred yards further back, opposite an estate road called Forth an Cos, or on the side road a few yards further up the hill (Kennall Park / Cot Wood). Please be careful not to block entrances.

There are Western National bus services linking Ponsanooth with Falmouth, Penryn, Redruth, Camborne and Truro.

The site of the Kennall Gunpowder Works is now leased to the CWT and is open to the public (except on the fourth Monday in February each year). Dogs MUST be kept on leads.

THE KENNALL GUNPOWDER WORKS

Explosives were important to the mining industry, and until 1809 they had to be imported into the county. In that year a gunpowder works was set up in a wooded valley at Cosawes, just east of Ponsanooth. (The site, now occupied by chalets and mobile homes, is visible in the distance on Round Walk 13: see page 183.) The Fox family, owners of the Perran Foundry (again see Round Walk 13) and responsible in conjunction with the Williamses for the creation of the Portreath Tramroad, were impressed by the success of Cosawes, and in 1812 they launched their own gunpowder factory here in Kennall Vale.

The site was ideal, being close to the mines, roads and a potential labour force at Ponsanooth, but well screened from the latter by trees (in fact, many more trees were planted to minimise blast impact in the event of an accident, and some massive granite walls were built for the same purpose), and having an excellent power-supply in the form of the Kennall River. "This river," wrote Hitchens and Drew in their "History of Cornwall", 1824, "from its source to its union with the sea runs about five miles and a half, in which short distance it turns thirty-nine water wheels all in active and full employ. It may be doubted, if within the same short distance another such stream can be found in England."

The enterprise at Kennall Vale flourished. It began on quite a small scale at the lower end, near Kennall House, but in 1844 a new section was added above, in Roches Wood. In the 1860s it employed fifty or more men; but after that its fortunes waned along with those of the mines themselves, and the invention of dynamite and gelignite in the 1880s hastened its demise, although it did not close completely on this site till about 1914. Later, a quarry was opened near the top end, and the ruined concrete buildings near the quarry-pit, now flooded, are relics of this. Transport within the gunpowder works was by horse-and-cart. The safety-record of the works during the hundred years of existence was remarkably good. The few serious accidents were fully reported in the local press; the best-known one was caused by a spark on the clothing of a woman bringing hot food into a mixing-house. The detailed story of the many processes involved in gunpowder manufacture, and of the Kennall Gunpowder Works in particular, is fascinating, and can be read in Bryan Earl's book, "Cornish Explosives" (Trevithick Society, 1978), and even more fully in the excellent archaeological report prepared for the Cornwall Trust for Nature Conservation (now the CWT) in 1985-6 by John R. Smith, obtainable from the Trust at Five Acres, Allet, Truro, TR4 9DJ.

You will be able to make more sense of what you see as you walk around the site if you have some idea of the steps in the manufacturing process. In very simplified form, these were as follows. The raw materials (charcoal, saltpetre and sulphur) were mixed in a rotating wooden barrel in a Mixing House, and taken to an Incorporating Mill, where the mixture was dampened and ground to a fine powder by two vertically-mounted millstones. Then it went to a Press House to be compressed into a "cake" about an inch thick; next this was broken (using wooden mallets) into lumps in a Breaking Down House, then reduced to granules in a Corning House, dried by means of piped steam in a Gloom Stove, and separated from dust in a Dusting House. Finally the granules were rounded and glazed (so that they could easily be poured into holes and were water-resistant - important in damp mine-workings - by being rotated in a drum with graphite in a Glazing Mill, before being packed in wooden crates. "Expense Magazines" were used for storage between processes. Most of these operations were powered by water-wheels, and much of the complex system of leats is still visible.

A TOUR OF THE SITE

It would take another book the size of this one to give you a proper "guided tour", so all I shall attempt is to point out the main features of historical interest. The Vale is, of course, also important as a nature reserve: for details of some of the plants and animals to be found here, see Appendix 1. One of Cornwall's leading naturalists, Frederick Hamilton Davey (1868-1915), was born in Ponsanooth and went to work at the gunpowder factory at the age of 11. See *Stars in the Grass* by Selina Bates and Keith Spurgin (Dyllansow Truran, 1994); the early chapters in particular make fascinating reading for anyone who has explored this place. "Some of his (Davey's) earliest nature observations," they write, "were made in the woods of Kennall Vale."

❶ As you walk along the path from the main entrance, you will catch glimpses of Kennall House in the valley-bottom. Most of the 1812 works was in what is now the private garden of the house, and little remains to be seen. After a few hundred yards, the first sizeable building on the left was a Packing House. Eight more buildings which originally stood just beyond this were destroyed when the quarry buildings were erected.

❷ Walk to the left here to see the flooded quarry-pit, one of the scenic attractions of the Vale. The concrete and brick-built ruined buildings and other structures nearby may not have the same visual appeal, but each had its part to play in the story of the quarry, and a fascinating story that was, as told by Peter Penpraze in *A Second View from Carn Marth.*

❸ Soon afterwards, turn sharp right on to the lower track leading back down the valley, where you get a good view of some leats and blast-walls. As you cross the bridge, the large building ahead was a Mixing House; the smaller one to the left was the Change House, where the workmen changed into pocketless woollen suits.

❹ Turn left to walk upstream. Now come the most spectacular industrial relics at Kennall Vale: the seven pairs of Incorporating Mills, each with its own leat to supply its overshot waterwheel, and each in turn a little more complete than the previous one. All of them can be entered from the upper level. The first three were part of the 1812 works; just beyond the third one (with water pouring from its leat in wet periods) is a pair of grindstones, the lower one in good condition. Notice the rendering of fine cement on the insides of the mill walls, designed to prevent explosive dust from clinging to them. The roofs have all gone; for safety reasons, these would have been light, wooden structures. The vestiges of a waterwheel at the last mill and the gearing inside date from about 1925-30, when a new wheel was installed to supply power for the quarry's first air compressor. The building beyond this was a Glazing Mill.

❺ Now cross the river again by the modern wooden footbridge and turn right to see the buildings at the top of the site (point 6 on the map). The largest of these was a Corning House, and is remarkable for the pit beneath it which once held the waterwheel. Nearby are a Dusting House and a store. (Visible over the wall at the top end of the site is an old paper mill, later used as a corn mill; it still has a large waterwheel in place, but unfortunately that cannot be seen from this angle.)

❻ The walk now returns to the main entrance by the path along which you first came.

Of course, there is far more here to discover. What you should do is arm yourself with John Smith's report and come back for a full day!

COMPLETING THE LINK TO THE SOUTH COAST PATH

The obvious way for walkers to get to Falmouth is to make use of the bus service: there is a convenient bus stop on Greenbank Road in Devoran. Another fairly easy option is to take a train from Perranwell Station, which is only a short walk from the Trail at the Devoran end. Purists, though, will see both these as cheating. For their sake, here are a few ideas about how the feat of reaching the coastal footpath on foot (or foot and ferry) might best be achieved. They boil down to two main options (via Falmouth or Portscatho), but in each case there are several choices of route to be made, and I have space only to give the bare bones. To follow the routes with confidence, walkers should arm themselves with the relevant OS maps (preferably from the Pathfinder series). My books, *Around the Fal* (for the Falmouth option) and *Around Mevagissey* (for Portscatho), would also be useful companions, both for route finding and also for background information. The latter book was out of print at the time of writing this, but still available in many shops; a successor, *From the Roseland to St Austell Bay*, has been published early in 1997.

OPTION 1: FALMOUTH VIA PENRYN OR THE FLUSHING FERRY

At the time this book went to press the only direct overland link between Devoran and Falmouth was the A39, one of the busiest roads in Cornwall. To walk beside it for any significant distance would be most unpleasant, if not lethal: indeed, one of the most dangerous sections would be the first mile-or-so, between Devoran and the Norway Inn at Perranarworthal. There has been some talk of creating a path along the foreshore, but it is hard to see how this could be accomplished, even if landowners agreed.

There is another way of getting to the Norway, using an attractive route with several points of interest along the way. For this, refer to the map and directions for Round Walk 13.

To join this route from the Devoran end of the Coast-to-Coast Trail, turn right as soon as you have crossed the wooden bridge over the Carnon River, mentioned at the top of page 61; this will bring you to the point referred to in the second line of section 9 in Round Walk 13 (page 187). A short diversion left now is recommended for those interested in looking at the buildings which originated as Basset Foundry, whose history is outlined in the italicised note on pages 186-7, but **for the walk to Perranwell and Perranarworthal turn right along the rough lane.**

For the next part of the walk follow the directions in sections 9 and 10 of Round Walk 13 (pages 187-8), and then section 1 and the first part of section 2 (pages 178-9). Cross the A39 and walk along Carclew Road, as suggested there, but instead of returning to the main road continue towards Carclew. (Some information about Carclew is given on page 198.)

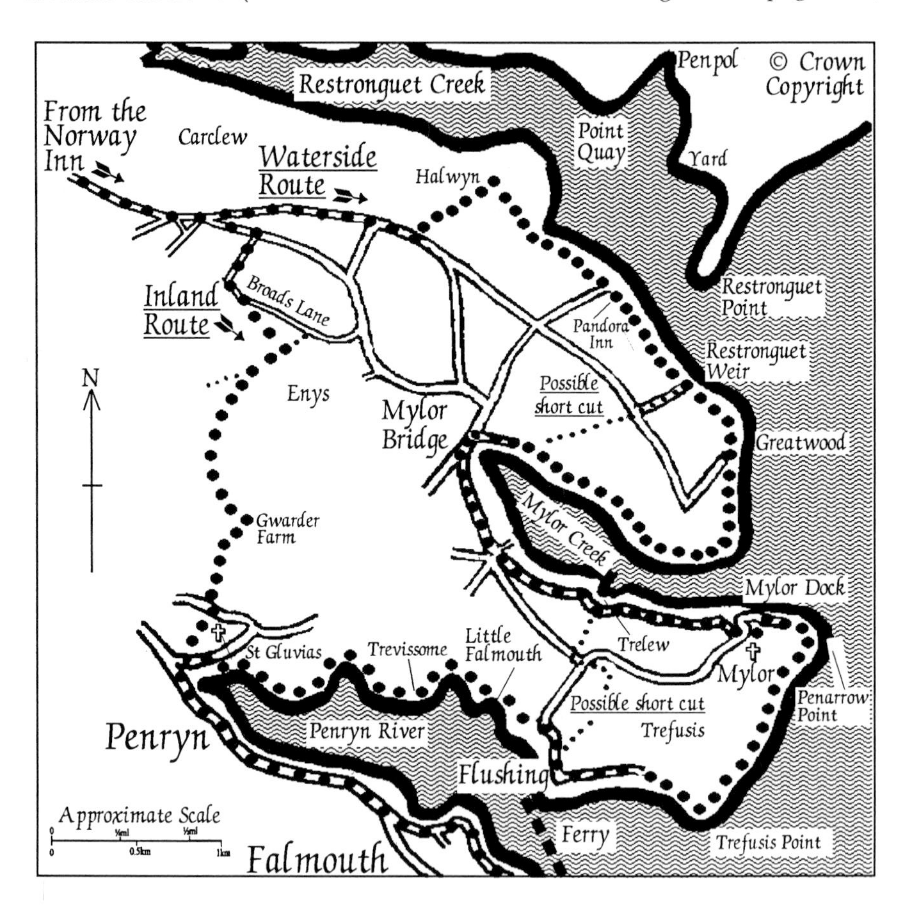

The road, which twists and turns uphill at first, can be quite busy, and as it is also rather narrow you need to take care, but otherwise it makes a pleasant walk, mostly amid mature trees and shrubs - some sections of it are a blaze of purple *Ponticum* rhododendrons in early summer. **After nearly a mile, turn left at the T-junction. Ignore the minor road on the right that comes next, but when you come to a fork,**

with Comfort Road going off to the right, you are confronted with several options. All of them are attractive, but they vary greatly in length.

Basically the choice is between an inland walk and a waterside walk, as the accompanying sketch-map attempts to show.

The inland route is clearly the most direct way if you intend to walk all the way into Falmouth; even if you want to take the ferry from Flushing it is the shorter route, although the waterside route is about the same length if you take both of the short cuts shown on the map.

Approximate distances (from the point where the two routes divide):

To Falmouth (Prince of Wales Pier) via inland route: 5 miles (8km)
To Falmouth (Prince of Wales Pier) via waterside route: 12 miles (19km)
To Flushing (Quay) via inland route: 5 miles (8km)
To Flushing (Quay) via complete waterside route: 8 miles (13km)

Inland Route

At the fork take the road on the right, signed to Comfort, then the first right turning, Broads Lane. About 500 yards along Broads Lane, take the first main left turning, a wide, stony track at the start of which are granite gateposts, and where in 1995 there was a "Private Road" sign. Go straight on later, where there is a private drive on the left and a stile on the right. Now watch for a stile on your left, with a sign about keeping dogs on a lead. Cross this stile, and from now on you will be guided all the way to Penryn by the yellow arrows of the Country Landowners Association and/or Public Footpath signs. During this part of the walk you are skirting the extensive grounds of Enys, a large estate with famous gardens, unfortunately very rarely open to visitors, although you can catch several glimpses of them from the path. **You cross a small stream on entering woodland after a relatively open section. Where a lane crosses, go left then immediately right through the first of many small gates which do duty instead of stiles in this district. Continue ahead beside the hedge on the right. After the next gate cross the drive and follow the yellow arrow by the left-hand granite post.** Now you can get a glimpse of Pendennis Castle almost straight ahead. **The path goes to the right of Gwarder farm, via more little, narrow gates. Next, keep by the hedge on the left. After another gate, follow the footpath sign left to Pencoose. After the farm, the lane brings you down to a road at the edge of Penryn. Turn left and then after 25 yards take the footpath on the right. Cross the next road, keep to the right of the main block of garages, and go on down the path where it resumes. This brings you out opposite the Volvo showrooms.**

For Flushing, turn left along the Mylor road, towards St Gluvias Church. Before reaching it, take the waterside path which starts near the

metal gates at the entrance to Islington Wharf. The path keeps quite close to the foreshore all the way; for details see *Around the Fal* (3rd edition) pages 16-19.

For Falmouth, **keep to the main road (A39), here named Commercial Road.** (There is a pavement all the way into Falmouth, and despite the traffic it makes an interesting walk, with many spectacular views of the Penryn River and Falmouth Harbour.) **After Penryn Bridge it continues through Ponsharden. At the third roundabout leave the A39, taking the road on the left (Falmouth Road, then North Parade) past the Falmouth Marina and the Greenbank Hotel. Continue along the High Street, at the end of which is Prince of Wales Pier. From there you can get the ferry to St Mawes and (in season) Place, in order to follow the coast path eastwards; or to "go west" carry on along the main street (Market Strand, Market Street, Church Street, Arwenack Street), eventually curving left along Bar Road past the entrance to Falmouth Docks. After that you can either walk round Pendennis Point or use Castle Hill to cut across to Cliff Road.**

Waterside Route

Continue along the main road towards Mylor Bridge for about 1km (rather over ½ mile). Ignore the lane on the left leading to Carsawsen, which is immediately followed by a minor road on the right; take the next farm track on the left, which runs down to Halwyn farm. On approaching the farm buildings, turn sharp-right. The path now continues downhill, giving fine views of Restronguet Creek, **and eventually reaches the waterside at the house named Tregunwith Wood. You now stay by the water all the way round to Mylor Bridge**, passing the Pandora Inn on the way. At Restronguet Weir you could take a short cut by going up the road, then continuing ahead along the signed footpath where the road turns right at Restronguet Barton. **From Mylor Bridge take the road towards Flushing, forking left at "Five Turnings" along the minor road which runs beside Mylor Creek.** At Trelew, where there is a little inlet, a valley path on the right provides a short cut to Flushing, as shown on the sketch map. **The creekside road eventually becomes a footpath before reaching Mylor Church. From Mylor Dockyard, with its marina and boatyard, the path follows the edge of the low cliffs all the way round to Flushing, and on from there to Penryn if you wish.**

OPTION 2: PORTSCATHO (OR THE COAST FURTHER NORTH) VIA THE KING HARRY FERRY

If you draw a straight line from Portreath to Devoran and then continue it eastwards it meets the coast at or very near Portscatho, and certainly for walkers who intend to head east on the coast path this option is the way to go unless they have a special wish to visit Falmouth. A very attractive walk links Devoran with Pill Creek at Feock, as described elsewhere in this book (Round Walk 15), and from there it's about 2.5km (1½ miles) to the King Harry Ferry by the most direct route, or about an extra kilometre (a little over ½ mile) if you include part of the National Trust's Trelissick Woodland Walk. Having crossed the Fal, you have a choice of routes to the coast: about 6km (nearly 4 miles) to Pendower via Philleigh village where the popular Roseland Inn is, or about 7km (4½ miles) to Creek Stephen, or about 8km (5 miles) to Portscatho, where you will find a pub, shops and a choice of accommodation. All three routes involve a mixture of country roads and field paths. Whichever way you go, there's no avoiding a certain amount of walking along the road which carries the ferry traffic, and since it's quite narrow this could be a problem. Fortunately, though, on the Feock side, where the traffic tends to be faster, you are on it only for a couple of hundred yards if you include the Woodland Walk. On the Philleigh side there is about half a mile on it, but here the twisting road generally precludes speeding. It's probably a good idea to walk on the left, since there's unlikely to be any traffic approaching you from behind until the next ferry comes in.

The ferry normally operates every 20 minutes, apart from Sundays in the winter.

The walk begins as described in section 9 of the Coast-to-Coast Trail plus Round Walk 14 as far as the start of the Old Tram Road (foot of page 195). Now follow the directions for Round Walk 15 as far as Pill Creek, Feock (start of section 8). Now instead of taking the sharp left turn signposted La Feock (near foot of page 206), continue along the road. Ignore the left turning at Higher Trevilla. At the T-junction turn right: this is the road to the ferry, so take great care. **Keep to the right-hand side, and soon you can leave the road by entering the grounds of Trelissick via the gateway on that side. Now you can either**

(a) (the shorter route) continue along the main path through the parkland to the buildings at Trelissick, which include a restaurant and shop. **A small door in the wall on the right side of the water tower returns you to the road, which now runs downhill to the ferry.**

Or (b) (the more attractive route, avoiding most of any further road walking on this side of the river) take the side path on the left, signposted Woodland Walk. This comes before the first of two cattle grids across the main path. The path winds down to a point where a little stream flows into a small creek. Don't cross the footbridge on the left but continue on the upper path as it curves right. After about half a mile of attractive walking with King Harry Reach down to the left, you will descend via a flight of steps to the road, and a short walk down that brings you to the ferry.

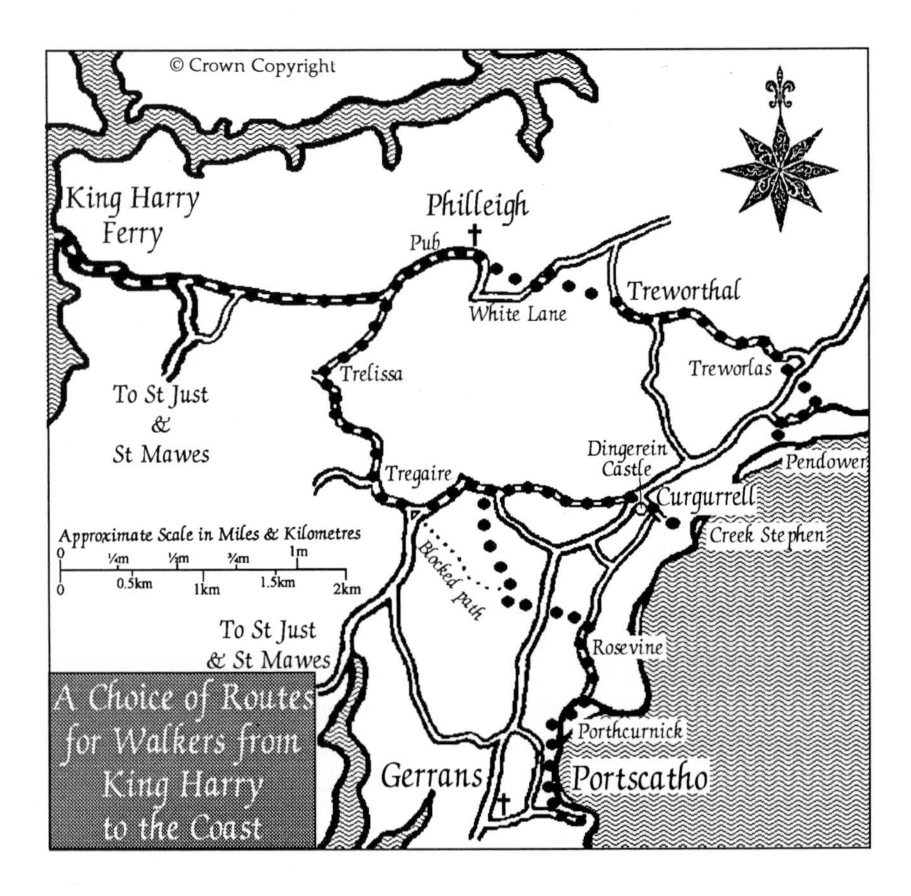

On the far side, walk with care on the road (preferably on the left, as suggested earlier), which runs mainly uphill among trees at first. After about half a mile, where the main road turns right continue ahead

on the minor road signposted to Philleigh. Nearly a mile further on, follow the road as it bends left for Pendower (and see the final paragraph for further directions); for Creek Stephen and Portscatho turn sharp-right on to a narrow but tarmacked lane marked "Unsuitable for motors"; after Trelissa it becomes a rough track. At the road turn left past Tregaire farm, the site of a manor of great historical importance. At the junction with the main road (A3078), you ought to be able to continue ahead on a footpath, but until and unless this has been restored you have to turn left and continue with great care along the road for about a quarter of a mile.

This is the second division of the ways.

For Creek Stephen, where the road bends sharp-right continue ahead on a bridleway which runs beside the Merrose Farm caravan park. At the main road cross, go a few yards to the right, then take the minor road on the left. (At the corner are the remains of the Iron Age fort known since late in the 18th century as Dingerein Castle, though any actual connection with King Gerent is very unlikely.) **Where the minor road turns right, continue ahead on the path past Curgurrell Farm to reach the coast path.**

If you wish to walk to Portscatho via Rosevine, cross the small stile on the right just before the sharp right-hand bend. The path runs fairly straight via a series of stiles, but turns left at Pollaughan farm and then continues along the farm drive to the main road. Cross that and follow the path ahead signed "Rosevine". Again there are several stiles, and also at least one patch which is usually very muddy. At the minor road turn right, down among the houses and hotels of Rosevine (a pretty name, but it appears to derive from the Cornish *ros-breyn*, "putrid moor"!), **to reach the coast path at Porthcurnick Beach, from which it's a short step to Portscatho.**

For the inland walk to Pendower, continue past Philleigh church, and just beyond Polglaze Farm (on the left) there is a footpath on the left which cuts off a corner in the road but tends to get a bit overgrown. Back on the road, having passed the houses at White Lane take the path on the right, which starts opposite a converted chapel. This brings you to the pretty hamlet of Treworthal. Continue along the road now for about half a mile. Shortly before this meets the main road, cross the stile on your right to join a short path across a field, cutting off a corner in the road; cross the main road with care and continue on the path opposite, via steps up to a stile. After a couple more stiles the path descends quite steeply to the coast path midway between the Pendower Hotel and the Pendower Beach House Hotel, at both of which you could get refreshments during the season.

APPENDIX 1
FLORA AND FAUNA OF THE MINERAL TRAMWAYS DISTRICT
by Dr Paul Gainey

An exhaustive study of the plants and animals of the whole area would require another book at least as big as this one, so I asked Dr Gainey to focus on two important sites visited on walks described in this book, both inland and both heavily influenced by industrial activity, but very strongly contrasted in other respects. Although of course the ecology of some other parts of this district, such as the clifftops in the north, the Fal estuary in the south and urban areas like Camborne-Redruth, is very different, the following studies should, between them, provide a useful guide to the natural history of the Mineral Tramways district as a whole.

The Wheal Busy site is included on the Coast-to-Coast Trail as well as on Round Walk 7, and a visit to Kennall Vale is described on pages 208-212.

Bob Acton

WHEAL BUSY

Disused metalliferous mining sites provide an unusual, and often hostile, man-made habitat in which a variety of characteristic animals and plants may be found. The Wheal Busy mining complex near Chacewater is an excellent representative example.

It is an ancient site which has largely escaped the ravages of modern re-landscaping and reclamation. Unfortunately, many of the mine shafts have been filled in and capped, thus denying many animals, such as the greater and lesser horseshoe, pipistrelle and natterer's bats a place to live. Also suited to the cool but constant temperature and stillness of air to be found in these shafts and adits were various species of spider, including the so-called cave spider and several species of hibernating adult butterflies such as the peacock and red admiral.

The derelict mine buildings, the engine houses and their chimneys, the arsenic flues and other such structures do, however, still provide a habitat for various species. The building blocks of the engine houses act as a suitable substratum for the adventitious roots of ivy, climbing ever skywards, to gain a foothold. The crumbling mortar between the blocks provides a markedly alkaline microhabitat because of its lime content. Several species of small fern, black spleenwort, hartstongue, polypody, wall rue and occasionally maidenhair spleenwort may be found living here. Also growing out of these joints are common species such as ivy-leaved toadflax and wall pennywort, alternatively known as navelwort. The upper levels of these engine houses supply resting places and nesting sites for birds such as jackdaws, crows, ravens and even peregrine falcons. Luckily some of the chimneys still act as roosts and hibernation sites for bats. Many other buildings associated with mining are derelict. Some, such as the flues and the structures associated with the stamps, have their floors and walls, what is left of them, grossly contaminated by impregnation with a cocktail of heavy metals such as copper and zinc or, as in the case of the condensing flues, arsenic. Ground nearby may be similarly contaminated. Despite this, a variety of plants, including species of moss and lichen, have colonised these rather hostile microhabitats.

Much of the Wheal Busy site is occupied by accumulated mine spoil tips. In many other areas these have been improved and replanted using visually more acceptable species. Through this action a significant proportion of such habitat has been lost for ever. Many of the spoil tips are bare of vegetation, especially of the larger plants such as trees. Other areas support only a very limited and specialised range of vegetation. There are several reasons why these areas should prove unattractive to plant growth. Much of the spoil contains metal sulphide ores which, over a period of time, undergo air oxidation, and in the presence of water, sulphuric acid is formed; hence, most plants that grow on these spoil tips are calcifuges, that is, lime-hating (acid-loving) species. Another reason is that the acid, once formed, can dissolve out heavy metals such as copper and zinc from the rock particles. Many of the plants present have had to evolve mechanisms in their root systems to deal with this toxicity problem. Finally, since most of the spoil material has originated from deep underground there is a distinct lack of certain elements such as nitrogen and phosphorus, both of which are required by plants for healthy growth. What few trees do grow upon the mine spoil are small even when quite old. At Wheal Busy oak, elder, ash, holly, pine, sycamore and hawthorn are to be seen. Of the shrubs in the spoil area, some are escapes from cultivation which have become naturalised, such as the small-leaved and Himalayan cotoneasters, and buddleia, which, as its alternative name of "butterfly-bush" suggests, attracts numerous species of butterfly to it during the summer months. Other naturalised plants such as Japanese knotweed and montbretia, which grow vigorously, also do well.

In places water accumulates to form permanent or semi-permanent pools. Very few animals or plants survive in such pools because of the toxicity and acidity of the water. Any vegetation is restricted to the pool margin where it may act as a landing place for blue-tailed, large red and emerald damselflies as well as common darter and golden-ringed dragonflies.

The damper areas support sallow, purple loosestrife, silverweed, pendulous sedge, a variety of rushes and the very attractive, albeit small, bog pimpernel with its delicate pale pink bell-shaped flowers. In the somewhat drier open areas creeping cinquefoil, various clovers, thistles and daisies predominate, sometimes interspersed with the rather beautiful common centaury. Here also various invertebrate animals may be found, such as the mottled grasshopper, green tiger beetle, grayling butterfly and several species of the aptly named mining bee. Turning over pieces of galvanise may reveal the presence of the common or viviparous lizard, a slow-worm or the occasional adder.

Many of the plants present on the mine spoil have evolved specialised features that aid their survival. Two dominant species are the common and the bell or purple heather. These, like most members of the plant family *Ericaceae* are calcifuges and find themselves well suited to the acidic soils. The roots of these heathers enter into a mycorrhizal (fungus-root) association with fungi in the soil. In this way they are able to supplement their mineral uptake with extra nitrogen and phosphorus donated by the fungal hyphae. There are several members of the family *Leguminosae* present, including two species of gorse, common and western, also broom, bird's foot and a variety of clover species. A general characteristic of this family is the presence of root nodules, small swellings on the roots which contain many symbiotic, nitrogen-fixing bacteria of the *Rhizobium* genus. These have the ability to convert atmospheric nitrogen into nitrate ions some of which are donated to the legume thus promoting healthier growth.

Present on the wetter areas, often among the heather, is round-leaved sundew. This is an insectivorous plant that has taken to capturing small insects for the purpose of gaining extra nitrogen. The leaves have many small, hollow hairs projecting from their surfaces. From the end of each of these glandular hairs exudes a minute globule of liquid containing a sticky substance which secures a recently-landed insect. Also present is a mixture of digestive enzymes which now begins the breakdown of the insect's body. Useful products are absorbed directly into the plant's tissues.

Other plants to be seen on and around the Wheal Busy site have adopted parasitic or semi-parasitic modes of living. Gorse, a common plant in this type of habitat, is occasionally seen covered by a mass of thin red stems with little clusters of small pink flowers at intervals along them. This is caused by a parasitic plant called dodder which lacks a root system of its own and derives all of its water and nutrients from the host. Also to be seen are lousewort, yellow rattle and, somewhat less commonly, yellow bartsia. These are all semi-parasitic plants: they have green leaves and are able to carry out photosynthesis to make their own food (sugars), but underground their roots tap into those of other plants, such as various grasses, for the purpose of water and mineral extraction.

Lichens, a group of primitive plants, also grow well and are relatively abundant on the spoil surface. Here they are found either in the more open, barer, areas or growing amongst the heathers. Members of the genus *Cladonia* are particularly successful and obvious. They look like a mass of intertwined, miniature, grey, grey-green or green twigs. At certain times of year they develop minute trumpet-shaped structures often tipped with a brilliant red colour, which make them distinctive and unmistakable. Lichens are, in reality, two different organisms, algae and fungi, living together in a symbiotic relationship. Together they are able to overcome the considerable problems associated with growing in this habitat.

Finally mention must be made of thrift or sea-pink and ivy-leaved bellflower, two of the more beautiful plants that grow in this habitat. Thrift, so characteristic of the Cornish coastline, has evolved a tolerance to heavy metals such as chromium, nickel, cobalt and others. As such it has a selective advantage in these heavy-metal-laden soils. The ivy-leaved bellflower is a smaller and more secretive plant which is present in relatively small amounts but is well worth the search if found.

KENNALL VALE

This area of woodland has also been subjected to the influence and activity of man in the past. As described elsewhere in this book, a gunpowder works here, starting in 1812 and continuing for over a century, harnessed the power of the River Kennall which falls rapidly through the steep, boulder-strewn valley. This was achieved by the construction of a complex of leats to drive waterwheels. Today many of the old buildings associated with the gunpowder works and the quarry of more recent date survive, and the site forms a Cornwall Wildlife Trust nature reserve covering some 20 acres. This mixed, broad-leaved woodland habitat very much contrasts with the Wheal Busy site.

The many trees present produce shade, especially when the leaf canopy is in position from early until late summer. The River Kennall and the leat system ensure a high humidity and dampness of soil. Finally, the woodland floor is covered by a relatively fertile, humus-rich soil formed as a result of countless years of leaf-mould accumulation.

Numerous tree species are present: ash, sycamore, sweet chestnut and beech, the last of which is dominant. Many of these trees were deliberately planted to act as a barrier to prevent excessive damage from shock waves and flying debris to the nearby village in the event of an explosion. Amongst the trees there is an under-storey of holly, hazel, rhododendron and laurel. Ferns of many types are abundant here: hard, lady, common male, golden male, broad buckler and hay-scented buckler ferns adorn the woodland floor and earthy banks, the moist, sheltered conditions very much suiting them. Some of the ferns - golden male, lady and broad buckler - form large shuttlecock-like arrangements with their fronds. Others - hartstongue, western polypody and black spleenwort - also grow out from the basic mortar found between the stones of the now derelict buildings. The western polypody, like the ivy, is also found as an epiphyte growing up, over and along the boles and boughs of some of the trees. In places the relatively rare Tunbridge filmy fern can be found growing on permanently wet, more-or-less vertical faces.

The very damp conditions are also responsible for the presence of a wide variety of snails, including the garlic, strawberry and great ramshorn snails, which are easily found. The garlic snail is readily recognised by the characteristic odour that is evolved when it is handled. Another gastropod mollusc, the river limpet, found on the undersides of stones in the river, testifies to the purity and oxygenation of the river water. The river itself and its banks have large boulders which are covered by an array of damp-loving moss and liverwort species. These boulders act as rest places for dippers and grey wagtails which can be seen flying up and down the river course all year round. During the summer months spotted flycatchers, blackcaps and chiffchaffs take up residence in the woods, whilst in the winter nuthatches, treecreepers and goldcrest wrens are often seen.

The complex system of leats is in a state of disrepair in many places. Leaking water has resulted in a number of very wet areas. Here plants such as marsh marigold may be found alongside pendulous sedge and the extremely poisonous hemlock water-dropwort. In other wet areas good stands of the alien plant called Indian balsam or policeman's helmet are to be found in late summer. The leaking, vertical walls of the leats are festooned with an almost complete covering of moisture-loving mosses and liverworts of many different species. Also growing out of these walls are ivy-leaved toadflax, opposite-leaved golden-saxifrage and wavy or wood bitter-cress. Huge clumps of the attractive western-oceanic moss species *Hookeria luscens* grow on the more earthy side of the leats, as does the rather rare south-western flowering plant, Cornish moneywort.

The floor of the woods supports shade-tolerant plants including carpets of bluebells, wood-sorrel, sanicle, pignut, bugle and enchanter's-nightshade. All of these plants are calcifuges and grow well on the acidic, humus-rich soils. The presence of great woodrush is perhaps an indicator of the past, when Kennall Vale would have been designated ancient or primary woodland.

Throughout the woods are a series of paths, originally built to bring in the raw ingredients of gunpowder - saltpetre, charcoal and sulphur - and then to take the finished product out. Today on the sides of these paths, ground-ivy, lesser periwinkle, lesser celandine, winter heliotrope, common violet, yellow pimpernel, dog's mercury and sweet woodruff may be seen. Sweet woodruff is a most uncommon plant in west Cornwall. The paths, which have been cut through the woodland, have created a series of open spaces or glades where the light intensity is somewhat greater, especially during the summer. These glades are particularly good places to see butterflies, including ringlet, comma, holly blue and the spectacular silver-washed fritillary. Other lepidoptera to be seen here include the rather beautiful peach blossom, swallow-tailed and drinker moths. Dragonflies also patrol these glades, two of the most impressive being the southern hawker and golden-ringed dragonflies. The relative abundance of night-flying insect life also attracts pipistrelle, natterer's and lesser horseshoe bats into the woods from surrounding buildings.

Finally, the rather dank conditions and abundance of dead and rotting wood and leaves produce an ideal habitat for saprobiotic fungi (those that feed on dead or decaying plants and animals). Some of these have been given rather intriguing names such as coral spot, dead men's toes, earthball and miners cramp balls.

* * * * *

For further, more detailed information on the metalliferous mining and the woodland habitats and their ecology, the reader is referred to the following:

Bere, R., *The Nature of Cornwall* (Barracuda Books, 1982) - pages 95-102 & 127-36

Haes, E.C.M. & Spalding, A., "The Insects on a Small, Isolated, Derelict Metalliferous Mine Site in Cornwall" (in *British Journal of Entomology and Natural History*, No. 9, 1996)

(Same authors) "Contaminated Land - A Resource for Wildlife: A Review and Survey of Insects on Metalliferous Mine Sites in Cornwall" (in *Land Contamination and Reclamation*, No.3, 1995)

Holyoak, D.T., *Report on a Survey of Bryophytes of some Derelict Mine Sites in Cornwall* (Cornish Biological Records Unit, Institute of Cornish Studies, Redruth, 1996)

Johnson, T., Payton, P. & Spalding, A., *The Conservation Value of Metalliferous Mine Sites in Cornwall* (Cornwall Archaeological Unit & Institute of Cornish Studies, University of Exeter, 1995)

Macnair, M., "Heavy Metal Tolerance in Plants, a Model Evolutionary System" (in *Tree* No. 2, 1987)

Sellars, B. & Baker, A.J.M., *Review of the Metallophyte Vegetation and its Conservation*, (N.C.C., Peterborough, 1987)

Smith, J.R., *Kennall Vale Archaeological Report* (Cornwall Trust for Nature Conservation [now the Cornwall Wildlife Trust], 1986)

Spalding, A., "The Importance of Metalliferous Mining Sites in Cornwall for Wildlife", in *Cornish Studies: Three* (Institute of Cornish Studies, Redruth, 1995)

Tanner, H. & Tanner, R., *Woodland Plants* (Impact Books, 1987)

See also MMS and SIG in the Further Reading list.

APPENDIX 2
CYCLING THE TRAMWAY TRAILS
by Nicholas Roberts
Schools' Off-road Cycle Leader (ESCA); Former Safety Officer & Senior Cycle Leader for Time Cycles

Given the length of the Mineral Tramways network, the best way to explore it must surely be by bicycle, especially if you are only spending a short time in the area. That said, I feel it would be helpful to offer some hints and advice to aid those whose off-road experience, or knowledge of the area, is limited.

Choosing the bike

First, and most important, choose the right bike! The general approach, so far, to the Tramway Trails has been to preserve their "wild" or "rural" nature as much as possible; thus although in some areas considerable work has been carried out to deal with deep mud or perennial flooding, the result is a surface similar to a well-maintained bridleway, not the smooth, graded surface often found on purpose-built cycle paths. Therefore, the only really suitable type of bicycle is the A.T.B. or "mountain bike". A good quality, purpose-built touring bike would cope with all but the roughest terrain, but such bikes do not come cheap!

Be careful if you are choosing a mountain bike, either for purchase or for hire; many such bikes offered at the bottom end of the market are really just basic road machines with straight handlebars, chunky tyres and a comfy saddle. Such bikes are fine until the going gets rough or steep, when their limited gearing lets them down. For cycling off-road, then, you really need a cycle with a triple chain-ring. "A what?" For those who don't know the jargon, the chainset is the group of toothed rings inside the right-hand crank, and a mountain bike should have three, to give it the low gears necessary to climb hills with loose or slippery surfaces.

Safety check

It of course needs no saying that your bike should for safety reasons be kept in good condition, but if you are hiring it is a good idea to check over a bike before paying, and it is certainly no bad thing to get into the habit of doing the same with your own each time before riding. There is no set procedure for doing this, but here is one often used by schools instructors like myself.

Moving front to back, check:

- that the front tyre is hard enough - it may look fine, but could be soft from a slow puncture;
- that the front wheel is firmly secured - especially important if the wheels have quick-release hubs;
- that the front brakes are working properly;
- that the handlebars are tight - place the front wheel between your knees, grip the handlebars and twist the bars sideways - there should be no independent movement from either handlebars or wheel;
- that the "front mech" - the gear changer for the chainset - is working properly;

- that the saddle is secure - again especially important if it has a quick-release mechanism;
- that the "rear mech", the gear changer for the cogs on the rear wheel, is working properly;
- that the rear brakes are working properly;
- that the rear tyre and wheel pass the first two checks;
- finally, that all reflectors are clean, and that all lights are working - if you have any. If you don't, be home before dark!

At this point I must stress the importance of saddle height. Children up to their mid-teens can suffer serious and permanent knee damage from riding with their saddle too high. Check with your local cycle shop, or better still contact the English Schools Cycling Association (ESCA).

Route classification

It has already been mentioned that the Mineral Tramways network is not being given a uniformly smooth surface, so it would be appropriate for this book to provide a guide to the state of the tracks, so that potential users may plan their rides accordingly.

I have chosen a simple system of route classification with four levels. It is a general guide only, not a yard-by-yard survey, but should nevertheless give a good idea of the condition of the Tramway Trails at the time of going to press. Please bear in mind that a few sections are still to be converted to bridleway, and so are as yet restricted to walkers; they are indicated in the body of the text.

The four levels of route are as follows:

- **A** - suitable for all ages/abilities to ride along. This classification includes stretches of metalled roads.
- **B** - also suitable for all ages/abilities to ride, but not as "polished" a surface as A. These stretches may be gravelly, have puddles to dodge (or splash through!) or some muddy patches.
- **C** - suitable for all persons with a moderate level of experience/ability to ride along. This classification includes stretches whose surface is rough but firm, or which are rather muddy. Those riders with limited off-road experience who decide, quite reasonably, to dismount should have no difficulty walking their bikes here, however.
- **D** - suitable only for persons with considerable experience or ability to ride along. This classification includes stretches where surface is rough and loose, and strewn with stones. These sections are likely to cause difficulties for the less fit even if they are walking their bikes.

There are very few D sections in the network. For those who may wonder, with justification, why such difficult terrain exists at all on routes intended for the general public, it is simply that, at the time of writing, these sections have yet to be dealt with in the works programme. They should be improved in the future, to at least B standard. But don't take this for granted! Recent upheavals - including the winding-up of Groundwork Kerrier, the organisation behind the creation of the network - brought about by local politics, have cast doubt over the whole programme of works, at least for the present.

For the time being, then, the state of the network is as follows.

The Coast-to-Coast Trail

Section	Grade	Notes
Portreath to Mawla	A	But bear in mind that the Tramroad trackbed is footpath only as far as Cambrose, and cyclists have to use the road, which tends to be busy, especially in the summer.
Mawla to top of Unity Wood	C/A	The first 400m stretch, though good and firm, is rather bumpy. Road (omitting Wheal Busy) from Wheal Rose to Killifreth.
Unity Wood	C	Inclined to be muddy, except in summer. Also, the gradient is quite steep near the lower end of the woods.
Bottom of Unity Wood to Todpool	A	
Todpool to Bissoe (Point Mills)	B	
Bissoe (Point Mills) to A38	A	But until the Mineral Tramways Spine Route through the former arsenic works site at the start of this section is raised to bridleway status, cyclists have to reach Bissoe Bridge via Hicks' Mill, as explained in the main text.

The Carn Marth Link, east to west

Section	Grade	Notes
Todpool, through Crofthandy & Carharrack, to the bottom of Carn Marth	A	For cyclists the best route is probably to go directly from Wheal Unity Gate to Crofthandy, omitting St Day.
East face of Carn Marth (Not really comparable with the north face of the Eiger!)	D	Some of this is public road, but the rest is narrow and clogged with loose stones, some large - a challenge even for experienced mountain bikers. For those happy to push, however, the effort is worth it, as the view from the top is magnificent.
Top of Carn Marth to Lanner Hill roundabout	B	The descent, however, is steep at first.
Lanner Hill roundabout to the Great Flat Lode Trail	A/B	This is mainly public road, but there is around 1km of off-road, which is B.

(Twelveheads to the bottom of Carn Marth via the Wheal Maid Valley and Carharrack: should all be of at least B/C grade, but the present doubts about rights of way in the Wheal Maid Valley make it an unsuitable route for cyclists.)

The Great Flat Lode Circular, heading anticlockwise (as described in Volume 1) from the point where the Carn Marth Link joins it, at Buller Hill Stables.

Section	Grade	Notes
Stables to Carn Brea Quarry	Mainly D	The first part is difficult because of loose stones, and there is a fairly steep descent into Church Coombe, with exposed tree roots and often muddy - very challenging to riders. The road is Class A, obviously, but the track climbing the eastern flank of Carn Brea is C: a bit rough at first, then muddy. The short final section, downhill to the Quarry, is D: very rough and loose.
Carn Brea Quarry to Tregajorran	B	
Tregajorran to the top of Carn Entral	A/D	A as far as the track at Brea Leats, a short stretch of which is D - narrow, stepped and uneven; and the steepish track up from Brea Adit to the top of Carn Entral is D simply because it is so overgrown. All these problems can be avoided, however, by keeping to the narrow road down into Brea village and up to Higher Condurrow.
Top of Carn Entral to Grenville New Stamps	B/A/C	Mostly good as far as the Brea-Troon road, then C - rather rough and narrow. Oh, and watch out for the llama!
New Stamps to Newton Moor	A	
Newton Moor to Treskillard	B	Very boggy crossing Newton Moor at times.
Treskillard to Buller Hill Stables	A	But you may have to get your bike over a couple of stiles towards the end!

* * * * * *

This, then, is the present state of the Tramway Trails at the time of going to press. There are a few short sections that most people wouldn't like to ride, but nothing that cannot be passed, dismounted if necessary, with a little effort. Of course, these stretches provide, until they are made more accessible, an enjoyable challenge for the more capable riders, who will particularly relish descending them. However, if you do choose to ride that way, please make sure before you set off that no-one is coming up, and WEAR A HELMET. This applies to all people riding a bicycle off-road. In other words, if you are using this network, then please be safe, be courteous, and, above all, enjoy yourself.

APPENDIX 3

REDRUTH & CHASEWATER RAILWAY:

The two storage yards
whose sites are visited on walks in Volume 1

Apologies to railway enthusiasts for not including these maps in the relevant volume. Please note that, in common with most of the other extracts from and adaptations of early maps that appear in this book, these two have been considerably simplified in the interests of clarity. Serious students of the subject should therefore consult the original maps.

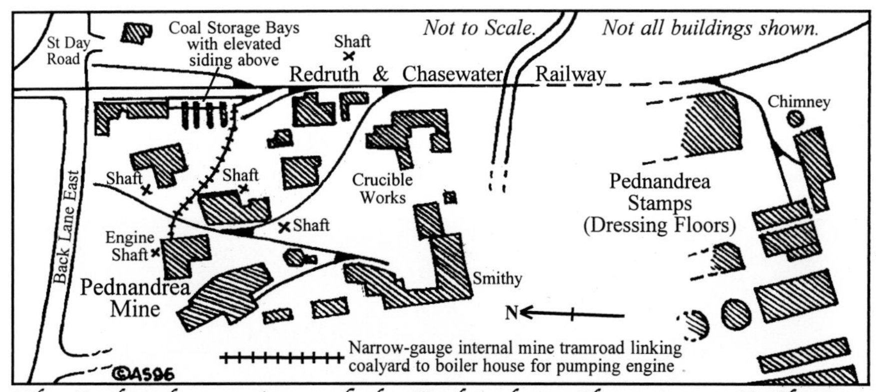

The Redruth terminus of the Redruth & Chasewater Railway
Map by A. Steenmeyer, based on 1st Edition OS (1880)

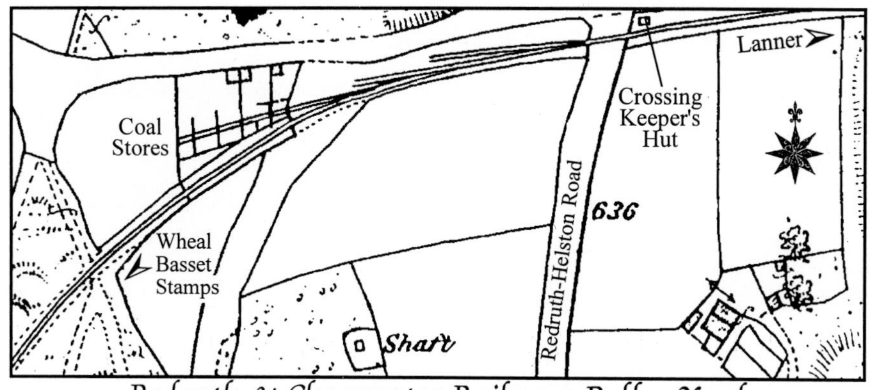

Redruth & Chasewater Railway: Buller Yard
Simplified extract from 1st Edition OS map (1880)

APPENDIX 5

GLOSSARY OF MINING & ENGINEERING TERMS

Supplement to the list in Volume 1

Cross-references (to items in the Vol. 1 Glossary) are indicated by the use of **bold type**.

ADIT (Revised entry) A drainage channel with its mouth or "portal" in a valley or on a hillside or cliff face. In deep mines, the water had to be raised by pumping to the level of the adit; this is why statistics often state the depth of a mine "below adit". Although some adits may have doubled as shafts by following the metal **lode**, and on occasions provided access for the miners, in Cornwall the term "adit" refers strictly to a drainage tunnel.

BOUNDS From the earliest times, Cornish tinners had the right to mine for tin and dig turves to smelt it in any unenclosed or waste land. The general practice, known as bounding, seems to have been to mark the area of proposed working by cutting three turves at each corner. From 1494, such tin-bounds had to be officially registered at the Stannary Court. For more detail see <u>TTB</u>.

BURNING HOUSE (Revised entry) A furnace or **CALCINER** (pronounced "cal-*sign*-er") where tin was made red-hot in order to burn off impurities such as sulphur and

Refined white arsenic before being ground and packed in barrels. The photograph is believed to have been taken at the Seleggan smelting works: see Volume 1 of this guide, pages 37-41. (Courtesy Paddy Bradley)

arsenic. If the arsenic was wanted, the fumes were passed through a long flue fromwhich the deposits were collected. Usually this was constructed in a zigzag formknown as a "lambreth" (labyrinth) with a tall stack at the far end to create a strong through-draught and also to reduce the damage caused by the noxious fumes thatissued from it. As the gas cooled in the lambreth, the arsenic condensed and formed crystals on the walls. When sufficient had collected, the calciners were stopped, iron doors in the lambreth were opened, and the arsenic "soot" was swept and shovelled out. Finally this was taken to a refinery to be roasted in furnaces like those used for smelting tin, linked to further condensing chambers, and ground into powder ready for sale. As well as arsenic, sulphur was obtained as a result of the refining process; some of that was used to manufacture sulphuric acid. Precautions to protect the arsenic workers were only rudimentary - wads of cotton wool in the nostrils and a cloth over the mouth, together with strict regulations about washing. Skin rashes and sores were common, especially in warm weather when the men sweated. In general, though, they seem to have remained surprisingly healthy, perhaps because they developed an immunity to the poison; it was even claimed that the arsenic promoted plump skin, a good complexion and thick, shiny hair. A **BRUNTON CALCINER** employed a slowly rotating hearth so that the ore could be roasted evenly and changed over at regular intervals. According to many historians, one factor which delayed final closure for many Cornish mines was the sudden increase in demand for arsenic during the early 1870s, when its value as an insecticide began to be understood, especially in controlling Colorado beetles on potato plants. Its use for several other purposes was already known; these included sheep dips, soap for cleaning leather, the clarification of glass, a process in the manufacture of lead shot, and pigments, particularly a brilliant green much used in Victorian wallpapers which became notorious when acidic pollution in city air reacted with it to produce deadly arsene gas. Although the arsenic trade declined during the 1880s there were revivals later, for example in 1906, during World War I (when arsenic was used to make poison gas), and again in 1923-4.

APPENDIX 6
FURTHER READING
Supplement to the list in Volume 1

The books are listed in alphabetical order of the shortened versions of their titles which are used when referring to them elsewhere in this guide.

BE — T.E.Crowley, *Beam Engines* (Shire, 1976 / 1982)

CE — Bryan Earl, *Cornish Explosives* (Trevithick Society, 1978)

CMD — Cyril Noall, *Cornish Mine Disasters* (Dyllansow Truran, 1989)

CV — Sheila Bird, *A Book of Cornish Villages* (Dovecote, 1988)

DDCV — Barry Simpson, *Devoran, A Different Cornish Village* (Author, 1990)

FRV — Ivy Edwards, with additions by Rachel & Elisabeth Rowlands, *The Family at Rose Villa* (privately published, 1988)

GIR — T.W.M.Darlington, *Glimpses into Renown: The Wayside Chapel Called Hicks' Mill - Gwennap Cornwall* (Author, 1991)

HAF — The Fal History Group, *History Around the Fal* (five volumes, the first published in 1980)

HoH — Edmund Vale, *The Harveys of Hayle* (D.Bradford Barton, 1966)

HMB — Adam Sharpe, with Nicholas Johnson & Rose Lewis, *A Guide to Conserving Historic Mine Buildings in Cornwall* (Cornwall Archaeological Unit, 1996)

HPG — C.C.James, *A History of the Parish of Gwennap* (Author, no date - probably late 1940s)

JT — Roger Burt, *John Taylor, Mining Entrepreneur and Engineer 1779-1863* (Moorland Publishing, 1977)

KCD — ed. R.Maber & A.Tregoning, *Kilvert's Cornish Diary* (Alison Hodge, 1989

MGC — Thomas Shaw, *A Methodist Guide to Cornwall* (Methodist Publishing House, 1991)

MMC — A.K.Hamilton Jenkin, *Mines and Miners of Cornwall*:
6: Around Gwennap (Truro Bookshop, 1963)
13: The Lizard - Falmouth - Mevagissey (Truro Bookshop, 1967)

MMS — (ed.) Nicholas Johnson, Philip Payton & Adrian Spalding, *The Conservation Value of Metalliferous Mine Sites in Cornwall* (Cornwall Archaeological Unit & Institute of Cornish Studies, 1996)

NC — Ronne Bere, *The Nature of Cornwall* (Barracuda, 1982)

OCI — H.L.Douch, *Old Cornish Inns* (D. Bradford Barton, 1966)

PV — Bob Acton, *The Landfall Book of the Poldice Valley* (Landfall, 1990)

SIG — Selina Bates & Keith Spurgin, *Stars in the Grass* (Dyllansow Truran, 1994)

SVCM — Bob Acton, *A Second View from Carn Marth* (Landfall Publications, 1991)

TIA — R.D.Penhallurick, *Tin in Antiquity* (Institute of Metals, 1986)

TTB — J.A.Buckley, *Tudor Tin Bounds, West Penwith* (Dyllansow Truran, 1987)

The magazine *Archive*, mentioned in connection with the Bain fleet at Portreath, is a quarterly publication devoted to industrial archaeology, illustrated with high-quality photographs and maps. It is published by the Lightmoor Press, 47-49 High Street, Lydney, Gloucestershire GL15 5DD.